Princeton Theologica

C000103046

Dikran Y. Hadidian

General Editor

29

# CHRISTUS FABER

## THE MASTER BUILDER AND THE HOUSE OF GOD

# CHRISTUS FABER

## THE MASTER BUILDER
## AND
## THE HOUSE OF GOD

*Behold the Man:*
*Rising Sun is his name.*
*From where he is, the sun shall rise,*
*And he shall build the house of the Lord*
(LXX Zach 6:12).

# BEN F. MEYER

PICKWICK PUBLICATIONS
ALLISON PARK, PENNSYLVANIA

Published by
*Pickwick Publications*
*4137 Timberlane Drive*
*Allison Park, PA 15101-2932*

**Library of Congress Cataloging-in-Publication Data**

Meyer, Ben F., 1927-
    Christus Faber : the master builder and the house of God / Ben
F. Meyer.
        p.    cm. --  (Princeton theological monograph series ;  29)
    ISBN 1-55635-014-7
    1. Jesus Christ--Historicity.    2. Bible.  N.T.  Gospels-
-Criticism, interpretation, etc.    I. Title.    II. Series.
BT303.2.M4664    1992
232--dc20                                                    91-45746
                                                                CIP

Pour Dionisaki,
source
jaillissante
de gaité,
de beauté,
de bonté

# CONTENTS

## PART ONE

# PART TWO

# FREQUENTLY CITED WORKS

Allison, *Ages*: Allison, Dale C., Jr. *The End of the Ages Has Come*. Philadelphia: Fortress, 1985.

Borg, *Conflict*: Borg, Marcus J. *Conflict. Holiness. and Politics in the Teaching of Jesus*. New York-Toronto: Mellen, 1984.

Burney, *Poetry*: Burney, Charles Fox. *The Poetry of Our Lord*. Oxford: Oxford University Press, 1925.

Dalman, *Words*: Dalman, Gustaf. *The Words of Jesus*. Translated by P. P. Levertoff. Edinburgh: Clark, 1902.

Dalman, *JJ*: Dalman, Gustaf. *Jesus-Jeshua*. Translated by P. P. Levertoff. London: SPCK, 1929.

Jeremias, *Parables*: Jeremias, Joachim. *The Parables of Jesus*. Translated by S. H. Hooke. London: SCM; New York: Scribner, 1963.

Jeremias, *Theology*: Jeremias, Joachim. *New Testament Theology: The Proclamation of Jesus*. Translated by John Bowden. London: SCM; New York: Scribner, 1971.

Jeremias, *Eucharistic*: Jeremias, Joachim. *The Eucharistic Words of Jesus*. Translated by Norman Perrin. London: SCM; Philadelphia: Fortress, 1966.

Lonergan, *Insight*: Lonergan, Bernard J. F. *Insight: A Study of Human Understanding*. New York: Longmans, Green & Co., 1957.

Lonergan, *Method*: Lonergan, Bernard J. F. *Method in Theology*. London: Darton, Longman & Todd; New York: Herder & Herder, 1972.

Lonergan, *Second Collection*: Lonergan, Bernard J. F. *A Second Collection*. Papers by Bernard J. F. Lonergan. Edited by William F. J. Ryan and Bernard J. Tyrrell. London: Darton, Longman & Todd; Philadelphia: Westminster, 1974.

Meyer, *Aims*: Meyer, Ben F. *The Aims of Jesus*. London: SCM, 1979.

Meyer, *Critical Realism*: Meyer, Ben F. *Critical Realism and the New Testament*. Allison Park: Pickwick, 1989.

Meyer, *Early Christians*: Meyer, Ben F. *The Early Christians: Their World Mission and Self-Discovery*. Wilmington: Glazier, 1986.

Riesner, *Lehrer*: Riesner, Rainer. *Jesus der Lehrer*. Tübingen: Mohr-Siebeck, 3rd edition, 1988).

# PREFACE

This book is a collection (but not a random collection) of studies of Jesus and the Church. Planned and executed over a two and-a-half-year period, the studies were conceived from the start as a unified effort to follow up on my own past work, especially *The Aims of Jesus* (London: SCM, 1979), while responding to current scholarship on a few selected, fundamental issues.

*Christus Faber/*"Christ the Artisan" alludes to a classic messianic image, the Messiah as master-builder of the house of God. This was among the most traditional and comprehensive ways in which Jesus described his mission. The mission was the eschatological ("end-time-oriented") restoration of God's people. Among the images that Jesus seized on to hit off facets of the mission were: the shepherd, the messenger, the physician, the teacher, the householder, the fisherman, the king, the architect and builder. Some of these (king, shepherd, architect) belong to the central fund of Old Testament messianic themes and represent maximally comprehensive images. From the oracle of Nathan, wellspring of classical messianism, the son of David (the original referent was, of course, Solomon) was chosen to build the house of God: *hû⁾ yibneh-ba⁾yit lišmî* = he shall build a house for my name (2 Sam 7:13a). So, when Simon confessed Jesus as the Messiah, Son of God, Jesus responded immediately with this image, extending it: he would indeed build the temple of the last days, and Simon would be the rock on which he built it. Again, at the trial before the Sanhedrin, it was the garbled report of Jesus' words on the building of the new sanctuary that led to the climactic question: are you the Messiah, the Son of the Blessed One?

At one time I hoped to give the lion's share of attention in this book to the history and theology of the temple. To my dismay I found that the current almost chaotic spectrum of opinion in Old Testament *Einleitung* (questions of the dating, provenance, history, etc. of the literary materials) made it not just difficult, but impossible, to carry the study through to my own or, no doubt, anyone else's satisfaction. Finally, reluctantly acknowledging that I did not know whose views to trust, and conscious that I could not hope to work out independent views of my own on these many issues, I gave up after a preliminary campaign of some years of research. In Part II, I do offer a swift sketch of the history and meaning of the temple. It is very limited and tends finally to accent elements that were to prove salient when, by both word and deed, Jesus would bring the temple theme to a climax.

For some time I have tried to bring to bear on biblical studies the resources of Bernard Lonergan's account of human intentionality, especially his work on knowledge and on method. The attraction of his account of knowledge lay especially in two spheres. The first is the sphere of concrete and precise detail in the retrieval of conscious human functioning (from perception and imagination/memory and feelings, through wonder—made thematic in questions and realized in satisfactory answers to them—to the existential subject's drive to values and hunger for authenticity).

The second is the sphere of human history. Lonergan's effort to lay new foundations for the long mishandled theme of "progress" converged, I discovered, at a deep level with the present set of studies. This presented an irresistible occasion on which to offer, in the essay "Jesus and the Church: Divine Solution to the Human Problem," the context in which the mission of Jesus in its full sweep and scope corresponds (generally and in particular detail) not only to Israel's hopes as attested in the scriptures but to "the human problem" as attested in human history. In the light of the affirmation of God, the fact of evil cannot fail to become "the problem of evil"; but by the same token the problem cannot fail to have a solution. Over and above the explicit treatment offered in this single study, the same solution tacitly pervades all the studies.

Other aspects of Lonergan's work, no less crucial, relate to method. Lack of a satisfactory account of knowledge has made itself felt in every aspect of hermeneutics and historical method. The history of interpretation has shown again and again that the many faceted enterprise called "the historical-critical method" could be and has been separated from and purged of philosophic commitments that had been gratuitously fused with them. Whenever one interprets, the process leads the interpreter into commitments in the mode of praxis that only philosophy can properly retrieve. When the methods of historically conscious philology are put to work, they function on philosophic bases, whether the interpreter is aware, fully or at all, of this inevitably operative fact. That many are not aware of this fact is betrayed time and again by the bewilderment of so many New Testament scholars at the chaos of conflicting results reached by scholars ostensibly at one on questions of method. Basic to the present effort is a critical realist hold on standard historical-critical methods.

This reflects Lonergan's phenomenology of knowledge and theory of objectivity. Critical realism is evident, first, in the heuristic definition of "the historical Jesus": the Jesus of ancient Palestine insofar as, intended by historical questions, he comes to be known through satisfactory answers to those questions. (It follows, of course, that I reject as spurious all definitions of the historical Jesus that, tinged with positivism or idealism, abstract from the reality of the historical figure, e.g., "the historian's image of Jesus"). Second, this realism highlights an indispensable contribution of history to the cause of religion: the framing of the transpositions of meaning that allow religious truths to be moved into new contexts, so surviving intact the reality of continuously changing contexts.

I do wish to respond to contemporary scholarship, but I have not tried to join others in contributing to the non-theological contexts in which historical-Jesus studies are so often set today. My effort, rather, is to accent just those data of the gospels that seem to me to be overlooked in those studies. A comment on the theological scene, however, and specifically on the radically changed theological context from the nineteenth to the twentieth century, may be in order. In the nineteenth century philologically sophisticated history turned out to be a new and potent tool in the service of causes, old and new. Applied to the Bible, it promised to reverse, definitively, the marginal advantage of a claimed "orthodoxy" over an imputed "heresy." Among the unacknowledged goals of German biblical scholarship was to establish that, in its Catholic form, Christianity from *Frühkatholizismus* through the Reformation to the present, had been an aberration and deception.[1] Gregory Dix put it in this neutral way: from F. C. Baur to Dix's own day the subsurface historical issue had always been "the 'identity' of the historic Catholic Church with the primitive Apostolic community."[2] Confessional competition, which is still, for good or ill, an underground force, has at last begun to yield in some measure to the more fundamental conflicts today: that between the age-old Christian conviction that the deep dimension of the drama of history turned on "the concrete and cumulative consequences of the acceptance or rejection of the message of the Gospel"[3] and the commonplace contemporary reduction of all religious claims to the status of interchangeable "paradigms" serving some human need. (To which should be added the conception of history as a totality, but from within a wholly secular horizon.)

Religious thinkers not so long ago dismissed the notion of religion as one among interchangeable paradigms as reductionist. If it has now become "commonplace," however, this is due to its adoption by a new generation of religious thinkers. The old difference between the irreligious and the religious has accordingly had to be redefined. It now tends to lie in how one answers the question about the need that religion meets. Is that need distinctive? Or is it reducible to familiar (moral, perhaps, but not necessarily transcendent) categories? Is the need basic, intrinsic to human beings or, on the contrary, a culturally contrived and optional extra? The view presented here is that a radical human deficiency—the human problem, which is not many but one—calls for a divine solution, which is also not many but one.[4] If the gospel is identical with that one solution, it follows that, at bottom, the drama of history does, in fact, turn on the full, cumulative consequences of accepting or rejecting the gospel.

What has emerged with new and powerful effect in the modern and contemporary age is a grasp of the dimensions of God's all-inclusive will to save. Clearly and incisively this has imposed itself on us. The normative way of salvation (it may be expressed, shorthand-fashion, by "baptism") remains exactly what it was and has been ever since the birth of the Easter Church. But in the light of developments, and especially in the light of our new grasp of the dimensions of historic change, development, and reversal, of the unpredictable and far-reaching diversity that human development entails, of the dynamics of progress and decline, it is clear that God's actually saving whoever would accept salvation—though it be by the grace of Christ—is simply free, unrestricted to the normative economy of salvation. It would consequently be greatly mistaken to conclude (on the premise of our primary concern with historical revelation) that the present inquiry is in the service of a narrow, exclusivist theology of salvation. It is a given of divine revelation that God wills the salvation of all (though we have no word on any guarantee of the salvation of all).

The all-inclusive divine will to save does not cancel the definitive and normative economy of salvation. In a recent novel V. S. Naipaul makes passing reference to the quest of "false consolation in the mind-quelling practices of a simple revealed religion."[5] By setting the quest of the normative economy of salvation within the immense horizons of God's universal saving plan and will, I wish on the one hand to affirm a certain genuine simplicity in Christianity, on the other to keep it free of the imputation of trammeling the free play and full range of both divine grace and of the human mind and heart and imagination. There is no obvious reason to suppose that Naipaul's remark is the product of close inquiry—it appears, rather, to be impressionistic—but it is not without some basis in history. Christianity has yielded more than once to temptations to narrowness and obscurantism. Yet this narrowness has been no more than the "shabby shell" disguising its authentic selfhood. The whole of the present inquiry is in the service of a religion and theology that aspires to pay reverence to the religions and philosophies of the whole human race, and understands that a Christianity that lives on the level of its own times will make religious practice and reflection an act of service both to God and to the whole human race. Discernment and courage have set the challenges to Christians in our time, whose Christianity—in its doctrines, devotions, reflections and practices—has become more and more mind-challenging, not mind-quelling.[6]

I have taken care to document as thoroughly as possible my use of the works of the late great Joachim Jeremias. In part this is simply the acknowledgment of a debt to an extraordinarily fine New Testament scholar. In part it is a detailed effort to specify, as a convenience to the reader, where Jeremias says what he says—this in tacit protest against a mini-tendency currently offering grotesquely inept and, on occasion, gratuitously odious interpretations of Jeremias's scholarly work. (Fortunately, this pseudo-scholarship has so far had negligible influence.)

Like *Critical Realism*, this book is opposed at once to a spurious (positivist) objectivism and to a spurious subjectivism, modern and postmodern. Both books are allied with the essays and essayists in *Lonergan's Hermeneutics*[7] (1989) as well as with that admirably open and critical hermeneutical movement that Peter Stuhlmacher has named "the hermeneutics of consent."[8]

I should like to make the following acknowlegments: four of

6 Christus Faber

the eleven essays presented here have already appeared in print and are reprinted with permission:

"Many (=All) are Called, but Few (=Not All) are Chosen," was published in *New Testament Studies* 36 (1990) 89-97.

"How Jesus Charged Language with Meaning: A Study in Rhetoric" was published in *Studies in Religion//Sciences Religieuses* 19 (1990) 273-285.(Presidential Address to the Canadian Society of Biblical Studies, Quebec, May 29, 1989, dedicated to William L Moran.)

"Jesus' Scenario of the Future" was published in *The Downside Review* 109 (1991) 1-15.

"The Church in Earliest Christianity: Identity and Self-Definition" was published in the *McMaster Journal of Theology* 2/2 (1991) 1-19.

A fifth essay, "Appointed Deed, Appointed Doer: Jesus and the Scriptures" was commissioned by the journal, *TRUTH*, and will appear in 1992.

B. F. Meyer
Les Verrières, Switzerland
July, 1991

# NOTES

1. John C. O'Neill, "The Study of the New Testament," in Ninian Smart et al., *Nineteenth Century Religious Thought in the West* vol. III (Cambridge: Cambridge University Press, 1985) 143-178, at 143.

2. Gregory Dix, *Jew and Greek* (Westminster: Dacre, 1953) 2.

3. Lonergan, *Insight*, 743.

4. Lonergan, *Insight*, 696-729 passim.

5. V. S. Naipaul, *The Enigma of Arrival* (New York: Viking, 1987; Harmondsworth: Penguin, 1988) 162.

6. The context of these words on God's all-inclusive will to save is not the reductionist "universal theology of religion" that a number of comparatists have excogitated; it is classical Christian soteriology in the expanded horizons of the present century.

7. S. E. McEvenue & B. F. Meyer (eds.) *Lonergan's Hermeneutics* (Washington: The Catholic University of America Press, 1989).

8. Peter Stuhlmacher, *Historical Criticism and Theological Interpretation of Scripture. Toward a Hermeneutics of Consent* (ed.) Roy A. Harrisville (Philadelphia: Fortress, 1977; with an introduction by James Barr, London: SPCK, 1979). See also B. F. Meyer, "Conversion and the Hermeneutics of Consent," in *Critical Realism*, 58-75.

# PART ONE

1

# ORIENTATIONS

Among observations, new and cogent, to emerge in the research of the past decade there have been: Hanna Wolff's retrieval of aspects of Jesus' personality, all grounded in the psychosexual integration that made him "the freest man" in antiquity;[1] Marcus Borg's retrieval of Jesus' attack on "the holiness paradigm" regnant in Israel;[2] and C. F. D. Moule's reflective distillation of "the gravamen against Jesus."[3] We have moreover profited from a resolute winnowing out of the more absurd proposals on Jesus,[4] an impressive treatment of the messianic-sapiential aspects of Jesus' teaching,[5] and a rich, if still unresolved, many-sided debate on the theme of the Son of man.[6]

But the phrase "new horizons" in the subheading is not meant to denote new observations, new developments, new proposals. It does not refer to anything new in research. Rather, it refers (in this era of intense focus on the reader) to possibilities in the life of the reader, i.e., to the reader's own horizons.

One's horizons change: not often perhaps, nor easily, but we do move from one set of horizons to another. Old horizons yield to new when it turns out that the old cannot accommodate some quite new and irresistibly persuasive truth or value. The theme and referent of the present study (long before the present writer or his readers came onto the human scene) claim to be just such a potent, ever-new truth and value.

We shall return in a moment to horizons. Meantime, there is the matter of saying what the purposes and emphases of the book are, partly in relation to recent research.

We begin with two observations, the first on "the restoration of Israel," the second, on the debate over eschatology.

We are building on what is now, I think, an established thesis: that "the reign of God" (*he basileia tou theou/malkûta* *de³laha³*)—the phrase as Jesus used it referred to the triumph of God at the end of time[7]—had in its first (as it would have in its final) manifestations an earthly side: the definitive restoration/salvation of Israel.[8] The two sides together, the triumph of God and the restoration of Israel, which entailed or included the salvation of the nations, defined the aims of Jesus. The point of his mission had been salvation in accord with the promise of the scriptures, i.e., by restoring his people and so saving the nations (through the assimilation to Israel that is caught in "the eschatological pilgrimage" of the nations).[9] If *this*, and not otherwise, was how God willed to establish his reign, the role of Jesus was precisely the role classically attributed to the royal Messiah: that of the messianic master-builder of the temple of the last days, for the son of David/son of God was appointed to build God's house (2 Sam 7=1 Chron 17; Hag 2; Zech 6).

It has seemed to me that the bond between the reign of God and the restoration of Israel, attested in the scriptures and reflected in the prayers of the Synagogue, offers the final explanation of why "new covenant," and hence "new temple" and "new cult," were thematically correlative to Jesus' all-commanding proclamation.[10] A main reason why such correlations, though clear to the ancients, have been so difficult for us to retrieve is our still common failure to savor our extraordinarily rich inheritances from Israel—the utter Jewishness of Christian origins and foundations.[11] —and the bonds, patterns, structures that obtain in that inheritance.

In this matter of legacy Greek tradition yielded perforce to the tradition of Israel. Gregory Dix showed why this was, sending a piercing shaft of light onto our half-aware image of the ancient world: there were no great penitents, he pointed out, in the Greek and Hellenistic sphere, nothing even remotely reminiscent of the depths plumbed by Jeremiah and the book of Psalms.[12] Looking back from our present vantage point, we are more alert than our predecessors (of, say, 1890-1940) were to the ambiguity, almost sinister ambiguity, of the drive to find Christian origins in the pagan world. Herman Gunkel, his colleagues and successors harbored far too narrow a conception of syncretism and, moreover, misidentified many phenomena in early Christianity as originally pagan and in their new context as instances of syncretism."[13]

Gospel data on Christian origins begin with John the Baptist and Jesus and from the start set the fulfillment theme in high relief, presenting distinct modes of fulfillment: the advent of an appointed time; the realization of promises and prophecies; the appearance of eschatological antitypes. In our view (and, perhaps, somehow conscious in John, in Jesus, and in their followers, as well), the actuality of fulfillment transcended the terms of the to-be-fulfilled. To those looking back from a historically conscious vantage point, it did so in the mode of *sublation* (not, to be sure, in Hegel's sense of synthesis resolving subsidiary contradictions, i.e., fulfillment trumping and cancelling the fulfilled, but in the sense that Karl Rahner and Bernard Lonergan attached to the word: fulfillment transforms and enriches the fulfilled, affirming and establishing it on a new basis). This sets a challenging task for whoever wishes to recover the horizons, perspectives, purposes of the gospel story's *dramatis personae.*

Before settling down to measure the challenge, however, one might find oneself taken aback by recent, confident charges of its irrelevance. Research taking an aggressive social-scientific tack has in the past few years made a point of bypassing such data, questions, and projects, calling them into question as abstract or artificial, and so doubtfully relevant to history. True, "fulfillment" themes are not a standard part of social-scientific inquiry. Nevertheless, the bond between the historian's desire to avail himself of social-scientific resources and this negative stance on data prominent in the gospels and apparently crucial to its *dramatis personae* seems gratuitous and easily reversible.

It has gradually become clear that what differentiates recent efforts to reconstruct the Jesus movement historically lies only partly on the level of technical resources, questions, and proposals. More decisively, it turns on value judgments in a broad sense. What claim does "theologically oriented" research make to historical realism? We might begin with a hard-headed historical question. What emerged, historically, from the Jesus movement?

What emerged, and immediately emerged, from the Jesus movement was the Church. Furthermore, the developmental process that issued in the Church was rectilinear. Rituals—baptism and "the (eucharistic) breaking of the bread"—were hallmarks of the movement in its earliest post-Easter form. These ascertainments create a certain *a priori* expectation, swiftly and massively confirmed by the relevant data, that the Jesus movement itself was irreducible to the socio-political reform or renewal movement proposed by some sociologically oriented research (Theissen, Borg, Horsley, others).

These reconstructions have often been accompanied by a sharp recoil from the evidence of apocalyptic eschatology. Entertained only occasionally in recent secondary literature (though everywhere affirmed or supposed by the sources) is the possibility that, since in his every word and symbolic act Jesus struck and sustained the distinctive note of *the climactic and the definitive*, he conceived his mission—from start to finish, wholly and entirely—in precisely that mode. This is among the underlying, if unacknowledged, issues in the debate over eschatology.

Dale C. Allison's dissertation, *The End of the Ages Has Come* made a significant contribution to this sphere of research. His main purpose was to account for the emergence of the early Chrisitian phenomenon of "realized eschatology." This he did by reference to the interpretation of Jesus' suffering and death as belonging to the great eschatological tribulation and of his resurrection as belonging to the eschatological resurrection of the dead. Along the way he dealt with alternative treatments of eschatology, arguing, for example, that the eschatology of the gospels and of Paul cannot be reduced to metaphor (as it had been by G. B. Caird and others). Allison argued that a merely metaphorical eschatology is improbably attributed to a person or movement promoting the expectation of "imminent" or "proximate" consummation.[14] I would add a further criticism of the hypothesis of metaphorical eschatology: it strips the mission of Jesus of a feature alien to the categories (provisional, pragmatic, etc.) of the modern and contemporary West, but intrinsic to the mission of Jesus, namely, "definitiveness." Jesus was the one after whom Israel was to await no other. (This "definitiveness," to be sure, did not make the accomplishing of his mission one whit less open to the traits that it bore, in fact, originality and finesse, imagination, resourcefulness and improvisation.)[15]

Social description and sociological analysis have impinged—in part eccentrically, in part constructively—on historical inquiry into Christian origins. The eccentricities have mainly derived from the still unresolved problem of correlating social-scientific frames of reference with "the participant viewpoints" of Jesus, his disciples, and the early Christians. Among signs of constructive reflection in this sphere of research is the critique that Richard A. Horsley has brought to bear on

Gerd Theissen's pioneer sociological analysis of the Jesus movement.[16] Horsley persuasively urged that Theissen's analytic project (structural functionalist theory together with its characteristic suppositions and applications) was inapposite to the illumination of the data of ancient Palestine and the New Testament. This, it seems to me, holds for Horsley's own project, as well. His analysis is better conceived and far better argued than Theissen's. On the other hand, it does not plausibly define the *raison d'être* of the Jesus movement, nor does it locate the perspective in which Jesus and his following had to do with hunger, poverty, sickness, demon-possession, and the like.

Still more fundamentally hampering recent historical-Jesus research and the inquiry into Christian origins has been a lethargic contentment with the wholly imaginary and implausible form-critical suppositions of Dibelius and Bultmann (1919 and 1921, respectively) on the origins of the Synoptic tradition.[17] The lack of a fully satisfactory, concretely detailed alternative helps explain, but hardly excuses this contentment. It is difficult to say what has kept the phantom communities of form-critical theory alive. We have no hint of evidence, independent of the form-critics' theorizing, that any early Christian community worked out its life-style, convictions, and policies in the form of stories about Jesus. Meantime, this form-critical mirage has undermined the search for satisfactory, i.e., exigent, ways of judging the historicity and non-historicity of gospel data.[18]

The present study supposes three categories of conclusions on the historicity of data: yes, no, and question-mark. There are some judgments of historicity and non-historicity that are quite certain, but the great mass of them belong within the range of modest to solid probability. I assume neither historicity nor non-historicity "till proved otherwise." This refusal to found judgments of gospel data on assumption *eo ipso* entails the need and legitimacy of the "question-mark" or suspended-judgment category. It also highlights the need for indices to non-historicity. No conclusion on the historical status of gospel data should be drawn on the basis of assumption. Non-historicity is as much in need of specific and positively persuasive argument as historicity is.

In what follows I have resisted the temptation to specify grounds for every instance of a historical judgment. The book will not, then be laden with notes on the historicity of data. Mainly, I rely on discontinuity of data with early Christian beliefs and practices and—a distinct index—on originality vis-à-vis Judaism. Where neither of these obtains, I do not feel compelled to drop the matter, but attempt to take account of subsidiary indices such as multiple and multiform attestaton, and personal idiolect and idiom. (This interest in the particularities of language and style is equally central to the indices to non-historicity.) I do not feel obliged to offer a fully articulated account of every datum. Above all, I see nothing wrong with leaving a considerable number of texts in the question-mark column. (A fuller treatment of these matters, including the important role that repudiation of the form-critical account of the origin of the Synoptic material plays in judgments of historicity may be found in the essay,"Objectivity and Subjectivity in Historical Criticism of the Gospels."[19]

Judgments on data are indispensable, but only a beginning. More important, finally, are ascertainments that ermege from new questions and new ways of bringing data into constellation. New understandings of data follow the realization that such-and-such data pertain to some pattern that had gone unrecognized. Several examples will be found in the chapters that follow, e.g., there is significant fallout from the retrieval of Jesus' conviction that *all* the scriptures must now come to *complete* fulfillment. Again, "flawless personal authenticity" (a term recalling existentialist buzzwords from mid-century but now newly defined in the context of intentionality analysis) emerges as a source both of Jesus' personal style and of his teachings. Again, Rudolf Pesch's insight into the crisis instigated by the prospect of Israel's rejection of the mission of Jesus offers the best explanation yet available of why Jesus was led to ask his disciples: "Who do men say that I am?"

It seems to me counterproductive to demand heavy attestation as a condition of historicity. Heavy attestation is welcome, but it is not to be expected in every instance of solid historicity. Research has too often found itself at sea when the sole reasonable explanation of a given set of phenomena appears to be lightly attested at best. But what is this hesitation except the old positivist prejudice that *data*, or *rules* relating to data, should be called upon to take the place of historical intelligence? Collingwood ridiculed the lack of imagination and intelligence reflected in this methical inhibition. In some instances, of course, this twofold poverty derives from a counterposition (an error of philosophic orientation). But in many others it is a defect corrected by coming to understand and exploit heuristic resources and procedures *over and above* the "indices to the historicity of (more or less isolated) data"—

over and above discontinuity, originality, multiform and multiple attestation, irreducibly personal idiom, and characteristic modes of speech.

Some examples of this bafflement: the issue of "the remnant (of Israel)." The word "remnant" does not occur in the gospels. Often this sort of negative observation is enough by itself to kill interest in a potentially significant issue. Parallel and related instances: the theme of the Church (the word "Church" shows up in the gospels only twice, both times in Matthew, both times in texts betraying the marks of either pre-redacitonal or redactional composition); the covenat theme (the word occurs only in the eucharisitic words); the atonement theme (the Greek word of "atonement, expiation" is absent from the gospels, and the theme is rare enough in the gospels that it, too, seems pracically limited to the eucharistic words); and the theme of election. *Eklogē/* election does not occur in the gospel literature. Still, as many have remarked, the issue has thematic status in the words of John and is repeatedly implicit in those of Jesus.)

Now, every one of these themes is not only authentic, that is not only had its place in Jesus' field of vision/horizon, but was *central* to his consciousness of mission, to its development, to the conflict that brought him to his death. It is not so much the mechanical application of indices to the historicity of data, but rather the line of argument reflecting an effort to understand the story, that terminates in positive judgments of historicity in these cases (though each case is distinct, and the probability of historicity is not equal in them all). It is by no coincidence that this comes to light exclusively in work free of positivist bias and other consciously or unconsciously cultivated illusions, and by the pervasive presence of a Pascalian *esprit de finesse* (I think especially of the work of Schürmann, Jeremias, Stuhlmacher, Hofius, Pesch, and others).

Among the numerous neurosis-like hangovers from the late-nineteenth-century positivist era has been a crabbed conception of "data." (In the 1930s Collingwood recalled the debate, not still raging then but still echoing, so to speak, in the minds of historians, over whether "unwritten sources" could be considered among the historian's legitimate data).[20] Accompanying this vapid approach to method has been the reductionof a few rules-of-thumb of ways of evaluating data. It is a melancholy observation that in current historical-Jesus research such habits easily survived the era of kerygma theology and still pass for "rigor." (The one thing worse is altogether skipping the appeal to criteria or indices in favor of intuition, literary or sociological.)

The intended accents of the present book come down to a few related themes: *election* as the *enjeu*, the "what-is-at-stake," in the response of Israel to John and to Jesus; Jesus' view of his contemporaries of the house of Israel, namely, as "lost sheep" (Matt 10:6; 16:24) or "sheep without a shepherd" (Matt 9:36=Mark 6:34; cf. Exek 34:5); the eschaton as an utterly transcendent order, which accounts for why "the Law and the prophets" are consigned to the pre-eschatological past of the life of Israel as its essential denomination; and the gap between prophetic knowledge (symbolic and schematic) and its real referents (non-symbolic events and non-symbolic time).

The chapters to follow will commend these related points. Here I shall offer a word on each of them.

Election: for both John the Baptist and Jesus of Nazareth the status of the nation in the eyes of God turned on its response to God's climactic and definitive call. No second-rank motif, this is a consciously basic component of both missions. Among the Baptist's most trenchant warnings was that "God can raise up sons to Abraham out of these stones!" (Matt 3:9=Luke 3:8). To overlook this is to miss a crucial element in the drama of both missions.

Leadership: the political government of Israel was shared by the Romans, who ruled Judea and Samaria, and the "ethnarch" Herod Antipas, who ruled Galilee and Perea (Transjordan) in dependence on Rome. The religious leadership was essentially the priesthood (in particular, the higher clergy, i.e., the high-priest and the priests in charge of the temple). Influential elites included the schools of piety: the Sadducees (counting among their constituents the Jerusalem aristocracy and the greater part of the higher clergy) and the Pharisees (chiefly of the merchant and artisan classes). *John and Jesus both disparaged these parties*, together with their leadership of sages or "scribes." Jesus' uncompromising view of this elite found expression in the image of the blind leading the blind (Matt 15:14b).[21] Like contemporary revisionist history, recurrent efforts to make Jesus a sympathizer of Pharisaism, or even indistinguishable from Pharisaism, not infrequently betray a tacitly programmatic component (no real conflict between Judaism and Jesus). Meantime, the issue of what historically brought Jesus to his death—the gravamen against Jesus—remains a vital and telling issue.

The eschaton: both of these prophetic figures proclaimed the end (resurrection, last judgment, final salvation) as imminent. Both conceived this final divine visitation in absolute and transcendent (apocalypticizing) terms. Current conceptions of Jesus (e.g., as "reformer" or leader of a "peace-party" in the politics of the time) seem hardly more persuasive than the many stillborn efforts of Liberal theologians from the mid-nineteenth century to the time of Albert Schweitzer, who reported on their scores of failed "lives." To judge from the language of both John and Jesus, the eschaton they announced surpassed by far all such pedestrian categories ad "reform." (This holds all the more for efforts to limit the aims of Jesus to the creation of a healthier society, with minimal reference to such "abstract" issues as election, judgment, and the like.)

Finally, there is the issue raised by the seventeenth-century deists and still left unresolved by their successors. Were John and Jesus "mistaken" about the end? How ought one to deal with the gap between the "visions" of these prophets and the reality of ongoing history? We would like to sort these matters out, and to do so in a way that allows us to go finally beyond the sphere of description to that of a prospective understanding and judgment on these missions.

We conclude by dealing briefly with the theme of horizons

"Horizons," the boundaries of my field of vision, are also, by metaphorical extension, the boundaries of all I know and care about. Within their limits I find insight exciting, argument cogent, value authentic. The strange thing, the frightening thing, is that all this—so basic, so indispensable—is not simply given to me, not simply available, guaranteed, automatic. It somehow depends on me, personally.  For, my horizons are the product of my life-history. And the correspondence of my horizons not only to the realities they disclose but to the real simply, i.e., to the order of what is intelligible, true, real, good, beautiful, holy is not simply delivered to me. I have no pledge whatever that *the real* and *what seems real to me* are one and the same. Yet—isn't this a face of life?—we must plead with one another to admit this bare possibility. So Augustine to Jerome: "It might just possibly be the case that what you think is not the same as what the truth is" (*Epistula 73*).

We are all aware that the human mind is not equally open to all ideas. It is quite unlike a great plaza

where all may come and go as they please. On the

> contrary, it is itself a unity, and it imposes unity on
> its contents—so much so that every apprehension of
> data involves, quite naturally and spontaneously, a
> kind of selection, and every selection in turn includes
> an initial structuring, and every structuring prepares
> and in a certain sense anticipates future judgments.[22]

Among the major flaws in naive realism is the identification of natural, given, common-to-the-species, "transcendental" horizons—the drive to the intelligible, the true, the real, the good; in short, the drive to being —with the horizons that (operationally, so to speak) happen to be mine.

My horizons are my own, but happily (and thanks precisely to the above-mentioned "drive to being") they are open to adjustment, improvement, change. Again, the literal act of seeing illuminates our metaphorical horizons. The line between land and sky that I see from any given vantage point changes as I move. So, too, as I move through time, as tomorrow becomes and keeps becoming today, keeps turning into a longer yesterday, my metaphorical boundaries change, too. I never, perhaps, altogether lose what I once found enthralling, but it invariably loses some, and sometimes all, of its hold on me. And so for everything, for every development, every bend and twist and turn, every forward step, every sudden or slow reversal.

Change *within* a given set of horizons is never so radical and reorienting as a change *of* horizons, a migration from one set of horizons to another. This kind of change is never wholly at my own disposition. I can take up writing poetry, but cannot simply, successfully, decide to be a genuine poet, any more than, by sheer will, I can be a high-diver, much less a world-class high-diver. I cannot even simply decide that, after half a lifetime as a democrat, I shall henceforward start thinking as a totalitarian—or vice versa. One can hardly alter a political allegiance within the spectrum of democratic options without passing through some densely compacted experiences, reconsiderations, revaluations. Far greater changes, such as a change of horizons, do not take place without some discernible cause or set of causes; but they also do not take place without some freely self-orienting act of my own. Hence, Joseph de Finance could name this exercise—that is, the changing of one's horizons—an act of "vertical liberty."[23] Self-orientation is a radical act. The test of its authenticity is a good conscience.

What normally brings about a change of horizons is the incapacity of the old, familiar horizons to accommodate some new ascertainment that imposes itself as a discovery. Here conflict, though not inevitable, is commonplace; for, although I am not entirely at the mercy of the horizons habitual to me, they do powerfully impinge on me. Temperament and cast of mind, values, preferences, and tastes, the whole of what has entered into and shaped my horizons may lead me to postpone attending to the new ascertainment, or to quash and partly forget it, or qualify it to death. But it may also happen—in fact, it happens again and again—that the new ascertainment will not be denied. Of course, there is also the possibility that the new ascertainment may be delightedly, even joyously welcomed, like the pearl of great price for whose sake the merchant sold all he had.

# NOTES

1. Hanna Wolff, *Jesus the Therapist* (Oak Park, IL: Meyer-Stone, 1987).

2. Marcus J. Borg, *Conflict.*

3. C. F. D. Moule, "The Gravamen Against Jesus," in *Jesus, the Gospels, and the Church* [W. R. Farmer Festschrift] (ed.) E. P. Sanders (Macon: Mercer University Press, 1987) 177-195. See also Moule's follow-up essay, "Jesus, Judaism, and Paul," in *Tradition and Interpretation in the New Testament* [E. E. Ellis Festschrift] (eds.) G. F. Hawthorn and Otto Betz (Grand Rapids: Eerdmans; Tübingen: Mohr-Siebeck, 1987) 43-52.

4. E. P. Sanders, *Jesus and Judaism* (London: SCM; Philadelphia: Fortress, 1985). I do not, however, commend Sanders's strictures against the work of Joachim Jeremias.

5. Riesner, *Lehrer*, 304-352.

6. See below, 125, note 9.

7. See Dalman, 135-139.

8. Meyer, *Aims.* Gerhard Lohfink, *Jesus and Community* (New York-Ramsey: Paulist; Philadelphia: Fortress, 1984); Sanders, *Jesus and Judaism.* The doctrine of the coming resurrection of the dead and the biblical imagery of new heaven and new earth, of the banquet of the saved with the patriarchs, and so on, ground the reference to "final manifestations" on earth of the triumph of

God. Peter R. Ackroyd, *Exile and Restoration* (London: SCM, 1968; Philadelphia: Westminster, 1975) provides a rich documentation of the thematic bonds, established in scriptures dating from the sixth century, among "new creation," the kingdom/kingship of God, the restoration of Israel, the new temple, the remnant of Israel, the new people, and so on. This sixth-century thematic constellation found its counterpart in the mode of fulfillment in the intentions, words, and symbolic acts of Jesus.

9. Jeremias, *Jesus' Promise.*

10. Jeremias, *Eucharistic,* 225-237, esp. 226 ("covenant" is Korrelat-Begriff of "reign of God").

11. J. Neusner thinks otherwise. See "The Absoluteness of Christianity and the Uniqueness of Judaism. Why Salvation is Not of the Jews," *Interpretation* 43 (1989) 18-31. The issue turns on the status attributed to the theme of "holiness, sanctification" (which, to be sure, was the reigning paradigm in Judaism before and after Jesus).

12. Gregory Dix, *Jew and Greek* (Westminster: Dacre Press, 1953).

13. Hermann Gunkel, *Zum religionsgeschichtlichen Verständnis des Neuen Testaments* (Göttingen: Vanderhoeck & Ruprecht, 1903). Rudolf Bultmann, *Primitive Christianity in its Contemporary Setting* (New York: World [Meridian], 1956) 177-203. Cf. Meyer, *Early Christians:*, 188-193.

14. Allison, *Ages,* 88. The argument has point, though it is not compelling. It is surprising that in an epilogue devoted to theological reflections on eschatology, Allison himself presents eschatology in metaphorical terms: religious interpretation of human existence must take account of polarities and contradictions; hence the use of eschatological language, etc. More fundamental and central, however, is that eschatology defines and establishes the mission of Jesus and the status of the Church as climactic, definitive, normative.

15. Originality: proclamation of the reign of God; symbolic acts like table fellowship with notorious sinners; the act of connecting symbolic acts (choice and sending of twelve; cures and exorcisms; table fellowship with notorious sinners) with the proclamation of the reign of God; Jesus' celibacy; his break with numerous parts of scribal halaka; valorization of depressed classes: *the simple* (including the socially insignificant, e.g., the poor; women; children), *the afflicted* (the ill, physically and psychically; the destitute; the miserable); *the outcast* ("sinners"). Finesse: non-use of grandiose rhetoric; avoidance or refusal of titles in public. Imagination: symbolic acts; extra-ordinary parabolic teaching. Resourcefulness and improvisation: in the face of refusal by the establishment and the prospect of national refusal, the laying of a new basis (acknowledgement of him as Messiah; his own expiatory self-offering) on which to prepare the disciples for a harsh future, which would include their renewed missionary appeal to Israel after his death.

16. Richard A. Horsley, *Sociology and The Jesus Movement* (New

York: Crossroad, 1989) 13-64.

17. Standard Bible Dictionaries provide information on the sociological dimension of the classical New Testament form-critics' account of the origins of the Synoptic tradition.

18. Given classical form-critical suppositions about the origins of the gospel tradition, an exigent use of indices to historicity and non-historicity appears to be otiose. The result is an easy lapsing into implausibility. Horsley, *Sociology*, 121f., for example, conjectures that the traditions on Jesus' initiatives toward notorious sinners—among the best instances of simultaneous discontinuity with early Christianity and originality vis-à-vis Judaism—are unhistorical. Burton L. Mack, *The Myth of Innocence* (Philadelphia: Fortress, 1988) exhibits throughout an approach to issues of historicity that borders on caprice.

19. *Critical Realism*, 129-145. Reprinted in D. L. Duggan (ed.) *The Interrelations of the Gospels* (Louvain, Peeters, 1990) 546-560.

20. Collingwood, *The Idea of History* (Oxford: Oxford University Press, 1946) 276-277. Collingwood located the key to the enlargement of historical knowledge in the well-stocked intelligence of the historian, not in the hunt for new data. The advance of knowledge, he argued, "comes about mainly through finding how to use as evidence this or that kind of perceived fact which historians have hitherto thought useless to them." *Idea*, 247.

21. Burney, *Poetry*, 133.

22. Bernard Lonergan, *The Way to Nicea* (Philadelphia: Westminster, 1976) 7.

23. Joseph de Finance, *Essai sur l'agir humain* (Rome: Gregorian University Press, 1962) 287-291.

## 2

## "PHASES" IN JESUS' MISSION

The earliest moments of Jesus' mission have not drawn the intense attention that they deserve. The main reason is that the relevant data derive from the Johannine tradition. Independent and fascinating, these data offer the first of many test-cases for the viability of John's gospel as a source of historical information, and provide a distinctive view of the setting in which Jesus' public career took shape. At the same time, they partly overlap with Synoptic data. Both resources locate the "call" of Jesus (the baptism alluded to in John 1:33b and depicted by the Synoptists) in the environment of the Baptist's mission. If, furthermore, John the Evangelist is right in having Jesus begin his active public career as a baptist (John 3:22), we are supplied with a compelling reason why the Baptist's arrest signaled a major juncture in Jesus' public activity. Though the Synoptists offer no more than the bare wisp of an acknowledgement of this transition, the transition calls for historical inquiry, insight, ascertainment.

Furthermore, we should take some account of the last phase of Jesus' earthly mission, of which recent analysis, literary and historical, has been lacking, and older analysis has left much to be desired. Everyone knows that in the organization of Synoptic narrative, the Caesarea Philippi pericopes are assigned a more or less cardinal role. But it seems that something is missing from the explanation of this basic fact. The fact is clear enough, but the "why" behind it is not at all clear. Below I wish to propose an answer to the question of what accounts for the cardinal role of the Caesarea Philippi pericopes. Purely literary considerations seem not to explain it. Are there elements of a historical explanation? Was there a historical development that has lain buried under the surface of literary phenomena? If so, what was it?

## Data on the Earliest Phase of Jesus' Public Career

Following the hieratic prose of the Prologue, the fourth Gospel depicts the opening of Jesus' public ministry under an implied heading: *hē marturia tou Iôannou*= "John's testimony" (John 1:19). "John's testimony" itself has a beginning: an interrogation of the Baptist by a Jerusalem delegation of "priests and levites" (John 1:19-28). This is followed by Jesus' entry onto the scene (presumably still at a ford of the Jordan in Transjordan, near Bethany) and John's testimony to him: "There is the lamb of God, who is to take away the sin of the world!" (John 1:29; cf. Isa 53:7,12).[1] Thus, it is from a distinctively Johannite (John-the-Baptist-related) angle of vision that the evangelist presents the figure of Jesus to the readership of the gospel. Moreover, the first disciples of Jesus (Andrew and an anonymous figure) are represented as having earlier been disciples of John (John 1:35-37).

The tendency of the Johannine text is, all agree, to narrow the role of the Baptist to a single task: to bear witness to Jesus (John 1:7,8,15,19,32,34) before all Israel (John 1:19,26,31; cf. 1:34,36), ultimately for the sake of mankind (John 1:6-9). This is witness to the fulfillment of scriptural witness: the moment has come for all the scriptures without exception to find their appointed realization. To be sure, the Baptist was well aware of his own place in the scenario of fulfillment. He looked to the future, but he knew that he himself already belonged to the privileged moment at which the scriptures were coming to fulfillment. When pressed, he presented this in the most self-effacing terms that the scriptures allowed. Who was he? The embodiment of the Isaian *qôl qôreˀ bammidbār*, "the voice calling out in the wilderness." That voice called out to comfort Israel, to announce the final restoration of God's people, to "reveal the Lord's glory" before the eyes of all flesh (=all mankind, Isa 40:5). John, however, may have cited the text atomistically, leaving its context aside. In either case, John's revelation, while it included the consigning of the chaff to the fire, had as its central feature the image of the wheat safely stored in the granary or barn. There was a deadly seriousness, but nothing thematically new, in the ruin of the unrepentent. There was a new and mysterious element, however, in the image of the-repentent-and-baptized being cleansed by a purifier who would "baptize" in wind (=the Spirit of God) and fire. This purifier would not be the Lord in person, but another—seemingly apoc-

alyptic-transcendental—figure; for, even apart from the mismatch between "God" and the imagery of "sandals" (Mark 1:7=Matt 3:11=Luke
3:16), there would be little point in John's protest of unworthiness vis-
à-vis God (Matt 3:11b=Luke 3:16b=Mark 1:7), but some point in his
protesting it vis-à-vis God's unknown agent appointed to mediate the
climactic saving act.

If we ask after the *raison d'être* of the Baptist's introducing
this figure into the scenario of the end-time, we might begin by excluding reasons other than this one: John was persuaded that the scriptures
themselves imposed it. It was an imperative of biblical fulfillment. But
if "scripture" is the key, what scripture was in question? We shall take
up three answers. First, we do not know. Second, the Messiah.[2] Third,
the Son of man.

It is true that we have no firm hold on an answer. But the possible candidates are narrowed down by a single clue: the figure in question was to have the decisive role in the judgment. We have it from
elsewhere that John awaited "the coming one" (Matt 11:3=Luke 7:19),
in all probability "the Messiah" (Ps 118:26). But the scriptures do not
assign the royal son of David a role in the judgment. John's own role
was to prepare Israel by repentance, confession, and a cleansing rite in
anticipation of an irresistible cosmic event. If the scriptures are our sole
plausible guide, what possible mediator of this event could there be,
other than the "one like a (son of) man"?

The figure originally intended by the symbol of the "one like a
(son of) man" was probably the angel/prince assigned to champion Israel: Michael (Dan 10:13,21; 12:1). Numerous scholars, beginning with
John A. Emerton,[3] have furthermore convincingly shown that the scene
of the Ancient of Days and of one like a man coming on clouds derived
from an age-old mythological scene featuring the father-god ᵓEl and
Baᶜl, "the Cloud Rider."

In the wake of the book of Daniel, the Baᶜl/Michael figure was
reinterpreted and merged with both the royal Messiah and the Isaian
Servant of the Lord.[4] Moreover, it may well have been on the basis of
the Daniel text itself that post-biblical tradition attributed the judgment-
role to "the Son of man," for (a) Dan 7:22 can be (mis)read to say that
the saints of the Most High were given not merely the winning verdict
in the judgment but the active role of judging (Dan 7:22, *wĕdînā᾽ yĕhîb
lĕqaddîšê ᶜelyônîn* = "judgment was given to [rather than for] the saints

of the Most High"), and (b) there is at least a functional correlation of the saints of the Most High with the one like a (son of) man" (Dan 7:13-14=7:17-18 =7:22b).

As for John the Baptist's references to the coming judge, his mysterious, figurative language (Matt 3:11-12=Luke 3:16-17; cf. Mark 1:8) strikes an apocalyptic note, and there is no scripturally attested candidate for a figure distinct from the Lord himself and associated with the judgment, other than the figure of the "one like a man" in Dan 7. If we compare the task of "the Man" in 4 Ezra 13 (judgment of the nations and restoration of Israel) with the task of the figure who "holds the winnowing fork in his hand" (Matt 3:12a=Luke 3:17a), they do seem to correlate. (This, to be sure, does not prove the existence in John's time of some extrabiblical tradition on "the Man" nor, much less, John's dependence on it. It helps us, however, to estimate how plausible it is that John should have associated this figure with the judgment about to take place.)

For us the most important point is not to establish that the Baptist correlated the roles of Messiah and Son of man; it is rather to confirm the positive probability of what the gospel of John proposes, namely, that Jesus was the Baptist's ally, leading a baptizing movement alongside John (John 3:22-26). This readily accords with the Synoptists, all of whom specify that the beginning of Jesus' independent public career had its point of departure in the arrest of John. The Synoptic gospels, however, do not explain why Jesus remained in Judea until after the Baptist's arrest. Somewhat implausibly perhaps, they leave it to be assumed that John's arrest quite coincidentally followed almost on the heels of the baptism of Jesus. By contrast, the fourth gospel offers the first limb of an explanation: Jesus in the first phase of his public career was in Judea as a baptizer already surrounded by a circle of disciples. The Synoptists have simplified here as elsewhere, opening the story with what in fact was the second phase of Jesus' mission, that of prophet, first in Galilee, of the reign of God (Matt 4:17=Mark 1:15).

If John was "the voice" alluded to in Isa 40:3, we are given a first clue to his appearance in the desert. He construed Isa 40:3a to read: "a voice crying out *in the desert*." Not only was the triumphal march of God to Zion to cross the wilderness,

Make straight in the desert/a highway for our God! (40:3b)

but the voice announcing this would itself ring out *in the desert.*

Might the Baptist's self-designation by reference to Isa 40:3 have been related to the passage on the *měbaśśēr* in Isa 52? We do not know and are not told. Since atomistic citation was common, we cannot with assurance attribute to John connections among texts. Moreover, the burden of the message of the *měbaśśēr* was the reign of Israel's God; but, as we shall see, the association of "reign of God" with John was a Matthean move (3:2), pre-redactional or redactional.

The call that John addressed to Israel had nothing of the "take it or leave it" character of a purely personal initiative. John was consciously a prophet: With his appearance prophecy, after long silence, returned to Israel.[5] Response to his call was not optional. On it hinged the status of Israel (Matt 3:9=Luke 3:8).

If the judgment be taken as the matrix of John's field of meaning, the probable nexus binding all the motifs of his preaching together was the well-established conception of Israel in the wilderness (Exodus to Deuteronomy) as the type of eschatological Israel. We have had a mass of learned conjecture on the conceptual resources explaining John's prophetic adoption of the baptismal rite. The late Bo Reicke offered an expert survey in one of his last essays.[6] It remains very difficult to know just how probably the resources of halakic and haggadic lore are brought to bear on John and his prophetic program. So far, the least unsatisfactory conjecture, perhaps, is that which relates John's baptism, on the basis of the typological correspondence of "beginning" and "end" (the *Urzeit/Endzeit* schema) to the generation of the wilderness. In this view, the generation of the wilderness was readied for the revelation and covenant of Sinai by a bath of immersion. Where in the scriptures is this said? It is not said, but simply inferred from the conclusion of the great covenant scene: "Then Moses took the blood and sprinkled it on the people" (Exod 24:8). The premise of the inference is that there is no sprinkling without previous bath of immersion (cf. *b. Yeb* 46b).[7] Further: we know that Paul found just such a baptismal "bath" in Israel's escape from Pharaoh through the sea (1 Cor 10:1-2). On the principle of correlation between beginning and end, Israel in the endtime was to be made ready for the definitive act of God by being bathed and purified.

If it is Israel that is judged, it is Israel that is saved; but as judgment entails the burning of the chaff, saved Israel—as well as Israel en route to salvation—is (with reference to "all Israel") a remnant: "the remnant of Israel." The data on John allow us to conclude with maximum probability that his purpose was to make ready the salvation of the remnant of Israel.[8] Elsewhere I have dealt with the objections, numerous but spurious, to this conclusion. Refusal of John's mission— a solid segment of the religious elite refused it—meant exclusion from restored and saved Israel. The responsive and repentant would be gathered like wheat; the recusant, burnt like chaff. In the open, eschatological remnant of those destined for acquittal at the judgment, God would bring his people to full and final restoration in the age to come.

## Transition from Phase One to Phase Two

The gospels (Mark 1:4; Matt 4:12; Luke 4:14) present Jesus as finding in the arrest of John a divine signal for himself (John was "delivered up [by God]," *paradothē,* Matt 4:12=Mark 1:14; and the response of Jesus was "under the power of the Spirit," *en tę dunamei tou pneumatis,* Luke 4:14). With his disciples (John 4:3; cf.1:35-51; 2:2,12; 3:22-24) he withdrew to Galilee and inaugurated a new moment in his mission: proclamation of the reign of God (Synoptic tradition). The gospels do not deal with the question (but historians should raise it): Why did Jesus cease to baptize? Why did he launch his new campaign? If the available data do not provide an answer, they at least make it clear (a) that Jesus took the baptismal rite to be decisively bound up with John's mission, but that (b) this was to be preliminary to another, fuller, more richly-faceted mission.

A certain limited light is thrown on the matter by a Synoptic text with significant variations: "Since the days of John the Baptist till now the reign of heaven has been subjected to violence, and the violent are taking it by force. For until John all the prophets and the Law foretold things to come . . . " (Matt 11:12-13). The Lukan (quasi) parallel: "The Law and the prophets [were] until John; since then the reign of God is proclaimed and everyone forces his way into it" (Luke 16:16).

Our interest focuses on the turning point of the ages. The era prior to the outbreak of the eschaton was one of promise, "the Law and the prophets"; and Judaism envisaged a new era that would endorse, ratify, enhance, fulfill the Law and the prophets. At Qumran "the sons of light," fully conscious of themselves as the community of "the new covenant," made it their chief business *to study the Law and the prophets*. Here we hear a different accent. The Law and prophets held sway "until . . ." Just how to fill out the rest of the "until . . ." clause depends on whether we judge the Matthean or the Lukan form of this logion to be original.

According to the Matthean text the days of John open the new era. This corresponds to a later rabbinic formulation which makes "until the days of" in the phrase "the prophets prophesy until the days of . . . " specify the moment of fulfillment.[9] But that this is the sense of the Lukan form is not at all sure. First, some literary observations. Elements in both forms that we can say from the start are secondary are italicised. The Matthean form: "Since the days of John *the Baptist* till now the reign *of heaven* has been subjected to violence, and the violent are taking it by force. For until John all the prophets and the Law *foretold things to come* . . ." (Matt 11:12-13). The Lukan parallel: "The Law and the prophets [were] until John; since then the reign of God *is proclaimed (euaggelizetai*=gospelled) and everyone forces his way into it" (Luke 16:16).[10]

A capital difference between the two texts lies in how they read "until" in the phrase "until John" (*heōs* in Matthew, *mechri* in Luke, translation variants of Aramaic *ʿad)*. Is it meant inclusively: "up to and including John"? Or exclusively: "up to but excluding John"? Jeremias offers an entirely convincing analysis:

> If *heōs/mechri* is meant to be inclusive . . . then the Baptist still belongs to the time of the old aeon. This was Luke's understanding. For he keeps stressing in Acts that the time of salvation began after the death [better: after the arrest] of John the Baptist (1:5; 10:37; 13:24f.; 19:4). On the other hand, the Matthean tradition understood the *heōs/mechri* exclusively, as the phrase *apo de tōn hēmerōn Iōannou* (11:12) shows. . . . The more difficult statement is without question that which sees the Baptist as the inaugurator of the new aeon. The early church had an understandable tendency to subordinate the Baptist to Jesus. Where he is set alongside Jesus we always have a sign of ancient tradition.[11]

While it is hardly possible to recover the whole primitive text, which

includes the still unresolved, famously enigmatic *crux* on the reign of
God "suffering violence," this much does seem recoverable, a distich in
synthetic parallelism and 4-beat rhythm:

> ⁾ôrāyĕtā⁾ ûnĕbî⁾ ayyā⁾ ʿad yômê yôhānān
> min hākā⁾ ûlĕhālā⁾ malkûtā⁾ deʾlāhā⁾[12]:
> The law and the prophets to the days of John /
> from then and henceforward the reign of God!

The antithesis ("Law and prophets" vs. "reign of God") is crystal clear.
Ambiguity respects certain particulars: first, whether ʿ*ad* is inclusive or
exclusive. The Lukan tradents opted for the first, keeping the Baptist in
the old aeon. The Matthean tradents opted for the second, which led
them to reformulate in Greek: "*apo de tōn hēmerōn Iōannou . . .* "
(Their discerning choice may have occasioned the tradition's attributing
to John an otherwise unattested proclamation of the reign of God; cf.
Matt 3:2). Second, there is an ambiguity about *how,* exactly, the Law
and the prophets mark the old aeon and how the reign of God marks the
new. Lukan tradents leave the first part unresolved, or perhaps they
thought that the notion of successive "economies" or "orders" was suffi-
ciently clear. (Luke later, will lightly specify the sense of the second
part by adding the verb *euaggelizomai.*) The Matthean option was to
specify the first part by *prophēteuein* (despite a certain awkwardness in
predicating this verb of the Law), and in the second part to highlight the
(to us baffling) "violence" motif.

The Lukan version, at least in order and wording, may well
have been closer to the original text than the Matthean version.[13] But,
as we have already observed, Luke's "is proclaimed/is gospelled" in the
second line may be dropped. It is good Christian idiom, but Jesus himself is not otherwise depicted as using the verb "to gospel/to break news
of salvation" (a word for which Luke has a marked preference) with respect to the reign of God. Further, the passive form of the verb is non-
retrovertible into Aramaic *(bsr* in *ithpaal* does not say "[X] is proclaimed," but "[X] is received/ heard").[14]

There is a dividing line, then, between the old age and the
new. Prior to that dividing line is the era of the Law and the prophets.
This era is ended and a new era launched with the fulfillment event that
is John's appearance in the wilderness and mission to Israel. The words

"the days" of John is an expression supplying for the lack in Semitic languages of an abstract vocabulary of "time." This term for "the time of the activity" of John is furthermore used formally: a given segment of time derives its specificity precisely from John and his mission. If therefore Jesus exercised a ministry of baptism (John 3:22) in some respects independent (John 3:26), still this ministry was defined by the Baptist and his purposes—no doubt a reason for the limited attestation of this aspect of Jesus' public life.

John's appeal to all Israel, launched (according to Luke) in A.D. 28,[15] climaxed, but in transcendent fashion, the time of the Law and prophets. "In transcendent fashion," because John began the era of final fulfillment. When the mission of John came to an end, one integral moment in the unfolding drama of eschatological salvation came to an end with it. Accordingly, the text presents a conscious periodizing: Jesus' reflection on the unfolding of phases in the economy of fulfillment. This alone—and this distich by no means stands alone (cf. the stream of images and thematic motifs setting the present off from the past in virtue of *present fulfillment:* e.g., Luke 7:22=Matt 11:5; Mark 2:19, 21-22; 4:21; 13:28-29)—would be enough to establish that Jesus' mission was eschatological through and through, and that in his own view he wholly belonged to the eschaton.

## The Third and Last Phase of Jesus' Mission

The arrest of John marked the end of the first phase in the scenario of fulfillment, and signalled the immediate opening of a second phase denominated by Jesus' independent proclamation in Galilee of the reign of God. By contrast, the third and last phase of his earthly mission belonged essentially to the esoteric tradition of Jesus' instruction of disciples. It did not signify the end of the preaching of the reign of God. It simply signified the disciples' halting entry into the *secret* of the reign of God.

This third and last phase of Jesus' earthly mission began with the leading question, "Who do men say that I am? . . . And who do *you* say that I am?" It ended with the Last Supper, the trial, the judicial murder of Jesus, his burial.

We do not know how long the ministry of Jesus lasted, nor in what year he died. (The years 30 and 33 have the best probability; neither date imposes itself.) What we do have from the Synoptic tradition is his prediction of coming death—for himself and for his disciples. How the historicity of the prediction is judged turns in large part on whether or not the critic has some grasp of its historic intelligibility.

The kerygma theologians, notably Bultmann, dealt with the prediction as prophecy after the fact (*vaticinium ex eventu*). Joachim Jeremias and Heinz Schürmann offered independent, circumstantially detailed arguments in favor of authenticity.[16] But a true breakthrough on the issue seems to me to have emerged only from a controversy among Catholic exegetes in Germany in the late 1970s on whether the "expiatory death" motif in the various forms of passion prediction (e.g., the eucharistic words) could be reconciled historically with Jesus' proclamation of the reign of God.

Anton Vögtle[17] and, still more emphatically, his pupil Peter Fiedler[18] argued that the two were incompatible. How make sense of a sudden new codicil—the addition of a new, unexplained further condition—to the previously unconditional offer of forgiveness summed up in the proclamation of Jesus? This manner of putting the question had a partly rhetorical ring—but it prompted Rudolf Pesch to offer a suddenly illuminating answer.[19] The motif of expiatory death arose from a newly crystallizing situation: that of Israel's refusal.

A premise insufficiently adverted to by Vögtle and his allies was the election-historical character of Jesus' mission. Like John, Jesus confronted the nation with a message in no way optional, which called for a response in no way optional. Hence an enormous risk. A mission geared to acquittal and life for Israel ran the risk of ending in condemnation and death for Israel. How were the refusers to be saved from themselves? Jesus' answer was the offer of his life, i.e., the will to go to his death in the service of forgiveness.

But was this a solution? It was a solution *only if this expiatory death were itself to be accepted by its beneficiaries.* This implied a distinctive post-Jesus mission to Israel.

New light is thus projected onto the classic question of historicity respecting the esoteric tradition from "Caesarea Philippi" to the end of the earthly story of Jesus. Here we have the historic and dramatic *principle of intelligibility* of this whole line of development. "Who do you say that I am?" no longer need be seen as the retrojection of a doctrinal interest of the post-Easter Christian community. The question, rather, was historically intended to prepare the disciples for the outbreak of the eschatological ordeal and for their witness-role in that ordeal.

The two motifs of "messianic confession" and "prediction of the passion" that together constitute the exchange "in the district of Caesarea Philippi" are related moments (distinct pericopes in Matthew and in Mark, merged in Luke) that find their full rationale in the second motif. Why this is hinges on a retrieval of context.

First, the proclamation of the imminent arrival/advance presence of the reign of God was by that very fact the proclamation of the restoration of Israel (hence one prayed in the *Qaddiš* that God "allow his reign to reign in your lifetime and in your days, and in the lifetime of the whole house of Israel"; cf. the eleventh petition of the *Tepillâ*).[20] But the joyous invitation to enter into Israel's climactic, definitive restoration had an inescapable counterpart: the exclusion of refusers from this same promised destiny.

Second, whether the nation—in solidarity with its leadership or not—were to accept or to repudiate the offer of God's chosen herald (Isa 52:7-9; cf. Mark 1:15=Matt 4:17) and shepherd (Ezek 34; 37; Zech 13; cf. Matt 15:24), *his* attention focused perforce on the remnant flock, large or little, that would accept the offer. In Jesus' scenario of the future,[21] the nation's repudiation of his mission would entail the outbreak of the ordeal of the end-time (Jer 30:5,7; Dan 12:1). In the sphere of significant human acts, the short time left before the end would be filled by the renewed mission of his disciples to Israel (Matt 10:23).[22]

Third, Jesus himself *would not be there* to direct and sustain this missionary witness. Here a key context has been widely overlooked. There are two missionary moments, not merely the one in the present of Jesus' earthly mission. The second would belong to the brief, fierce moment of the eschatological ordeal. It is this second mission that is bound up with motifs of hatred and calumny "because of me" (Matt 10:21; cf. Matt 5:11=Luke 6:22), with persecution and martyrdom (Matt 10:19-23; cf. Mark 8:35=Luke 9:24; cf. Luke 17:33; Matt 10:39; 16:25; John 12:25). Now, this scenario was never realized in the way it had been envisioned.[23] Two things accordingly have happened. First, the evangelists have telescoped words on the second mission with those on the first (Matt 10 has drawn on material from Mark 13) despite the inconcinnities and oddities that this has entailed. A result in our time, from Schweitzer to the present, which even the most clairvoyant gospel redactor could not have foreseen: super-literalists (Schweitzer himself was an example) were led to suppose on the basis of 10:23b that, when sending out his disciples, Jesus expected the Son of man to come within days, so that, were the disciples to return to Jesus—*no Son of man having come*—Jesus might suffer a nervous breakdown. More fanciful spirits, having no hold on any concrete context in which words like Matt 10:23b might make historical sense, dismissed them as inauthentic and explained their presence in the gospel as reflecting an imaginary Jewish-Christian debate on the legitimacy (not of a Torah-free mission—that kind of debate did in fact take place—but) of a mission to gentiles. Others offered a "telescopic" account of the discourse in Matt 10: two missions were indeed envisioned here. The first was in Jesus' public life, in Galilee. The second was the post-Easter Christian mission to the Jews of Palestine and to the gentiles of the Mediterranean basin. Here the interpreters split, some assuming that Jesus foresaw the world mission and took these words to be authentic, others sceptical of such foreseeing. They agree, however, on what Matt 10:23b *referred to*: namely, to this Christian missionary effort and, under the image of the coming Son of man, to some such "fulfillment event" as the fall of Jerusalem. What these views have in common is lack of hold on Jesus' own scenario of the future and, in consequence, lack of hold on the problem that the instruction of the disciples from Caesarea Philippi on was designed to solve.

        To sum up: there came a time in the career of Jesus when he foresaw and took account of the prospective failure of his mission to win over all Israel. Repudiation of his mission would bring his death, so launching the ordeal. But the death would be an expiatory death. The remnant flock saved in and through it would indeed survive the ordeal to welcome the day of "the Man" and the advent of the reign of God. Meantime, following the outbreak of the ordeal, his disciples were to shoulder the task of proclaiming the reign of God that would in one sense reverse, in another endorse, the saving death of Jesus. Remaining bound to the land of Israel they—many of them—would follow him to martyrs' deaths. *Jesus' present task was to alert them to the coming ordeal and to equip them for a task that would belong to it.* The first step was a leading question: "Who do men say that I am?"' It was meant to lead not only to acknowledgement of his messianic identity, but to a double prospect: repudiation by the nation, vindication by God.


# NOTES


1. The reference to the Hebrew text of Isa 53:12 is certain in virtue of the precise correspondence between *ho airōn tēn hamartian tou kosmou* (John 1:29) and *hû᾿ hēṭ᾿ rabbîm nāśā᾿* (Isa 53:12). The Johannine singular *tēn hamartian* (as Joachim Jeremias noticed many decades ago) is the earliest (if indirect) attestation of the Massoretes' singular *hēṭ᾿* (in contradistinction to the plural of the LXX and 1QIsa, which reads *ḥṭᵖy*).

2. Recently, Volker Hampel, *Menschensohn und historischer Jesus* (Neukirchen-Vluyn: Neukirchener Verlag, 1990) 222-226.

3. John A. Emerton, "The Origin of the Son of Man Imagery," *Journal of Theological Studies* 9 (1958) 225-242.

4. Sufficient grounds are unavailable for positing a pre-Danielic Son-of-man tradition; a tradition did, however, grow up out of Daniel 7—how swiftly it is difficult to specify. The Similitudes of Henoch probably date from the second half of the first to the opening of the second Christian century, most scholars today preferring the latter date. On the nature of the tradition, see Johannes Theisohn, *Der auserwählte Richter* (Göttingen: Vandenhoeck & Ruprecht, 1975). Also, Hampel, *Menschensohn* (see above, note 2) 41-48.

5. Rudolf Meyer, to be sure, attempted to pioneer a new reading of biblical and rabbinic texts, one that would dispense with the notion of the dying out of prophecy in the post-Exilic period; see TDNT VI, 812-828. His reliance on several improbable rereadings, however, make the proposal dubious. Ragnar Leivestad, "Das Dogma von der prophetenlose Zeit," *New Testament Studies* 19 (1973) 288-299, traces the sources of this conviction, to which the scribes of the time of John and Jesus held.

6. Bo Reicke, "The Historical Setting of John's Baptism," in *Jesus, the Gospels, and the Church* [W. R. Farmer Festschrift] (ed.) E. P. Sanders (Macon: Mercer University Press, 1987) 209-224. See also Jerome Murphy-O'Connor, "John the Baptist and Jesus: History and Hypotheses," *New Testament Studies* 36 (1990) 359-374.

7. See Jeremias, *Theology*, 44, with references to his earlier treatments of the issue.

8. Meyer, *Aims*, 117-122.

9. Billerbeck I, 601-603.

10. Dalman, *Words,* 139-143.

11. Jeremias, *Theology,* 46-47.

12. Dalman, *Words,* 141.

13. For a different view, W. G. Kummel, " 'Das Gesetz und die Propheten gehen bis Johannes'—Lukas 16,16 im Zusammenhang der heilsges-
chichtlichen Theologie der Lukasschriften," in *Verborum Veritas* [G. Stahlin
Festschrift] (ed.) 0. Böcher and H. Haacker (Wuppertal: Brockhaus, 1970) 89-
102, at 94-98.

14. Dalman, *Words,* 140.

15. Meyer, *Aims,* 281, note 1. Reicke, "John's Baptism" (see above,
note 6) offers reasons for dating John's death at A.D. 32.

16. Jeremias, *Theology,* 276-299; Heinz Schürmann, "Wie hat Jesus
seinen Tod bestanden und verstanden? Eine methodenkritische Besinnung," in
Schürmann, *Jesu ureigener Tod* (Freiburg: Herder, 1975) 16-65.

17. Anton Vögtle, "Todesankündigungen und Todesverständnis
Jesu," in *Der Tod Jesu. Deutungen im Neuen Testament* (ed.) Karl Kertelge
(Freiburg: Herder, 1976) 51-113.

18. Peter Fiedler, "Sünde und Vergebung im Christentum," *Concili-
um* 10 (1974) 568-571.

19. Rudolf Pesch, "Das Abendmahl und Jesu Todesverständnis," in
*Der Tod Jesu* (see above, note 17) 137-187, at 183-185; also, *Das Abendmahl
und Jesu Todesverständnis* (Freiburg: Herder, 1978) 103-109.

20. On the Qaddiš see I. Elbogen, *Der jüdische Gottesdienst in seiner
geschichtlichen Entwicklung* (Frankfurt: Kaufmann, third ed., 1931; repr.
Hildesheim: Olms, 1967). Text and comments in Dalman, *Words,* 99-100. The
eleventh petition in the *Tepillâ:*

> Restore our judges as of old and our councillors as in the beginning; /
> Remove from us sorrow and sighing, and reign over us, O Lord, you
> alone.

21. Meyer, *Aims,* 202-209; also, "Jesus' Scenario of the Future,"
*Downside Review* 109 (1991) 1-15; reprinted here as chapter three.

22. Joachim Jeremias offered an adroit effort to break the impasse between two competing interpretations of Matt 10:23b, that of Heinz Schürmann,
"Zur Traditions- und Redaktionsgeschichte von Mt. 10,23," *Biblische Zeitschrift* 3 (1959) 82-88; repr. in Schürmann, *Traditionsgeschichtliche Untersuchungen zu den synoptischen Evangelien* (Dusseldorf: Patmos, 1968) 150-156;
and that of Werner Georg Kümmel, "Die Naherwartung in der Verkündigung
Jesu," in *Zeit und Geschichte* [R. Bultmann Festschrift] (ed.) Erich Dinkler
(Tübingen: Mohr-Siebeck, 1964) 31-46. Schürmann (whose view I overconfi-
dently adopted in *Aims,* 44) removed the word entirely from the missionary
context. Kümmel presented a solidly argued philological case for inferring the
missionary context of the word, but (a) mistakenly separated it from Matt

10:23a; (b) mistakenly denied its character as a consolation word; and (c) failed to locate the referent of the word in a mission operative after the outbreak of the eschatological ordeal. Jeremias improved on both: Matt 10:23 is a unity; its reference is to the persecution of the disciples; but, "Why do the disciples not go outside the country? The answer can only be that their commission binds them to Israel" (*Theology*, 136). Jeremias might well have added that the saying belongs to the esoteric instruction of the disciples after Caesarea Philippi, as, in all probability, the allusion to the Son of man shows, and that is supposes a missionary appeal to Israel that will have traits transcendinq the mission to Galilee sketched in Matt 10.

23. On the (in principle, inescapable) gap between (a) the symbolic scenario characteristic of prophetic knowledge and (b) the reality that actualizes it; between (a) symbolic images such as the eschatological pilgrimage of the nations and (b) the reality of the world mission; between (a) symbolic time and (b) real time, see "Was Jesus Mistaken?" in Meyer, *Aims,* 242-249.

## 3

## JESUS' SCENARIO OF THE FUTURE

For many years Johannes Weiss's rediscovery in 1892 of the meaning of eschatology (an insight fleshed out in the second, much fuller edition of his book in 1900)[1] passed for a great breakthrough. In recent years we have heard the announcement of its reversal made ever more frequently and confidently. First of all, some of the original recoil from scandal that greeted Weiss has staged a comeback. (The scandal in fact was not altogether original to the 1890s. A number of deists early in the history of modern biblical studies caught wind of it, and argued that if Jesus could be wrong about the coming of the end of the world, he could be wrong about many other things, as well.) Second, Weiss himself made it clear in 1900 that, eight years after the publication of his discovery, he was still unequal to the task of integrating it into a theology for the present. We might add that since then no such integration has imposed itself in generally accepted fashion among New Testament scholars (though the translation of eschatology into existentialist categories mounted a surprisingly potent generation-long appeal for general acceptance). Third, the most far-reaching negative result of the debate has been the incapacity of biblical scholars, and especially of practitioners of historical-Jesus research, to define the various contexts in which future events signified by words and acts of Jesus might be convincingly placed. The problem has been the failure to get hold of Jesus' own scenario of the future.

The purpose of this study is to survey, briefly, the grounds for reaffirming Weiss's discovery; to review a particular proposal, developing Weiss's view, for the reconstruction of Jesus' scenario, that of C. H. Dodd, as revised by Joachim Jeremias; to fill out the scenario and make it concrete by recovering "the eschatological ordeal" as the context for numerous sayings of Jesus about the historical future; and, finally, to commend an already available (if still to be fully and finally developed) solution to the theological problem that Jesus' future scenario raises.

## Reasons For Thinking That Weiss Was Right

Why should we think that Johannes Weiss was right about Jesus' expectation of the imminent consummation of history? We may
break down the more or less immediately accessible reasons into three
categories. First, many gospel texts attest that Jesus expected the imminent consummation of the present world order, and that he understood
the new order to be established by this consummation (the reign of
God) as transcendent or post-historical. Second, this expectation con-
forms with and fits aptly into the close, controlling context of "an immediate before" (John the Baptist) and an "immediate after" (*hebraioi,
hellēnistai,* Paul), which similarly express the expectation of the imminent consummation of history. Third, this body of evidence ("before Jesus—Jesus—after Jesus") itself belongs to the larger context of ancient
Israel's prophetic tradition, which universally exhibits the traits of *imminent expectation.*

First, then, we shall consider some gospel texts, starting with
public traditions and afterwards moving to private or esoteric traditions.
Words (a) that were addressed to an undifferentiated public—hence, in
principle, to Israel at large—and (b) that made thematic the imminent
consummation of time and history, include especially the independent
proclamation that Jesus, following the arrest of the Baptist, made in
Galilee and, eventually, all over Israel (Mark 1:14f.=Matt 4:17; Mark
1:38=Luke 4:43; Mark 1:39=Matt 4:23=Luke 4:44; Mark 1:45). He
proclaimed, in synagogues and out-of-doors, the fulfillment of God's
promises and of Israel's hope (Luke 4:16-30; cf. Luke 4:44; also Mark
1:21=Luke 4:31; Mark 6:2=Matt 13:53).

In Jesus' usage *hē basileia tou theou/malkûtā᾽dē᾽lāhā᾽* gives
these proclamation texts their character, evoking the absolutely climactic and definitive salvation of Israel (and, as we shall see, of the nations
in dependence on Israel). This, to be sure, is by no means because
words such as "the *malkût* of God" could not be used except to desig-
nate the age to come; on the contrary, it has long been widely known
(probably thanks most of all to Gustaf Dalman, who established the
matter late in the last century in *Die Worte Jesu*),[2] that Jewish tradition
attests these words in other senses. Indeed, Dalman showed how *differ-*

*ent* ordinary Jewish usage was from that of Jesus, and ranged under Jesus' originality the absolute eschatological sense with which he invested the words *hē basileia tou theou/ malkûtāʾ diĭĕmayyāʾ*.[3] This expression and its equivalents took on an absolute ("end-of-the-world") sense from the convergence of various end-of-the-world motifs that Jesus associated with them. For example, in some of the great apocalyptic beatitudes he connected *hē basileia tou theou/malkûtāʾ dēʾlāhāʾ* with a climactic and definitive reversal of the conditions of historical existence.

Above all, the parables that he drew on in bringing the sense of "the reign of God" into sharp focus are not only instructive, but compelling. They make the point that the present moment is more than a great moment; it is *the* great moment. At stake is not only the life of individuals, but the life of the last generation of history. The present is more than an opportunity; it is *the only opportunity.* After the present moment, the deluge—of which the biblical deluge was only a sign and type: after us, the Judgment of the World!

The parables, admittedly, are not directly or mainly bent on spelling out a scenario of events; they are bent on mediating a real, as distinct from merely notional, grasp of the present moment, with a view to eliciting a decision in favor of the reign of God (more concretely, in favor of the restoration of Israel coming to realization in those who met Jesus' proclamation, symbolic acts, and teaching with a "Yes."). Hence, it is not so much this or that single parable that counts as evidence; the evidence, rather, lies in the pattern by which, in the "reign of God" parables in particular, the reign is "unpacked" by the judgment motif.

The reign of God is not like ten bridesmaids, but like a wedding (Matt 25:1); not like a householder, but like a distribution of wages (Matt 20:1); not like a man who sowed good seed, but like the harvest (Matt 13:24); not like an earthly king, but like the settlement of accounts (Matt 18:23).[4] The central moment in the parable of the ten bridesmaids is the image of the sudden arrival on the scene of the groom and his party. It dramatizes the need to look ahead, to plan, to act intelligently, so as have the lamps ready at the moment of his arrival. It is thus to be ranged among the "crisis parables." The harvest in the parable of the Sower is the end-time, when it will be revealed how stunningly successful the mission of Jesus had been! The distribution of wages and the settlement of accounts are meant to evoke J-Day, the great Assize and Judgment of the world (to be followed, assuredly, by the banquet of salvation). And, it is important to recall, there is only one judgment of the world, for which "the men of Nineveh" (Matt 12:41=Luke 11:32) and "the queen of the south" (Matt 12:42=Luke 11:31), and the citizenry of the cities of evil—Tyre and Sidon and Sodom of old (Matt 11:21f.=Luke 10:13f.)—are raised from the dead.

There is a repeated public announcement that time is short between the present moment in Jesus' public career and the globally conceived consummation, e.g., "the reign of God" (Mark 1:15 and its many parallels and quasi-parallels; the "this generation" texts: Mark 8:12a, b.38; 9:19;13:30; Matt 11:16=Luke 7:31; Matt 12:39,41f.=16:4=Mark 8:12=Luke 11:29-32; Matt 12:45, 23:36; Luke 11:50; 17:25, which refer to Jesus' contemporaries and usually evoke the danger of destruction that they face in the impending ordeal and judgment. The judgment in question is that in which they will be condemned by the queen of the south and the men of Nineveh, by the people of Tyre and Sidon and Sodom. This judgment is not put off into the distant future but is imminent: the sign of the coming consummation is precisely "this present moment" (Luke 12:56).

The present of Jesus' career was itself borrowed time (Luke 13:6-9). Time was short between Jesus' suffering and the outbreak of the ordeal over all Israel (Luke 23:28-31), just as it would be short between his judges' condemnation of him and the condemnation of his judges by "the [Son of] Man" (Luke 22:69, where *apo tou nun=min kaddûn*=soon;[5] cf. Mark 14:62=Matt 26:64). The time is short between the outbreak of the ordeal and its resolution by the advent of the day of salvation (Mark 14:58=Matt 26:61; John 2:19; cf. Mark 15:29=Matt 17:40; Acts 6:14).[6] Jesus' message to Antipas equivalently said that Antipas could do nothing to bring about Jesus' death before the moment when Jesus himself would bring his career to its appointed completion (*teleioumai*, Luke 13:32). (The exact sense of this completion remained unspecified, but it was soon to come.)

To his disciples, in private, he gave the repeated instruction that time was short between the now of his public career and the outbreak of the eschatological ordeal (Luke 12:49f.; Matt 26:18; Mark 14:42; cf. Lk 11:4c=Matt 6:13a; John 14:19a; 16:16a). He put no interval at all between his own sufferings and their share in them (e.g., Luke 22:36f.; Mark 10:39=Matt 20:23). The ordeal, however, would be brief (e.g., "three days") in the word on the new sanctuary), for God had already decided to abbreviate it for the sake of the elect (Mark 13:20=Matt 24:22). Putting the matter more concretely: In the course of their desperate missionary task (offering the kerygma of salvation in the face of the imminent end, and driven from pillar to post by persecutors), before they would have completed their missionary task in all the towns of Israel, the day of "the [Son of] Man" would come (Matt 10:23). Some of his followers present on the spot, he told them, would not taste death before seeing the reign of God come in power (Mark 9:1).

We turn now to the controlling context of "before" and "after." John the Baptist addressed all Israel, warning his contemporaries that judgment was imminent (Matt 3:10=Luke 3:9), and summoning them, in the face of this judgment, to repentance (Mark 1:4; Matt 3:7-10=Luke 3:7-9), to the confession of sins (Mark 1:5=Matt 3:6), and to a ritual act of washing meant to seal the repentance and mark the repentant for acquittal at the judgment. To outsiders, and in his own view as well, John's mission belonged to the eschatological scenario. That the eschaton was conceived as absolute is secured as solidly probable by the transcendent terms in which "the coming one" (Matt 11:3=Luke 7:19f.; John 1:15, 27)—hardly identifiable, except perhaps in apocalyptic tradition—and his work are described. The coming one will wash the repentant "in the holy Spirit and in fire."

> His winnowing fork is in his hand,
> and he will clear his threshing floor
> and gather his wheat into the granary,
> but the chaff he will burn with unquenchable fire
> (Matt 3:11f.=Luke 3:16f.).

The text unmistakably evokes "last judgment" and definitive division, a motif that interlocks easily with the typology, pervasive in the Johannite tradition in the gospels, of "first and last" (as it was in the beginning, so shall it be in the end).[7]

If the Baptist constitutes the relevant "before," the earliest community constitutes the relevant "after." Here a full treatment of evidence is out of the question; summary indications with references to further treatment must suffice. The Aramaic-speaking followers of Jesus (called *hebraioi* in Acts) obviously derived their expectations from Jesus. If they neither launched a world mission nor found its launching

by others to be self-evident, this was in all probability due to their expectation of the pilgrimage of the nations to Zion on the appointed—
and, they thought, swiftly approaching—day.[8] The *hellēnistai* cultivated an eschatology of their own; but, like that of the *hebraioi*, it too envisaged the early end of the world. Oscar Cullmann, writing in the af-
termath of World War II, well described the psychology of this belief,
offering the analogy of a population still living in war conditions, but in
the consciousness that the war's decisive battle had already settled that
its side would win. In these circumstances the tendency was to expect
an end to the war soon. The early Christians, he observed, wondered
what God's point could possibly be in prolonging the course of history.[9]
These early Christians were clearly heirs of Jesus' own expectation of
the early end.

Further, we know that Paul seriously hoped to live to see the
end of the world. From his first (1 Thess 4:13-17) to his last letter (Rom
15:17-29) he kept intact his lively expectations of an early end of time.
In 1 Cor 15:50 he cited a pre-Pauline couplet on how entry into the
reign of God (or into immunity from decay), namely at the parousia,
was conditioned by the antecedent need of transformation of both the
living and the dead. There followed Paul's disclosure of an eschatological secret: the living as well as the dead would be transformed at the
parousia (1 Cor 15:51-52). "For the trumpet will sound, and the dead
will rise imperishable, *and we* [the living] *shall be changed*" )1 Cor
15:52). Here, clearly enough, he aligned himself with those who would
still be living at the parousia. Later, in 2 Cor 5:2-5 (cf. Rom 8:18-27,
esp. vv. 22-23; 1 Cor 15:50-55, esp.vv. 53-54), though aware that his
survival was by no means sure, Paul still harbored the hope of arriving,
still living, at the parousia and, with the rest of the living, "putting on"
immortality.[10]

To conclude the case for Weiss's view: It has often been remarked by Old and New Testament scholars alike, that the tradition of
prophecy in Israel always strikes the note of imminence. There is no
prophecy of the distant future. Let two scholarly testimonies suffice. In
his study of the *Wirkungsgeschichte* of Hab 2:3, August Strobel showed
how post-biblical Judaism dealt with the problem of "delay" in the fulfillment of biblical prophecy.[11] (Too many New Testament scholars
had mistakenly supposed that the so-called "delay of the parousia" was
peculiar to the prophecy of Jesus.) On the contrary, "delay" was a re-

current phenomenon in the history of biblical prophecy. Again, apropos of his study of the program of restoration in Ezekiel, Jon D. Levenson remarked that in the Hebrew Bible generally "the eschata are always held to be imminent. Israel recognized no distant end to history."[12] In other words, the phenomenon of prophecy had an invariable—mythical or symbolic—thrust. What this means is that, quite independently of whether Jesus conceived the end in absolute or non-absolute terms, his prophecy—if, as history-of-religions phenomenon, it was in any sense significantly aligned with that of the prophets of Israel—bore on the imminent future. In the light of the evidence that we have reviewed above, there is little doubt (I would say) that the prophecy of Jesus belonged to absolute eschatology. But whether absolute or not, it bore, like all biblical prophecy, on the imminent future. Neither Testament shows us prophets entertaining a compound, temporally disjoined perspective, both imminent and non-imminent.

In the light of the above briefly presented and yet relatively massive and convergent evidence, one wonders on what grounds (other than preference) an historical investigation might conclude that, unlike the Baptist and unlike his own disciples and other early Christians, Jesus did *not* expect the consummation of history in the near future.

Still, those who have rejected Weiss's recovery of Jesus' expectation of the imminent end of the world have seen all these texts before, and have doubtless had pointed out to them that biblical prophecy bears on the imminent future. They have neither conceded nor repined; rather, they have contrived numerous ways of rendering this seemingly compelling evidence quite harmless.

One way is to point to the non-absolute eschatology of the Old Testament. It is true that few Old Testament texts are eschatological in an absolute sense, for Dan 12:2f. is the only entirely unambiguous biblical affirmation of specifically human life beyond history. On the other hand, it ought to be acknowledged that the kind of theme found in Dan 12:2f. has contributed to the shaping of a significantly new state of the question. In the second century before Christ a new sort of eschatology made its way into Israel's ancient tradition.

Another tack has been to subvert the seemingly cogent evidence of imminent judgment by positing a division between "judgment" and "judgment": when judgment is imminent it is not final; when it is final it is not imminent. The distinction, however, seems to serve no purpose other than to avoid "imminent final judgment." That it con-

tributes to the solution of no other problem and illuminates no other issue or set of texts surely makes the proposal suspect.

Finally, a number of scholars seem to have installed themselves in what the followers of Karl Popper call an unfalsifiable position: for, they have thus far failed to specify credible conditions which,
if fulfilled, would show that Weiss was right (followed by the judgment
that, in fact, these conditions have not been fulfilled). By refusing to
specify some credible x or y or z—had it been a part of the historical
record—as evidence that might have made Weiss's case, they have refused to treat the matter in terms of evidence. In short, they are saying
that no conceivable evidence could have made Weiss's case; or, whatever the evidence, Weiss was wrong. This leaves the critics of Weiss liable to the suspicion that their view is burdened with an *ideological* element.

## The Hypotheses of C. H. Dodd and Subsequent Commentators

In his slim, brilliant monograph of 1935, *The Parables of the
Kingdom*,[13] C. H. Dodd took up our question directly. After an introduction to the topic of parables (ch. one), he collated the evidence of
the gospels, and especially that of the parables, on "kingdom" and on
the historical future that Jesus envisaged (ch. two). He followed this
with a treatment of texts that could not be fitted into the *historical* future, but required a new, *post-historical* framework or context. The historical future made up an "eschatology of woe," comparable to that of
many of the prophets of Israel: suffering and death for Jesus himself
and some of his followers, disaster for the Jewish people, capital, and
temple. An apocalyptic, post-historical future portrayed—following the
imagery of the Day of Judgment—an "eschatology of bliss," e.g. the
new temple built "on the third day."

Dodd's most striking single observation was that the gospel
texts did not differentiate and relate resurrection and second coming;
this led him to propose that originally the two were conceived globally,
as one and the same: the Day of the Son of Man. He proposed the conjecture that whereas Jesus had referred to a single event, his disciples,
after the resurrection, made a distinction between two events, "one past,

His resurrection from the dead, and one future, His coming on the clouds. . . . Thus the eschatological scheme of primitive Christianity was constructed."[14] Dodd further noted the convergence of this view with that of Wilhelm Weiffenbach (1873), as reported in Schweitzer's *Leben-Jesu Forschung.*[15]

Joachim Jeremias presented Dodd's view of the future sayings of Jesus, revised and refocused, in an appreciative review article.[16] He eliminated much of the conjecture that had accompanied Dodd's proposal and abandoned the distinction between "historical events" presented in "the prophetic manner" and "supernatural events" presented in the "apocalyptic manner." All the events, historical and post-historical, were conceived as elements in a divinely initiated supernatural sequence; at the same time, the whole belonged qualitatively to the tradition of the prophets. Above all, Jeremias omitted the entire effort that Dodd had mounted to take the sting out of his own reconstruction by distinguishing between symbol and symbolized and then reducing what had been symbolized to "[totally] realized eschatology." In Jeremias's reconstruction, on the contrary, there was no recoil from the maintenance of a real future—both for Jesus and for the Church, whether ancient or modern. The force of the resurrection was positively to guarantee the future coming of "the [Son of] Man."

Apparently unaware of Jeremias's treatment of Dodd's effort, Dale C. Allison, Jr., in a doctoral dissertation of 1982, published as a monograph in 1985,[17] offered a thoroughgoing treatment of the eschatology of the gospels. Apart from the issue of when the ordeal or tribulation began, Allison supported Jeremias's view with a cicumstantially detailed account of relevant gospel texts and their parallels in Judaic intertestamental and rabbinic texts.

In *The Aims of Jesus*[18] I urged five advantages of this theory. First, it did not do away with any data, but confronted all the relevant data together, searching for an intelligible pattern therein. This effort was rewarded by arrival at a wholly intelligible whole vision of things (the now of the ministry, followed by the outbreak of the eschatological ordeal, which would finally be brought to an end by the Day of the Son of man—at once, resurrection, parousia, pilgrimage of the nations, judgment, banquet of the saved).

Second, the theory did not yield to the common temptation to tinker with the ever-present motif of imminence.

Third, it showed how the standard New Testament schemes of

eschatology had come into existence, namely, *ex eventu:* the Easter experience of the disciples (or the resurrection of Jesus) took place without the end of history, the judgment, and so on. This straightforward negative ascertainment, together with the firm conviction that the whole prophecy of Jesus was to be retained, generated perforce the parousia theme as a distinct entity bound up with the final coming of the reign of God.

Fourth, the theory provided the key to the interpretation of every text that required to be located in the context of Jesus' own scenario of the future. This included notably the so-called parousia parables, the three-days sayings, texts on the Church, etc.

Fifth, the theory had hermeneutical significance. Negatively, it represented a clean break with the naive practice of retrojecting the interpreter's view of "fulfillment events," e.g., the fall of the temple in A.D. 70, into the historical Jesus' view of the future. Positively, it allowed for the emergence of exegetical and historical problems, some of which we shall deal with here.

The scheme of the future envisaged by Jesus' sayings might be represented as follows:

| 1. Repudiation, suffering death of Jesus | NOW | ORDEAL | REIGN OF GOD |
|---|---|---|---|
| 2. Day of "the [Son of] Man": judgment | | | |

## How Referents of Future Sayings Fit into Jesus' Scenario

Two further aspects of Jesus' scenario of the future call for attention. First, his allusion to and affirmation of the eschatological pilgrimage of the nations; second, his affirmation of the messianic remnant in which alone Israel was to find eschatological restoration. The first derives its solid probability from the explanatory power it brings to bear on the general issue of how Jesus regarded the destiny of the gentiles.[19] The second is not only an inference from a mass of data (two in particular: the correlation between "reign of God" and "restoration of Israel";[20] and the role and impact, in Jesus' view and in his intention, of the response of Israel to his proclamation[21]). The affirmation is also attested by gospel texts: the word to the "little flock" (Luke 12:32), the *Petros/Petra* (*kêpā²*) word of Jesus to Simon (Matt 16:17-19), and the eucharistic words (Mark 14:22-25=Matt 26:26-29; Luke 22:15-20; cf. John 6:48-51).[22] The messianic remnant was already in existence, but only at the coming of God's reign would it be revealed as the sanctuary of God belonging to the new creation (Mark 14:58=Matt 26:61; John 2:19).

In our present context—namely, the scenario in accord with which the historical Jesus intended his words on the future—this "remnant," or Church, belonged to all three of the moments that made up that scenario: the present moment/the ordeal/the day of "'the [Son of] Man." The "now" of Jesus' public career was delimited by an imminent future: the outbreak of the eschatological ordeal.

> I have come to kindle a fire on earth,
> and how I wish it were already burning!
> I have a baptism to be baptized with,
> and how I am torn until it be accomplished!
> (Luke 12:49-50).

This ordeal (*ho peirasmos/nisyônā²*) was the sole context for Jesus' words on the specifically historical future. That future would be launched by his own destiny of repudiation (*apodokimasthēnai*) and death (e.g., Mark 9.31=Matt 17.22=Luke 9.44).[23] Inasmuch, then, as Jesus envisaged his followers as the messianic community[24] (family, household, sanctuary, flock), the Church had a hidden life in the present, would have a dramatic life in the ordeal, and would be vindicated and glorified with Jesus at the coming of the reign of God.

The reason why this is regularly overlooked today is not far to seek. The early Church itself changed the sense of texts bearing on the future by accommodating them to its own new scenario. And according to this scheme, the Church was specifically located in the interim between resurrection and parousia. But this interim, according to which the Church was post-paschal and pre-parousiac, *did not figure in Jesus' scenario*. The Church's scheme, it must be remembered, was imposed by events. That is, in the actuality of history the resurrection differentiated *ex eventu* two moments that Jesus had signified as one. With the actuality of the resurrection, the historical Jesus' undifferentiated symbolic scenario of the future was necessarily rendered obsolete—or rather was now differentiated in accord with historic actuality, for what had been signified symbolically was now in process of actual realization. All Christian scenarios and salvation-historical schemes henceforth differentiated the time of salvation as having been opened by the resurrection of Christ and as to be closed by his parousia or second coming. Such was the era of the Church. The one flexible element—an element, that is, which could be diversely located—was "the eschatological ordeal." The views that won out in the end located the ordeal in the future prior to the parousia.

The New Testament writers either suppose or explicitly affirm this scheme and fit into it all the words and acts of Jesus that bore on the future. The parables, for example, that originally warned of the imminent outbreak of the ordeal were now made to call for watchfulness in the face of the coming parousia.

But originally the little flock of the Messiah headed for rejection would be a sanctuary built on rock, proof against the ordeal (Matt 16.18)—so, a rock of refuge during the coming crisis; its prayer (addressed to ²abbā²) specifically envisaged the outbreak, soon, of the ordeal. Its rite (of bread and wine) would be a rite precisely for the ordeal.

The last two points might be spelled out more fully. The first petition of the ²abbā² prayer that Jesus taught his disciples was a call for the consummation, when the world would acclaim the saving act of God ("Let Thy name be hallowed!"), i.e., the advent of his reign. Indeed, once the ordeal had broken out, this call would be all the more pressing, a cry to the Father for "'Thy reign'" (*malkûtāk*), for God's coming triumph over present evil. "God can *shorten* the time of distress for the sake of the elect. . . "[25]; similarly, the petition "our bread of tomorrow give us today!)"[26] would be all the more deeply meant once the ordeal would have broken out. Even now, in Jesus ministry, the suppliant stood in consciously dire need, hungering now for the bread to come—the banquet of salvation.[27] The same would hold for the petition for forgiveness: "and cancel our debts as we (here and now) cancel those of our debtors."[28] The ordeal would only intensify this petition, for it would have brought the judgment that much closer. Finally, the time of eschatological distress becomes thematic in "and do not let us fall victim to the ordeal"[29]; that is, when the great test or temptation comes, save us from apostasy under pressure; save us from our persecutors, yes, but save us from ourselves!

As for the ordeal as the projected context of the rite that came to be called the eucharist, it is especially suggested by the so-called remembrance mandate (Luke 22:19; cf. 1 Cor 11:24-25). True, we cannot establish with certainty the historicity of this word; nevertheless, its historicity appears to lie in the large middle range of probability.[30] It is also true that the remembrance mandate as Paul interprets it in 1 Cor 11 has for its primary object the commemoration of the saving death of Christ and that the resurrection is tacitly included. (Otfried Hofius has recently made both points in exemplary fashion.)[31] But supposing the historicity of the mandate, its original sense remains to be fixed.

The normal way of settling such matters is by appeal to parallels. Parallels, in fact, may be found both for the instance in which it is God who does the remembering and for that in which it is the human beings who do the remembering. But Jeremias showed that in religious and especially cultic contexts in the literature of Palestinian Judaism, whether Greek or Semitic, the first is the more usual. In that case, the *eis anamnesin* refers to something being brought before God—a bequest (Zech 6.14), the bread of the presence (LXX Lev 24.7), the sounding of trumpets at a sacrifice (Ecclus 50.16) etc.—that he may remember, either *in bonam partem*, to have mercy, or *in malam partem*, to condemn or punish.[32] In the present instance the *touto poieite,* or "'do this," enjoins a ritual act, namely, the "taking" of the bread, the invocation/blessing/ thanksgiving, and the speaking of the interpretative word on the bread, and its distribution. The following *eis tēn emēn anamnēsin* signifies, "that God may remember me": namely, *by bringing in the day of salvation* or, in other words, by the public vindication of Jesus: his resurrection, enthronement, and advent (as the Messiah, the Son of the Blessed One and "the [Son of] Man") with his angels, signalling the end of the ordeal, the assembly of the world for judgment, the banquet of the saved.

If the eucharist "in memory of me" soon came to signify the Christian ritual act of remembering Jesus' death and resurrection, this, like so many other quasi-automatic post-paschal reinterpretations (parousia becomes a discrete event; crisis parables become parousia parables; the ordeal is transposed to an increasingly indefinite future), derives from the unforeseen isolatedness that qualified the actuality of

Jesus' resurrection. This holds for practically all words on the future
historic life of "the Church."[33]

## Response to the Objection that Jesus had been "Mistaken"

Elsewhere I have traced the diverse strategies and tactics
adopted by those theologians who acknowledge that the historical Jesus
proclaimed the reign of God in the sense of absolute eschatology and
who have attempted to answer the objection that immediately springs
from this and that the deists were the first to pose: Had not Jesus been
mistaken, and had he not accordingly forfeited his status of infallible
revealer? I shall not repeat the survey of opinions here, but shall merely
rehearse what seems to me (so far, at least) to be the uniquely reasonable way of dealing with this issue.

There are some distinctive features that are recurrent in biblical prophecy. First among them is the prophet's insistence that he
speaks for the LORD. He does not speak his own word or on his own
behalf. In the gospel literature we have: " . . . the word which you hear
is not mine but the Father's who sent me" (John 14:24). What the
prophet wills is to speak precisely God's message, not his own. All else
is functional to this.

Second, it belongs to the phenomenon of biblical prophecy
that messages bearing on the future be expressed in symbols. (There is
a kind of mimicry of this when, in apocalyptic texts, the writer presents
the apocalyptic seer as depicting the supposed future—but actually
well-known past—in sometimes stiltedly symbolic language.) What we
have called the historical Jesus' scenario of the future exemplifies this
symbolic feature. His word on the future intended a symbol-charged
two-act drama of crisis and resolution. The crisis was the eschatological
ordeal to be opened by his own repudiation and suffering. The resolution was the day of "the [Son of] Man" bringing the ordeal to an end
with the triumph of the reign of God. As mentioned above, Jesus also
adopts symbolic prophecy from the scriptures, e.g., the pilgrimage of
the peoples to Zion, which is assimilated to the resolution phase of the
coming two-act drama.

The thesis I propose bears on the nature of prophecy. In prophecy, what the symbol intends is what God, for whom the prophet

speaks, intends. This apparently never enters the horizons and perspectives of the prophet in the form of determinate knowledge of the future. The question "Was Jesus mistaken about the future?" should accordingly first be reformulated as follows: Did Jesus have determinate knowledge of what God intended by the symbolic scheme of things that Jesus had been commissioned to announce? The answer to this question seems quite clearly to be, no. The same question should be put respecting all prophets of the biblical tradition. In every instance the same answer appears to be forthcoming.

The deists would have considered these observations a kind of cheating. The observations do indeed imply that, regardless of what measure of enlightenment we may have achieved, it does not equip or position us to pronounce on prophecy. Why should it? Why should we suppose that our access to critical knowledge puts us in possession of resources equal to the phenomenon of prophecy? Above all, why should we think of prophecy, in so far as it bears on the future, as a kind of empirical-knowledge-by-anticipation? Nothing in the literature of prophecy suggests that prophetic knowledge has this character. We should not naively imagine that any prophet ever had before his inner eye the kind of scenario that history, on cue, might literally follow.

It is instructive to notice how the early Church took account of the disparity between Jesus' prophecy and its own experience. It muddled through. It did not take the tack that we are taking, by posing the question of the nature of prophetic knowledge. We have in the texts of the New Testament, e.g., in Acts and in Paul, some evidence of how they re-presented to themselves the prophetic theme of the pilgrimage of the peoples. In Acts 2 the presence in Jerusalem of representatives of the whole world is apparently understood as a realization of the theme of the great pilgrimage. Paul, e.g., in Rom 15.19-29, offers his own distinctive actualization of the same prophetic theme.[34]

When all is said and done, Christians of the long pre-critical period from the New Testament to the deists managed to bring to the construal of the prophecy of Jesus a far fuller measure of *l'esprit de finesse* than have critics from the Enlightenment to the present. The opening paragraph of the present short study recalls that Johannes Weiss confessed his inability to integrate "the reign of God" in the absolute eschatological sense into a theology for the present. But the Church across the centuries—utterly disinclined (unlike modern scholars) to reduce to fiction the objects of future hope—succeeded without strain in the project that so baffled Weiss. The "reign of God" was the object of that all but indestructible human longing which comes alive when the last wisp of ordinary hope for the present life disappears. Josef Pieper called it "fundamental hope." It was not bent on anything that one could "have," but only on "being" and "selfness," the salvation of the person.[35] Christians of all eras, beginning with Paul in 1 Cor 15, have correlated their fundamental hope with the real future signified by "the reign of God" (see "reign of God" in 1 Cor 15:24,50).

The present effort to deal with the question that arises from the disparity between the language of absolute eschatology and the reality of fulfillment—the lone resurrection of Jesus, the launching of a missionary effort to the whole world, the ongoing reality of a hard history—does not directly impinge on *the question of fact* respecting the terms of Jesus ' proclamation, namely: Did it belong to absolute eschatology as Weiss, Dalman, Schweitzer, and their successors have maintained? Or was this simply a mistaken supposition, an illusion of which the dissolution—by recourse to a merely metaphorical eschatology— pertains to an alleged contemporary renaissance in Jesus studies?[36] A reasonable answer, one that cuts the ground out from under the prematurely triumphant question of the deists, may encourage some to confront the data of the gospel literature undistracted by the simplistic and irrelevant thesis—a bogey, but one that has been repeated over and over again by scholars who, perhaps, should have known better—that Jesus was mistaken. All prophecy speaks in the idiom of symbol. There is an irreducible disparity between this idiom and the actuality of events. The disparity is not well described as error. None of the prophets were mistaken, least of all the greatest of them.

## NOTES

1. Johannes Weiss, *Die Predigt Jesu vom Reiche* Gottes (Göttingen: Vandenhoeck & Ruprecht, 1892; 2nd ed. 1900; reissued 1964). E.T. of 1892: *Jesus' Proclamation of the Kingdom of God* (eds.) R. H. Hiers and D. L. Holland (London: SCM, 1971).

2. See Gustaf Dalman, *Die Worte Jesu* (Leipzig: Hinrichs, 1898, 2nd ed. 1930; reissued Darmstadt: Wissenschaftliche Buchgesellschaft, 1960); E.T., *Words,* 96-101.

3. Dalman, *Words*, 135-139, a passage that still stands with only slight corrections. (Dalman, 91-93, mistakenly fixed on *malkûtā᾽ šĕmayyā᾽*, rather than *malkûtā᾽ dĕ᾽lāhā᾽*, as Jesus' original expression; but this expression was first used a generation or more after the time of Jesus, as Jeremias has observed.)

4. Jeremias, *Parables*, 101.

5. Dalman, *Words*, 311, offers, as retroversion of *kai apo tou nun*, ûmikkĕ̂an/ûmin kaddûn: "and soon."

6. See B. F. Meyer, "The 'Inside' of the Jesus Event," in Meyer, *Critical Realism*, 157-172.

7. Conscious symbolism: not only the pelt clothing that recalled Elijah, but above all the encircling wilderness and the water-rite, both of which connected the present moment with Exodus traditions. See Jeremias, *Theology*, 43-45.

8. Meyer, *Early Christians*, 53-66 on the *hebraioi*; 67-88 on the *hellēnistai*.

9. Oscar Cullmann, *Christ and Time* (Philadelphia: Westminster, 1950 ).

10. B. F. Meyer, "Did Paul's View of the Resurrection of the Dead Undergo Development?" in *Critical Realism*, 99-128, at 114-116.

11. August Strobel, *Untersuchungen zum eschatologischen Verzögerungsproblem auf Grund der spätjüdisch-urchristlichen Geschichte von Habakuk 2, 2ff.* (Leidon-Köln: Brill, 1961).

12. Jon D. Levenson, *Theology of the Program of Restoration of Ezekiel 40-48* (Missoula: Scholars Press, 1976) 53, note 33.

13. C. H. Dodd, *The Parables of the Kingdom* (London: Nisbet, 1935; reprinted London-Glasgow: Collins [Fontana] 1961).

14. Dodd, *Parables*, 76.

15. Dodd, *Parables*, 76, note 24.

16. Joachim Jeremias, "Eine neue Schau der Zukunftsaussagen Jesu," *Theologische Blätter* 20 (1941) col. 216-222. See also, J. Jeremias,"'Die Drei-Tage-Worte der Evangelien" in (eds.) Gert Jeremias, H.-W. Kuhn, and H. Stegemann, *Tradition und Glaube* [K. G. Kuhn Festschrift] (Göttingen: Vandenhoeck & Ruprecht, 1971) 221-229.

17. Allison, *Ages*.

18. Meyer, *Aims*, 204-206.

19. See the structure of the argument in J. Jeremias, *Jesus' Promise to the Nations* (London: SCM, 1958).

20. See Meyer, *Aims*, 128-137.

21. See Meyer, *Aims*, 195-197.

22. See Meyer, *Aims*,210-215 on "remnant"; 215, 309 on the "little flock" saying; pp. 185-197 on the *kêpā᾽* word; the article cited above, note 6, on

the sanctuary riddle; and on the eucharistic words, B. F. Meyer, "The Expiation Motif in the Eucharistic Words: A Key to the History of Jesus?" *Gregorianum* 69 (1988) 461-487, esp. 479-486.

23-. Jeremias, *Theology*, 280-282.

24. See Jeremias, *Theology,* 168, on the likelihood that behind *ekkle-sia* in Matt 18:18; 16:18, stood *'ēdā/ēdtā*'. Jeremias applied a finely differentiated literary criticism to Matt 16:17-19, but from *Golgotha* (Leipzig: Pfeiffer, 1926) to his last works, he maintained the substantial historicity of the text.

25. Jeremias, *Theology*, 140.

26. On the translation of the text see Meyer, *Early Christians* 21-22, note 7.

27. See Jeremias, "'The Lord's Prayer in the Light of Recent Research" in Jeremias, *The Prayers of Jesus* (London: SCM, 1967) 99-102.

28. See "The Lord's Prayer," 102-104.

29. See "The Lord's Prayer," 104-106.

30. Here we have an instance in which a given exegesis is evidence of historicity. For if the text of the remembrance mandate is to be read in the sense commended by the exegetical argument in Jeremias, *Eucharistic* 237-255, it is archaic, pre-paschal, historical.

31. Otfried Hofius, "Herrenmahl und Herrenmahlsparadosis. Erwägungen zu 1. Kor. 11,23b-25," *Zeitschrift für Theologie und Kirche* 85 (1988) 371-408; repr. in Hofius, *Paulusstudien* (Tübingen, Mohr-Siebeck, 1989) 203-240.

32. *Eucharistic*, 246-249.

33. These include notably Mark 10:42-44 and Matt 16:17-19. On the first text see T. W. Manson's detached note on the text in *The Teaching of Jesus* (Cambridge: Cambridge University Press, 1967, a reprint of 2nd ed. of 1935) pp. 313-315. On the second text, see Meyer, *Aims*, esp. 304, note 48.

34. See, e.g., Roger Aus, "Paul's Travel Plans to Spain and the 'Full Number of the Gentiles' of Rom XI 25," *Novum Testamentum* 21 (1979) 232-262.

35. Josef Pieper, *Hope and History* (London: Burns and Oates, 1969) 24-26.

36. Marcus J. Borg, "A Renaissance in Jesus Studies," *Theology Today* 45 (1988) 280-292.

## 4

# APPOINTED DEED, APPOINTED DOER:
# JESUS AND THE SCRIPTURES

Of the many indices to Jesus' consciousness of his mission to Israel, three kinds are especially revealing: his identification of himself and his disciples as eschatological antitypes of Israel, her kings and prophets; his allusions to divinely appointed eschatological "measures" (of time, of evil, of revelation) being filled to the brim; and his pointing, as to "signs of the time," to the enactment in his own activities of God's promises of salvation for the end-time. We begin with the observation that these three facets of the consciousness of Jesus exhibit a point of convergence: a full awareness of being charged with the climactic and final mission to Israel as promised and previewed in the scriptures.

Second, we shall *independently* (i.e., without dependence on the foregoing) establish this same conclusion by a cumulative and convergent argument drawing on five data in the gospel narratives, the historicity of which has won universal agreement. These are: Jesus' proclamation that the reign of God was at hand; the fact that Jesus spoke and acted "with authority"; that he was widely known as and was a wonder-worker; that he "cleansed"—or mounted a "demonstration" at—the Jerusalem temple; and that he died crucified, condemned by the Romans as "the king of the Jews." From these as yet disparate and unelucidated data I propose to argue to the main currents of the gospels' christology. All the themes belonging to these main currents, according to the argument, derived from Jesus and reflected his grasp of the scriptures as bearing on his own mission.

The form of the argument is as follows: the above-mentioned data, of which the historicity is all but universally accepted, establish Jesus' consciousness of being charged with God's climactic and definitive mission to Israel in view of the imminent consummation of history,

or the reign of God. *But to speak of a "climactic and definitive mission"
in the context of the imminent consummation of history is to imply the
imminent consummation or fulfillment of the whole of eschatological
promise and prophecy.* It follows that we ought positively to expect to
find on Jesus' part not only an eschatological consciousness, but one
marked by *the awareness of present fulfillment,* a phenomenon without
parallel in ancient Israel.[1]

Crucial to the argument is the ascertainment that, like his contemporaries, Jesus understood the great soteriological themes of the
scriptures as prophetic, that is, as awaiting fulfillment from the moment
at which the end-time would break out. This is why we should positively expect the bearer of God's climactic and definitive mission *to focus
on and to coordinate these themes.*

The sheer sweep and power of the argument—from the consciousness of an eschatological mission, through the necessity of all the
scriptures to come to fulfillment, to the main currents of the messianol-
ogy or christology of the gospels—invite us to press it for its validity,
i.e., to test the sufficiency of its premises and the cogency of its logic.
Do the gospels, in fact, exhibit the requisite data? Do they confirm that
Jesus, like others who looked for the dawning eschaton, read the scriptures as prophecy awaiting its moment of convergent fulfillment? Is
there any plausible escape from the argument?

Finally, this argument evokes an antecedent expectation that
the profusion, the positive explosion, of christological speech following
on "the Easter experience of the disciples" will have been rooted in Jesus' own self-understanding. We shall accordingly conclude by entertaining the question of whether this expectation is confirmed.


## Three Sorts of Indices to Jesus' Consciousness of His Mission

Three words—the temple riddle (Mark 14:58=Matt 26:61=
John 2:19; cf. Mark 15:29=Matt 27:40; Acts 6:14), the response to Antipas (Luke 13:32), and the Jonah saying in response to the demand for
a "sign" (Matt 12:39=Luke 11:29; cf. Mark 8:12; Matt 16:4)—share a
set of sharply profiled traits that reflect the Jesus of history: first, a context of clash with authoritative or elite forces in Israel; second, the

"three-days" motif, which evokes (in consciously enigmatic fashion) the divine governance of the life and fate of Jesus;[2] third, a consequent and unmistakable note of perfect confidence. Jesus clearly regarded the looming crisis (or eschatological ordeal) in the light of its subjection to God's royal sovereignty.

Two of these sayings present "types" of salvation: the sanctuary (*naos*/Heb.: *hêkāl*/Aram.: *hêkĕlāʾ*) of the temple is presented as a type of the messianic community of salvation, transfigured in the reign of God.[3] Jonah, saved from the sea-monster, is presented as a type of one raised from the dead, returning (at the great consummation, the day of "the [son of] Man") to confound those who pressed Jesus for a "sign." There would be no sign but that one![4] Both sayings thus belong to the series of words presenting Jesus and his disciples as eschatological antitypes of familiar biblical figures: Moses (Matt 5:17, 21-48; cf. John 6:14; 7:40), David (Mark 12:35-37=Matt 22:41-46=Luke 20:41-44; Mark 2:25-26=Matt 12:3-4=Luke 6:3-4), Solomon (Matt 12:42=Luke 11:31), Elisha (Mark 6:35-44=Matt 14:15-21=Luke 9:12-17), Isaiah (Mark 4:12=Matt 13:13; Luke 8:10), the Servant of the Lord (Mark 10:45=Matt 20:28; Mark 14:24c=Matt 26:28b; Luke 22:20c; John 6:51), the one like a [son of] man, and the tribes and prophets of Israel (Mark 3:13-14=Matt 10:1-2=Luke 6:13; Matt 5:12=Luke 6:23). The typological interpretation of the early Church was not an independent development; it was grounded historically in Jesus' own use of typology. The two typological texts adduced here (the riddle of the new sanctuary and the sign of Jonah) are, in particular, words of Jesus;[5] nor is the eschatological character of the antitypes open to reasonable doubt.

Second, we meet the motif of divinely appointed measures of all things and its specific application to the eschaton in the Markan form of the public proclamation: *peplērōtai ho kairos*/the time is fulfilled—or filled full. Though the verb is used variously of time, the probable image here is a great vase that with the years has been slowly filled until at last it is full to the brim.[6] As Paul Joüon pointed out long ago,[7] the parallelism of *peplērōtai* and *ēggiken* suggests that the latter (substratum: *qĕrabat*) means "has arrived." The whole is aligned closely with the "today" and "fulfilled" motifs in Luke 4:21 ("Today this scripture has been fulfilled [*peplērōtai*] in your hearing").

Elsewhere Jesus applied the same "filling-up-to-the-appointed-measure" motif to "evil" and to "revelation." "This evil generation" (of unbelievers and killers of God's envoys) will find itself overwhelmed by the rapidly approaching ordeal/tribulation, when God will exact from it the blood-debt for all the murders recorded in the scriptures from first to last (i.e., from Cain's fratricide in Gen 4 to the stoning of Zechariah in 2 Chron 24:20-25; Matt 23:34-36=Luke 11:49-51). "Fill up, then, the measure of your fathers!" (Matt 23:32), spoken to men already set on the death of Jesus (Matt 21:45-46), is a bitterly ironic summons to bring to completion with this prospective crime the last wave of evil allotted to history.

By contrast, the final measure of revelation allotted to Israel is bestowed, now at last, through the agency of Jesus. "Do not think that I have come to annul the Law [or the prophets]; I have come, not to annul but to complete" (Matt 5:17).[8] This motif of the eschatological completion of God's revelation is carried through in the following antitheses (Matt 5:21-22, 33-34, 38-39, 43-44) as well as in the accounts of Jesus' teaching in general, e.g., in the move from Moses's provisional legislation on divorce (Deut 24) to the eschatological restoration of the ideal of paradise (Gen 2:24 ) enacted anew for the already inaugurated restoration of Israel (Matt 19:3-9=Mark 10:2-10) . In short, Jesus here presents himself, in accord with popular messianic tradition, as the prophet like Moses, bringing Israel the final measure of revealed truth.

Third and last, when John in prison sent the question to Jesus, "Are you he who is to come [Ps 118:26], or shall we look for another?" Jesus allowed his actions to speak for him; in the urgent staccato of two-beat rhythm, he answered: "Go and tell John what you hear and see:

> blind men see,
> cripples walk,
> lepers are cleansed,
> deaf men hear,
> dead men are raised,
> and good news is broken to the poor!"
> (Matt 11:5=Luke 7:22-23).

Jesus is saying that his own public activity in Israel must be read as the superabundant fulfillment of eschatological promises (Isa 35:5-6; 29:18-19; 61:1).[9] He had come as the messianic consolation of Israel (Isa 40:1; Tg Isa 33:20). Like the answer to the high-priest in the Sandedrin trial (Matt 26:64a; cf. Luke 22:70d), Jesus' response is averse to claims (in manner), while entirely affirmative (in substance).

It seems to me that these three phenomena—self-identification as eschatological antitype, the claim that in him and his mission the divine "measures" assigned to the eschaton were being brought to completion, and, finally, the specific invitation to interpret his public activity as the fulfillment of eschatological promise and prophecy—are inexplicable except as attesting a unique consciousness: that of mediating God's last, climactic visitation of his people. (We are looking back from two millennia later; this should not distract us into supposing that the Jesus of the public ministry envisioned a long history still to come.)[10] The historicity of the texts is solidly probable and their central meaning appears to be perfectly clear. Let him who has ears hear. But since the music of these texts apparently falls outside the auditory range of many professional listeners, I shall propose a distinct and independent consideration of texts equally intelligible and still more widely acknowledged to be historical, namely, the five data listed in the introduction to this essay.

## Did Jesus Announce the Imminent End of History?

We take it that scholarship has copiously established the historicity of the proclamation of Jesus. The one relevant issue that has not found universal agreement bears on its eschatological character. When Jesus spoke of the imminence of the reign of God (*basileia tou theou/ malkûtâ² dē² lāhā²*), was this meant to signify the imminence of the end of history? Starting a hundred years ago with Johannes Weiss, this question has periodically appeared to have been settled in the affirmative—only to be upset by some new effort of revisionist scholarship.

In 1935 C. H. Dodd offered a brilliant reconstruction of Jesus' scenario of the future, which included an affirmation of the imminent end of history.[11] But Dodd followed his reconstruction with a historico-hermeneutical account of what it finally meant. The account, under the name "realized eschatology," left nothing still to be expected in the future, whether by Jesus or by the believer today. (In this Dodd was followed by T. F. Glasson[12] and J. A. T. Robinson,[13] who worked out this view with such consistency that its latent defects became patent.)

Meantime, in an article little noticed (it appeared during the Second World War in a journal that ceased publication before the war was over), Joachim Jeremias offered a positive appreciation of Dodd's historical reconstruction, adding a number of corrections and refinements, and dropping Dodd's unhelpful attempt to free Jesus from the liability of a mythical view of the future.[14]

In the post-War period, existentialist kerygma theology also had its say. Ernst Käsemann attempted, like Dodd, to save Jesus from the luggage of apocalyptic expectations, but forgoing Dodd's laborious indirection. Without flinching at the necessary literary and historical surgery on the gospels, Käsemann directly attributed to the historical Jesus an exclusively realized eschatology.[15]

Yet another rescue attempt was mounted by George B. Caird.[16] Caird did not contest that Jesus spoke the language of apocalyptic eschatology. The issue was whether he meant this language literally or metaphorically. According to Caird, Jesus expected a metaphorical end of the world. On the literal plane this corresponded to the end of the current era in human history. (Disciples of Caird today include Marcus Borg and N. T. Wright.)[17]

Several of these efforts to interpret the proclamation of Jesus came under critical review in 1985 by Dale C. Allison, Jr., in a monograph based on an earlier doctoral dissertation.[18] Allison conclusively showed that many of them (those especially of Glasson, Robinson, and Caird) were unsalvageable. His account (though he was apparently unaware of this) was largely a reprise of Joachim Jeremias's 1941 reconstruction of Jesus' scenario for the end-time. Indeed, Jeremias's brief presentation was in certain details more exact,[19] though Allison's monograph provided a fullness of treatment—in the framing of the question, the survey of the gospel sources, and the repertory of relevant intertestamental and other Jewish literature—that far surpassed the reach of Jeremias's short review-article.

Having recently taken up anew the question of Jesus' future scenario,[20] I shall not review the entire question here. Let it suffice to say that Johannes Weiss was right at least about Jesus' expectation of the imminent end of the world. Just prior to Jesus, the Baptist proclaimed the imminence of the last judgment. Just after Jesus, Paul repeatedly indicated his hope and expectation of the imminent parousia of the Lord. In the interim between the Baptist and Paul, Jesus affirmed that the last judgment, for which the men of Nineveh and the queen of the south were to be raised from the dead, was on the brink.[21]

What Weiss and Schweitzer missed, and what Dodd caught, was the present realization in Jesus' own time of at least part of Israel's heritage of eschatological promise and prophecy. To this should be added the nascent Christian community's unambiguous affirmation of the era of fulfillment as having *already arrived.* Both in Jesus himself and in the Easter community of his followers there were two facets of the eschatological consciousness: first, a consciousness of eschatological promise/prophecy "already fulfilled"; second, the complementary consciousness of promise/prophecy "still to be fulfilled." Together these facets of eschatological consciousness commend, as the most useful terminological rubric both for the views of Jesus and for those of the post-Easter Church, "eschatology inaugurated and in process of realization."

## Four More Data Acknowledged to be Certainly Historical

No one doubts the historicity of Jesus' proclamation of the reign of God. Similarly, the historicity of the following data is secure:

(1) Jesus impressed his contemporaries of one who spoke and acted "as having authority" (*hōs exousian echōn/kĕšallîṭāʾ*, Mark 1:22=Matt 7:29=Luke 4:22; Mark 1:27=Luke 4:26). What sort of authority? Not, emphatically, the authority of the professionally trained theologian (cf. Mark 11:28=Matt 21:23=Luke 20:2); rather that of a charismatic wielding supernatural power over demons, a power that he could and did sovereignly transmit to his disciples (Mark 3:15=Matt 10:1; Mark 6:7=Luke 9:1). More, Jesus acted as one bearing the authority to remit sins (Mark 2:10=Matt 9:5=Luke 5:24)—in short, like the plenipotentiary of a new, independent economy of salvation.[22]

(2) Once, when some Pharisees delivered a threat against Jesus' life, allegedly from Antipas, Jesus coolly responded with a memorable word on his invulnerability until the moment of God's choosing, when he would indeed be subject to the onslaught of Satan:

> Behold, I drive out demons
> and perform cures
> today and tomorrow,
> and on the third day I complete my course
> (Luke 13:32).

Since the three-days motif connotes God's sovereignly appointed plan, the sense of the text is: "(Tell that fox that) I cannot be touched until the divinely appointed time." Quite incidentally, however, the saying defines the public career of Jesus under the rubric of exorcisms and cures, thus significantly adding to the sum of testimonies to Jesus' career as a wonderworker.

Central to these testimonies is a series of sayings: (a) the double *māšāl* on Beelzebul and the advent of the reign of God (Matt 12:27-28=Luke 11:18-20); (b) the *māšāl* on dynasties and households divided against themselves (Mark 3:24-26=Matt 12:25-26=Luke 11:17-18); (c) the *māšāl* on the binding of the strong man (Mark 3:27=Matt 12:29=Luke 11:21); (d) the inference that, if (in the context established by Jesus' proclamation) it was by God's power that he drove out demons, the reign of God had already (virtually)[23] come (Matt 12:28=Luke 11:20). This last motif epitomizes at least one of the many facets of Jesus' wonderworking.

(3) The historic drama of the cleansing of the temple, as I have recently argued elsewhere,[24] has been underplayed both by the gospels themselves and by recent historical-Jesus research. The historicity of the event is not in doubt. The meaning of the event is clearly many-faceted.[25] In the present context, however, the critical point is not so much to unpack these many facets as it is to note how the cleansing is charged with an implicit claim to plenary authority over the destiny, the definitive restoration, of Israel. A secondary matter is the provenance, in the public life of Jesus, of the riddle on the new sanctuary. It seems to me to belong, with mid-range probability, to the follow-up on the cleansing of the temple. This follow-up was hardly the question of *exousia/rĕšût* i.e., theological authority (Mark 11:27-33=Matt 21:23-27=Luke 20:1-8); it must rather have been the demand for a sign, as John presents it (John 2:18-19). But whatever the precise source of this word, it is clear that in Jesus' riddling answer (something like: "Destroy this sanctuary / and after three days I will build it"; cf. John 2:19 and Mark 14:58), the "authority" was that of the son of David/son of God (2

Sam 7:12; 1 Chron 17:11-13; Ps 2:7; 110:3; 4QFlor 11) commissioned to build God's house (2 Sam 7:13-14; 1 Chron 17:12-13; Hag 1:1-2; 2: 20-23; Zech 6:12-13). Inasmuch as "God's house" in texts like these was open to signifying God's eschatologically restored people (*ekklē-sia/ʿēdtāʾ*), and since this is precisely the sense of the new sanctuary in Jesus' word, the cleansing itself as well as this word (which, in the present hypothesis, immediately followed on the cleansing) showed that Jesus understood the restoration of Israel to belong to his mission—indeed, as its central task.[26]

(4) In the light of the above ascertainments, the *titulus* on the cross, "the king of the Jews," makes excellent historical sense. In the passion story the key religious question (as shown by Mark 14:61=Matt 26:63; cf. Luke 22:67) had been whether Jesus would acknowledge his claim, up till now exclusively implicit in the public forum, to be the appointed agent (the Messiah) of the appointed eschatological act (the restoration of Israel). When the Sanhedrists presented this question to Pilate, they gave it a political twist. The *titulus,* doubtless a product of Pilate's own malicious irony, is a solid index to the crime of which Jesus was accused: pretention to royal dominion. The *titulus,* besides being well attested (Mark 15:26=Matt 27:37=Luke 23:39=John 19:19), interlocks easily with the other data on the Sanhedrin's effort to bring about the suppression of Jesus.

Our purpose is not to deal on its own merits with each of the five data adduced here; it is rather to point to the fact that, taken collectively, they converge on Jesus' consciousness of being the bearer of a divinely appointed, climactic and definitive, mission to Israel. Once again, consider these data cumulatively: (a) Jesus proclaims the imminence of the divine saving act celebrated in the prophets as the eschatological restoration of God's people. (b) But he does not just announce it. His public performance, including teaching and wonderworking, strikes his contemporaries as maximally authoritative, the authority deriving directly from God. (c) When threatened by Antipas—just as when questioned by the Baptist—his response points to his career as wonderworker: it accords with the divine plan and proceeds under its protection (Luke 13:32) and it fulfills the promises of the scriptures (Matt 11:5=Luke 7:22-23). (d) When "reign of God" is taken in the sense that Jesus intended, namely, as God's definitive act of salvation,[27] its correlates include "new covenant, new sanctuary, new cult."[28] The thrust of the symbolic action at the temple accordingly appears to intend the end of the old (Mosaic) dispensation and to intimate some new, implicitly messianic, dispensation. (e) The last wisp of remaining ambiguity is dissipated by the *titulus* on the cross. The conclusion that we find imposed on us (again, not from these five data taken singly but from the five taken cumulatively and collectively) is that Jesus did indeed think of himself as called to a climactic and definitive mission to Israel.

## The Scriptures Must be Fulfilled

Many years ago John Downing, in an article on Jesus and martyrdom,[29] offered an apparently irrefutable observation: Jesus, by his proclamation of the imminent coming of the reign of God, implicitly defined himself as God's last voice, the last prophetic envoy to Israel. "He was the last prophet," argued Downing, "for men's reactions to him and to his preaching determined their eschatological destiny (Luke xii.8 and par.)."[30] Or, in the expression of Amos Wilder, Jesus' role was "that of mediator of God's final controversy with his people."[31]

Keeping in mind this motif of "*last* envoy, *last* prophet" (which Jesus himself made thematic and emphatic by his warnings to the crowds that time was running out, that the great judgment was on the brink), we should perhaps bring it into relation with the biblical conception of God's word and of his fidelity to his word.

YHWH could be counted on. Thus, when Joshua's work was done, the narrator of his story writes:

> So YHWH gave unto Israel all the land
> that he swore to give unto their fathers,
> and they possessed it and inhabited it;
> and YHWH gave them rest round about
> according to all that he swore unto their fathers;
> and there stood not one of their enemies against them;
> YHWH delivered all their enemies into their hand.
> There failed not aught of all the good things
> that YHWH had spoken unto the house of Israel.
> All came to pass (Josh 21:42-43; English versions: 21:42-45).

The key word is "all." YHWH gave Israel all the land he had promised, and he gave them rest according to *all* he had sworn. Of *all* their enemies not one withstood them; YHWH delivered them *all* into their hands. Of *all* the good things that he had said, not one failed. In a word, *hakkol ba* : all came to pass.

This passage is not only repeated again and again in fragmentary fashion in the texts that follow in the book of Joshua; it also epitomizes the biblical theme of YHWH's *sedaqah*/righteousness and his *_emûnah*/fidelity, motifs endlessly recurrent in the scriptures. We are moreover in the presence of a massive index to the way in which Israel would come to understand promise and prophecy for the end-time. The whole of it, all without exception, would come to pass. That specifically included the salvation of the nations by assimilation to eschatologically restored Israel.

The background to new developments in the reading of the scriptures might be sketched in a few strokes. The traumatic events of the sixth century—the loss of king and aristocracy in 597, the far more violent and severe losses in the capture of Jerusalem in 587, another deportation in 582; return followed by disillusionment; rifts and factions in the Judean restoration—are diversely reflected in the new foundations laid by prophecy (Trito-Isaiah and Deutero-Zechariah) and by the reforms of Ezra and Nehemiah. The true restoration of Israel became a leading theme and an ongoing, contentious issue. The transcendent terms into which Trito-Isaiah and Deutero-Zechariah transposed the restoration theme opened the era of proto-apocalyptic, remotely preparing the scene for new forms of faith-literature.

The Macedonian conquest of the East similarly instigated new developments in the way indentured Israel envisaged the salvation of the nation. The probable influx from the eastern diaspora of mantic wise men (not the representatives of proverbial wisdom such as we find in Ben Sira) may well explain the origins and salient features of the book of Daniel.[32]

In Qumran we find a systematic way of reading the scriptures, one facet of which is the specification of "the (prophetic) meaning" (*peser*), which focuses on the community, its origins, status, and destiny. The biblical books partly retain their original sense, but by the time of Jesus they (the prophets in particular) were read as pointing toward definitive fulfillment at the outbreak of the end-time. Qumran furnishes

the fullest data on this;[33] but we find it also in intertestamental literature,[34] in the targums,[35] and in John the Baptist (e.g., John 1:23 on Isa
40:3; cf. Mark 1:3= Matt 3:4=Luke 3:4).

Paul, looking back, would say, "Whatever promises God has
made, their Yes is in him" (2 Cor 1:20). Similarly, Jesus himself, repu-
diating the charge of annulling the scriptures, claimed rather to bring
them to completion and fulfillment (Matt 5:17=Luke 16:17; Matt
11:5=Luke 7:22).

In the introduction to this essay we sketched an argument according to which a consciousness like that of Jesus, i.e., of one charged
with a climactic and definitive mission to God's people, should lead us
to expect to find in him a phenomenon otherwise unexampled in ancient Israel: the conviction that God's promises for the end-time *were
already being fulfilled.* Now we may be more specific. We should expect to find that, as time passed and the fulfillment of the whole-to-be-
fulfilled was inaugurated and underway, Jesus should somehow indicate (a) that some of this whole-to-be-fulfilled had now, already, found
fulfillment; (b) that some of it was now finding fulfillment (i.e., during
his public career); (c) that some of it was about to find fulfillment; and
(d) that, since the prominent, perhaps dominant, end-time scenario
(e.g., Dan 12:1-2) posits a distinction between the great affliction and
its cessation (e.g., with the resurrection of the dead), all the rest, i.e.,
whatever of prophecy remains still outstanding (including the very resolution of the ordeal) would find fulfillment when the mission of Jesus
would be crowned by the advent of God's "reign."

In point of fact, we find among the data of the gospel story the
full confirmation of this multiple expectation. (a) After Antipas's execution of the Baptist, we learn that in Jesus' view God had already fulfilled the Elijah promise/prophecy (Mal 3:23-24; English versions: 4:5-
6; Ecclus 48:10) *in the mission of John.* (b) Earlier, by way of answer
to the Baptist's query, Jesus pointed to his own career of wonderworking and proclaiming as bringing prophetic oracles of salvation to fulfillment here and now. (c) Again, he instructed the inner circle of his disciples that he was destined by prophetic necessity to be repudiated and
killed (in accord with the role of the Servant of the Lord who, to be
sure, was equally destined to be vindicated and glorified; see Mark 9:31
and its many parallels);[36] moreover, the disciples were to share in this
suffering, which would signal the outbreak of the eschatological ordeal.

(d) Finally, once the tribulation or ordeal had run its fierce but brief course, he would complete his work as the Davidic master-builder of the new sanctuary (i.e., of the people of the new covenant) (Mark 14:58=Matt 26:61=John 2:19; cf. Acts 6:14), a saying that, again, inescapably implied the total reversal of his personal fate. This would be the moment at which the gentile world would be judged and saved (Matt 8:11=Luke 13:29).[37]

These data of fulfillment—not exhaustive, but merely representative of the full picture offered by the gospels—are telling. They meet our expectation that, given the kind of consciousness of mission that we can with assurance affirm of Jesus, and given the ancient Judaic view of the scriptures as having the aspect of prophecy to be fulfilled in the eschaton, we should expect to find in him the conviction that *in this last climactic mission to Israel. and therefore in the bearer of this last, climactic mission the scriptures—all the scriptures without remainder—had of divine or prophetic necessity to come to fulfillment.*

## Jesus: Proximate Source of the Messianology of the Gospels

If the scriptures had prophetically spoken, as Jesus was fully persuaded that they had, of God's decisive saving act, namely, the restoration of Israel, of the *měbaśśēr* or herald who was to announce it (Isa 52), of the prophet like Moses who was to reveal its demands (Deut 18:15,18), of the Davidic Messiah anointed to accomplish it (2 Sam 7; cf. 4QFlor), of the Servant who would extend it to the ends of the earth (Isa 49:6), of the one like a (son of) man whose triumph would seal it (Dan 7), it follows that we are faced immediately with prophecies and promises which, precisely as that last moment, called inescapably for fulfillment.

How might we form an idea of what, in the scriptures, Jesus took to be soteriologically significant, to call for fulfillment? The clues must be sought in the gospel texts. After an initial period of public activity as the ally of the Baptist until the latter's arrest (John 3:22-26),[38] Jesus inaugurated his own independent public career in Galilee (Mark 1:14=Matt 4:12=Luke 4:14) with the public proclamation, made especially in synagogues but also out-of-doors: "The reign of God is at hand/has arrived!" (*ĕggiken hē basileia tou theou/qĕrabat malkûtà᾽ dē᾽*

*lāhā'*). To many who heard it, these words surely recalled the *Qaddiš* prayer ("may he allow his reign to reign. . . . ") recited weekly in the Synagogue and just as surely evoked the news of salvation epitomized in the cry *mālak 'ĕlōhāik*, "your God reigns" (Isa 52:7). This accordingly suggests that Jesus spoke in the voice of the Isaian *mĕbaśśēr/ euaggelizomenos*—a figure interpreted at Qumran in "messianic" terms: "one anointed with the Spirit" (11Q Melch 18).[39] In Isaiah, then, Jesus found both his career as proclaimer of salvation and the essential burden of his proclamation.

Though, as it happens, we have no confirmatory textual index, it is highly probable that, like the ordinary people among his contemporaries, Jesus took the promise of a prophet like Moses (Deut 15:15,18) to await its fulfillment in the end-time—and concretely to find this fulfillment in his own act of bringing to completion the last measure, the fullness, of revealed truth (Matt 5:17).

It is quite out of the question that Jesus should not have been aware of the many strands of biblical tradition promising a new David or son of David appointed to mediate God's act of restoring his people. Let it suffice to refer to the riddle of the new sanctuary (Mark 14:58=Matt 26:61=John 2:19) with its biblical antecedents on the one appointed to build God's house (2 Sam 7:12-13; cf. 1 Chron 12:13-14; Hag 2:20-23; Zech 6:12-13). There are, of course, many other texts that show Jesus' hold on motifs of royal messianism (e.g., the Caesarea Philippi scene;[40] the royal entry into Jerusalem;[41] repeated use of shepherd imagery[42]).

So far as the Isaian Servant passages are concerned, we find at least two pieces of evidence for Jesus' awareness especially of the last, great passage as soteriologically significant prophecy. These two crucial texts are Mark 10:45=Matt 20:28 (the ransom word, which specifies the beneficiaries of the ransom as "many" [cf. Isa 52:14-15; 53:11-12], and for which Peter Stuhlmacher has provided both a striking exegesis and a persuasive argument in favor of historicity[43]), and Mark 14:24=Matt 26:28 (the word over the cup, which brings together two motifs of Isa 53: the "pouring out" of the Servant's life [Isa 53:12] and, again, the "many").

The two most significant indices to Jesus' keen awareness of the great apocalyptic scene of Daniel 7 are, first, his references to the thrones for the court of judgment (Dan 7:9-10) in Matt 19:28=Luke

22:29 and, second, the "little flock" saying in Luke 12:32, where the motif of transferring to the disciples a share in royal dominion is derived from Dan 7:27.[44] We might add that the Lukan form of Jesus' words in the Sanhedrin scene (Luke 22:69), which takes nothing from Dan 7 except the term "Son of man," is probably prior to the parallels in Mark and Matthew and probably authentic.[45]

Our conclusion is that Jesus, in the consciousness of election to a climactic and definitive mission to Israel, sought and found in the scriptures the specifications of God's eschatological deed and the specifications of his own role as the chosen instrumental doer of that deed. By ineluctable logic these scriptures could not, in Jesus' view, fail to find fulfillment in the drama of his own mission and in its swiftly approaching climax—the ordeal and its resolution. All the scriptures must find fulfillment, whether in the now of his mission or in the rapidly approaching ordeal and final triumph. If the Baptist had fulfilled the Elijah role, Jesus with his disciples was to fulfill the roles of servant of the Lord and Davidic builder of the house of God. Moreover, though Jesus never simply relaxed that altereity which typified his words on the Son of man,[46] picturing him, for example, as witnessing for or against men in accord with how they had stood vis-à-vis Jesus (Mark 8:38; Matt 10:33=Luke 12:9), it is ultimately inescapable that he understood himself as destined to perform the triumphant role of the Son of man. It is an attractive hypothesis that, adopting a deliberately ambiguous use of *bar ᵊnāšâᵓ*/Son of man, he applied it both to "man" in general and to himself (in his "prediction of the passion," in Mark 9:31 parr.).[47] If Luke 22:69 is an authentic word, we are given a hint of Jesus' focus on Ps 110; this in turn grounds the hypothesis that he provided at least a hint (e.g., Mark 12:35-37a=Matt 22:41-46=Luke 20:41-44) that he himself, now the lowly son of David, but soon to be transcendently enthroned—David's "lord"—at the right hand of God.[48] This, of course, correlates and converges with the role of the Son of man on the "Day when the Son of man will be revealed" (Luke 17:30; cf. 17:24,31). Nevertheless, for the disciples only "the Easter experience" would definitively break down the altereity that somehow differentiated between Jesus and "the (Son of) man." (In the light of that breakdown, it is amazing that the original form of the sayings, which exhibit it, should have been so well preserved in the tradition.)

The procedure of the above argument, one that puts a premium on the value of heuristic anticipations, has been consciously and inevitably schematic. First, we acknowledged evidence for Jesus' firm personal conviction of election. He was a man with a mission; the mission bore on, belonged to, the climactic and definitive saving act of God. Jesus accordingly found himself called to function as God's (intimately instrumental) agent with respect to what the scriptures defined as the final restoration of Israel, comprehending (by assimilation to Israel) the salvation of the nations. Second, to this we added the observation that Jesus could not have failed to expect that the sum total of scriptural promise and prophecy was bound by divine necessity to come to fulfillment in connection with his own mission. Third, we consequently found ourselves in the position of being able to articulate a set of significant anticipations: that the accounts of Jesus should yield evidence (a) of eschatology inaugurated and in process of realization; (b) of eschatology in accord with the schema of crisis to be followed by resolution (Dan 12:1-2; cf. Isa 53) and hence of some elements of fulfillment postponed until the moment of resolution; (c) on Jesus' part, of some reflection on and correlation of such soteriological themes (interpreted as prophecy) as the herald of salvation, the awaited prophet, the royal Messiah, the Servant of the Lord, and the one like a man in Dan 7; (d) on the disciples' part, of the probably fragmentary, only partly thematic, and gradually developing knowledge or realization of the eschatological roles of Jesus. Fourth, we found that these anticipations were solidly met by the data of the gospels. Fifth, we concluded that Jesus himself had been the principal source of the earliest post-Easter messianology/ christology.

We should add that in this reconstruction Jesus is seen as intent on listening to the scriptures for the orientation of his life and mission. We do not, however, find in him one constantly and restlessly engaged in adjustments, revisions, changes of heart and mind. The paucity of messianic self-revelation accorded on the part of Jesus neither with simple ignorance nor with any supposed sense of personal ordinariness, but with an economy of revelation that withheld the secret of his person and destiny out of realism and wisdom respecting his listeners. Hence the special importance that accrues to the esoteric traditions in the gospels. It should be added that the disciples were neither swift nor deft in construing the intentions and paradoxical self-disclosures of Jesus. The conditions of the possibility of accurate comprehension were not given except with the so-called "Easter experience." But what this experience generated in the disciples was not the celebration of new, previously unknown messianic and soteriological themes. *All* had been repeatedly adumbrated, if not made thematic, by Jesus.

## Conclusion

We have offered the reader an experiment, a mode of investigation (moving from heuristic anticipations to the interpretation of data) hitherto little used in biblical criticism,[49] though it has been successfully brought to bear on other fields.[50] Its principal advantage is that the orientation of the investigation, made explicit from the start, derives less from the undiscussed preferences of the investigator (which in some measure are always present, albeit most variously in how, from scholar to scholar, they relate to the purity of the desire to know) but from a grasp of procedures spontaneously operative in ancient Judaism. The orientation in question here derives from the manner in which Jesus and his contemporaries typically read the scriptures. We moved (a) from the evidence of Jesus' conviction of personal election to a mission bearing on God's climactic saving act (b) through the scriptures, read as prophecy reserved for eschatological fulfillment, (c) to the anticipation, *and its satisfaction*, of a many-sided, scripturally prophesied role and destiny. To the chosen one scripture revealed in advance the saving mission and its bearer—deed and doer alike in all their variety.

Among the limits of this procedure two are noteworthy: its schematic character and its essential incompleteness vis-à-vis the reality of Jesus and his mission. (Where do we find in the scriptures so much as a hint of Jesus' initiatives toward notorious sinners? Where do they foretell his heavy accent on forgiveness and the rejection of resentment and vengeance?) Its two main strengths are also noteworthy: the orienting principle of the inquiry is a set of verifiable observations about antiquity which markedly diminish that ever widening gap between ourselves and the suppositions operative in ancient Judaism but not among us. Of these we tend to be oblivious or amnesiac, or at least we systematically minimize them. The result is to find that data— unambiguous in context—tend, without that context, to grow dim and almost to vanish before our eyes in a cloud of ambiguity. Those who suppose that scholarship consists in a leisurely cultivation of ambiguity and in recoil from "closure," including the closure intrinsic to framing arguments and drawing conclusions, are likely to repudiate the procedure either with cool disdain or the vehemence of offended ideology.[51] Those, on the other hand, who think that historical inquiry should devise new ways of heading for historical conclusions may well find some merit in the procedure.

# NOTES

1. On whether the realized element in the eschatology of Jesus and of earliest Christianity has any true parallel in ancient Judaism, see Allison, *Ages*, 91f. Here Allison significantly nuances the account of "realized eschatology" in David Aune, *The Cultic Setting of Realized Eschatology in Early Christianity* (Leiden: Brill, 1967). But despite his fine contribution to the main issues, Allison himself has been led to suppose that *T. Job* 39:9-40:6 might offer a true parallel to the realized eschatology of the resurrection of Jesus. In presenting the "resurrection" of Job and his children, however, the writer of the testament never steps out of the narrative world of Job into that shared by writer and reader. This does not hold for NT texts on the resurrection of Jesus, as 1 Cor 15:3-8 unequivocally shows by its accent on available living witnesses to whom the risen Christ had appeared. Moreover, this difference grounds another: the impact attributed to Jesus' resurrection vs. the total lack of impact of the "resurrection" of Job.

2. Joachim Jeremias, "Die Drei-Tage-Worte der Evangelien," in *Tradition und Glaube* [K. G. Kuhn Festschrift], eds. Gert Jeremias, H.-W. Kuhn, H. Stegemann (Göttingen: Vandenhoeck & Ruprecht, 1971) 221-229, at 227.

3 . J. Jeremias, "Die Drei-Tage-Worte"; B. F. Meyer, "The 'Inside' of the Jesus Event," in Meyer, *Critical Realism* 157-172.

4. Joachim Jeremias, "Iōnas," in eds. Kittel and Friedrich, *Theological Dictionary of the New Testament* III, 406-410 .

5. Respecting Jesus' use of typology, a detailed special study is still lacking; meantime, see R. T. France, *Jesus and the Old Testament* (Grand Rapids: Baker, 1982 [1st ed., 1971] ) 38-82. The historicity of the temple riddle in the Synoptics is guaranteed by discontinuity (the Synoptics nowhere attribute the word to Jesus); that of the sign of Jonah is less compelling, but the uniqueness of the Lukan form and the seeming difficulty that the tradition had in understanding it exactly are telling indices to historicity.

6. Franziskus Zorell, *Lexicon Graecum Novi Testamenti* (Paris: Le-

thielleux, 1931) "*plērōma*, " 1079; see also "*pleroō,* " 1076 . For Mark 1:15 it follows that *kairos* here is not punctiliar but equivalent to *chronos.* Among recent treatments, see Joel Marcus, "('The Time Has Been Fulfilled!' Mark 1.15)," in *Apocalyptic and the New Testament* [J. L. Martyn Festschrift], eds. J. Marcus and M. L. Soards (Sheffield: JSOT, 1989) 49-68. On the theme of eschatological measure: R. Stuhlmann, *Das eschatologische Mass im Neuen Testament* (Göttingen: Vandenhoeck & Ruprecht, 1983).

7. Paul Joüon, "Notes philologiques sur les Évangiles, " *Recherches de science religieuse* 17 (1927) 537-540, at 538.

8. Jeremias, *Theology*, 82-85.

9. "Superabundant," especially inasmuch as the Isaian texts on which Jesus drew do not include reference to raising the dead.

10. Meyer, *Aims*, 202-208.

11. C. H. Dodd, *The Parables of the Kingdom* (London: Nisbet, 1935; repr. London-Glasgow: Collins [Fontana] 1961) ch. 2 and 3.

12. T. F. Glasson, *The Second Advent* (London: Epworth, 3rd ed., 1963).

13. J. A. T. Robinson, *Jesus and His Coming* (Philadelphia: Westminster, 2nd ed., 1979).

14. Joachim Jeremias, "Eine neue Schau der Zukunftsaussagen Jesu," *Theologische Blätter* 20 (1941) 216-222.

15. Ernst Käsemann, "The Beginnings of Christian Theology" in Käsemann, *New Testament Questions of Today* (London: SCM, 1969) 82-107; "On the Subject of Primitive Christian Apocalyptic," *Questions*, 108-137; "Sentences of Holy Law in the New Testament," *Questions*, 66-81.

16. George B. Caird, *Jesus and the Jewish Nation* (London: Athlone, 1965); *The Language and Imagery of the Bible* (Philadelphia: Westminster, 1980).

17. Borg, *Conflict; Jesus: A New Vision* (San Francisco: Harper, 1987). Also: "An Orthodoxy Reconsidered: The "End-of-the-World Jesus'," in *The Glory of Christ in the New Testament* [G. B. Caird Festschrift] (eds.) L. D. Hurst and N. T. Wright (Oxford: Clarendon, 1987) 207-217.

18. See above, note 1.

19. Two points are relevant. First, Allison found fault with Dodd's (and so equivalently with Jeremias's) view that an important root of early Christianity's realized eschatology was the realized eschatology of Jesus' words, e.g., that the reign of God had come, already, to Israel in and through his cures and exorcisms. But, so far as I can see, Allison has not found a way of supporting this denial. Second, in his many historical-Jesus studies Jeremias repeatedly affirmed that Jesus understood his coming suffering to inaugurate the eschatological ordeal (e.g., in *Parables*, 220: Jesus' suffering "represents the beginning of the final tribulation . . . " The metaphor Jeremias used in *Neutestamentliche*

*Theologie I. Die Verkündigung Jesu* (Göttingen: Vandenhoeck & Ruprecht, 1971, 2nd ed. 1973) 231, was that his suffering would constitute *der Auftakt* (the first syllable, first beat, opening phase, prelude) of the eschatological ordeal. The choice of the term "prelude" in the English translation, however, led Allison, 118, (a) to suppose that in Jeremias's reconstruction Jesus took his own suffering to precede, but not to belong to, the ordeal; and (b) to find fault with Jeremias's failure to prove the view thus mistakenly attributed to him. (For his own part, Allison took the tribulation to be already underway during Jesus' ministry [117-128]). See how some of the most relevant texts (e.g., Matt 26:18; Luke 12:49; 13:33; John 12:19; 16:16a) are read in Jeremias, "Drei-Tage-Worte" and *New Testament Theology*, 127-141.

20. Meyer, "Jesus' Scenario of the Future," *Downside Review* 109 (1991) 1-15; reprinted here as Chapter 3.

21. See, e.g., Allison, *Ages*, 111, note 40.

22. A point made cogently by N. T. Wright in a text (as yet unpublished) delivered at a McMaster University seminar, December 14, 1989, on hermeneutics and the historical Jesus.

23. The scholastics, building on the Aristotelian distinction of potency and act, differentiated within "act" between what was formally and what virtually actual—a distinction often appropriate to the advance presence of God's reign.

24. B. F. Meyer, "The Expiation Motif in the Eucharistic Words: A Key to the History of Jesus?" *Gregorianum* 69 (1988) 461-487, at 481-484.

25. Among these facets was one that, recently and independently, J. Neusner and I inferred from the negative stance toward the cult implicit in Jesus' demonstration at the temple, namely, that the counterpart of the temple cleansing must be—the Last Supper. See J. Neusner, "Money-Changers in the Temple: The Mishnah's Explanation" *New Testament Studies* 35 (1989) 287-290; Meyer, "Expiation Motif," 482-484.

26. Hence the thesis that "to predicate 'Messiah' of Jesus in the sense he himself intended is to grasp the 'inside' of the Jesus event as the single task of re-creating Israel—and the nations by assimilation to Israel—in fulfillment of the scriptures." Meyer, "The 'Inside' of the Jesus Event," in *Critical Realism* 169.

27. The case was made by Dalman, *Words*, 96-101, who differentiated this from other senses of the phrase in ancient Judaism.

28. See Johannes Behm, "diathēkē," in (eds.) Kittel and Friedrich, *Theological Dictionary of the New Testament* II, 124-134, esp. 128, 132-133; Jeremias, *Die Abendmahlsworte Jesu* (Göttingen: Vandenhoeck & Ruprecht, 3rd ed., 1960) 217f.: the (new) covenant is "Korrelatbegriff zu *basileia tōn ouranōn*." ET *Eucharistic* 226. But what holds for new covenant holds for new sanctuary and new cult. On the pre-Jesus tradition respecting the new temple/

sanctuary see E. P. Sanders, *Jesus and Judaism* (London: SCM, 1985).

29. John Downing, "Jesus and Martyrdom," *Journal of Theological Studies* 14 (1963) 279-293.

30. Downing, "Martyrdom," 286f.

31. Amos N. Wilder, "Eschatology and the Speech-Modes of the Gospel," *Zeit und Geschichte* [R. Bultmann Festschrift] (Tübingen: Mohr-Siebeck, 1964) 19-30, at 29.

32. John J. Collins, *The Apocalyptic Vision of the Book of Daniel* (Missoula: Scholars, 1977) 56f.

33. Though there are numerous good general expositions, e.g., Otto Betz, *Offenbarung und Schriftforschung* (Tübingen: Mohr-Siebeck, 1960); M. P. Horgan, *Pesharim: Qumran Interpretations of Biblical Books* (Washington: BBA, 1979), to understand concretely the Essenes' style of interpreting, special studies of individual texts, e.g., William H. Brownlee, *The Midrash Pesher of Habakkuk* (Missoula: Scholars, 1979), are indispensable.

34. See John Barton, *Oracles of God* (Oxford: Oxford University Press, 1986); Christopher Rowland, "The Inter-Testamental Literature" in (eds.) J. Rogerson, C. Rowland, B. Lindars, *The History of Christian Theology. II. The Use of the Bible* (Grand Rapids: Eerdmans, 1988) 153-225.

35. In the present context, see especially Bruce Chilton, *A Galilean Rabbi and His Bible* (Wilmington: Glazier, 1984) and Bruce Chilton, *The Isaiah Targum* (Wilmington: Glazier, 1987).

36. Jeremias, *Theology* on Mark 9:31 and its many parallels, 281-286.

37. Still valuable: Bengt Sundkler, "Jesus et les païens," *Revue d'Histoire et de Philosophie religieuses* 16 (1936) 462-499; J. Jeremias, *Jesus' Promise to the Nations* (London: SCM, 1958); Jacques Dupont, "'Beaucoup viendront du levant et du couchant . . . ' (Matthieu 8,11-12 Luc 13,28-29," *Sciences Ecclésiastiques* 9 (1967) 153-167.

38. On Jesus as "baptizer," Meyer, *Aims*, 122-124.

39. Joseph A. Fitzmyer, "Further Light on Melchizedek from Qumran Cave 11," in Fitzmyer, *Essays on the Semitic Background of the New Testament* (Missoula: Scholars, 1974) 245-267.

40. Meyer, *Aims*, 185-197.

41. Meyer, *Aims*, 168-170, 199.

42. Messianic shepherd imagery: Ezek 34:23-24; 37:24; Zech 13:7-9; cf. 12:10; 13:1-6. On the imagery in gospels: Gustaf Dalman, "Arbeit und Sitte in Palästina vi," *Beiträge zur Förderung christlicher Theologie*, series 2, 41 (1939) 249-250, 253-255.

43. Peter Stuhlmacher, "Vicariously Giving His Life for Many, Mark 10:45 (Matt. 20:28)," in Stuhlmacher, *Reconciliation, Law, and Righteousness* (Philadelphia: Fortress, 1986) 16-29. Now also Volker Hampel, *Menschensohn und historischer Jesus* (Neukirchen-Vluyn: Neukirchener Verlag, 1990) 302-

342.

44. Otto Betz, *Jesus und das Danielbuch. II. Die Menschensohnworte Jesu and die Zukunftserwartung des Paulus (Daniel 7,13- 14)* (Frankfurt: Lang, 1985). Betz takes a negative view of Daniel's influence. On the two texts adduced, see Jeremias, *New Testament Theology*, 205, note 4; and 265.

45. B. F. Meyer, "How Jesus Charged Language with Meaning: A Study in Rhetoric," *Studies in Religion/Sciences Religieuses* 19 (1990) 273-285, at 285, with note 32; repr. here as Chapter 6.

46. Jeremias, *Theology*, 265f. and, still more relevantly and incisively, 275-276.

47. See above, note 36.

48. On the sense of the pericope on David's son and David's lord, see Jeremias, *Theology*, 259, 276.

49. An exception (though perhaps not an altogether successful one) is the collaboration of Wilhelm Thüsing and Karl Rahner, *A New Christology* (New York: Seabury, 1980).

50. An example is the argument from human problem to the heuristic specification of the divine solution in Lonergan, *Insight,* 687-730.

51. The recoil from the closure proper to judgments of credibility and to beliefs pervades Northrop Frye's transactions with the Bible in *The Great Code* (New York-London: Harcourt Brace Jovanovich, 1982). If ideology is the rationalization of alienation, this is ideological, transparently alienated as it is from religious belief, which Frye conceives single- and narrow-mindedly as headed for religious war. See my essay, "A Tricky Business: Ascribing New Meaning to Old Texts," *Gregorianum* 71 (1990) 743-761.

5

## "MANY (=ALL) ARE CALLED,
## BUT FEW (=NOT ALL) ARE CHOSEN"

The conviction that God is good, that he takes "no pleasure in the death of the wicked" (Ezek 18:23), that he "desires all men to be saved" (1 Tim 2:4), and that Christ gave himself as a ransom for all" (1 Tim 2:4), belongs to the main thrust of Christian soteriology. Although there have been soteriological pessimists (Thomas Aquinas, the Angelic Doctor, was an optimist on the salvation of the angels, but a pessimist on the salvation of human beings) and optimists (Karl Barth construed Paul's universalist teleology as a flat guarantee of universal salvation), most Christians have had to content themselves with an affirmation of God's at least antecedently universal salvific will, with the hope for the salvation of many and even of all, and with a straightforward agnosticism respecting whether the finally lost will be "any" or "many" or something in between. But in the word of Matt 22:14 (l.v. 20:16), Jesus himself speaks, and he seems (a) to evoke election =predestination=salvation, (b) to reduce the number of the elect=predestined=saved to "few," and (c) to suggest that the differentiation between the called and the elect is not the outcome of human acts but of divine decision. All three factors—final salvation is at stake, few are saved, and this by God's sovereign decision—say why this word has been a *crux interpretum*.

The last of these three factors may be disposed of first. Just as, when the human subject responds positively to Jesus, this is ascribed not to his act of faith but to God's act of revelation (Matt 11:25=Luke 10:21; Matt 16:17), so here the accent falls not on the human subject's decision and perseverence in it, but on God's sealing of it by "election." This style of thought and expression highlights the primacy and ultimacy of God's love, while supposing (though not defining) the role of the human subject's free self-determination. So far as Matt 22:14 is concerned, this solution is illuminated and confirmed by the double parable to which it is attached.

The first factor, respecting whether salvation is at stake, is not quite so easily dispatched. Still, it must be admitted that the word *eklektoi* does indeed evoke eternal salvation, for, unlike the use of *bahar* through most of Old Testament literature, the horizons of election in the gospels make room not only for God's this-worldly governance of and predilection for his people, but for an economy and predilection with next-worldly connotations, too (Mark 13:20, 22, 27=Matt 24:22, 24,31).

Despite the variety of exegetical experiments, the truly critical issue remains the motif of the "few." The few chosen=predestined=saved calls to mind the "few" who find the narrow gate that leads to life by contrast with the "many" who enter by the wide gate that leads to destruction (Matt 7:13-14; cf. Luke 13:24). Jesus, on the other hand, when asked, "are the saved to be few?" (Luke 13:22) does not answer, except by urging whoever wonders about such things to "strain every nerve" to enter into life (Luke 13:24) while there is still time (v. 25). Elsewhere, moreover, he envisages the saved not as a few but as a great multitude (Mark 4:8=Matt 13:8=Luke 8:8; Mark 4:32 =Matt 13:32b=Luke 13:19; Matt 22:10=Luke 14:23b).

The effort to escape what seems to be Jesus' view of the saved as "few" has taken two main forms. The first differentiates between the terms of goals of election; the second limits the field of vision to Israel. According to the first form, many are called, few chosen, with respect, not to eternal salvation, but to the community of restored Israel (=the Church).[1] It is doubtless true that "restored Israel" dominates the foreground of Jesus' vision of things.[2] Nevertheless, those "simple" (*nēpioi*) who by the prevenient goodness and favor of God (Matt 11:25-26=Luke 10:21; Matt 16:17) accepted Jesus' eschatological offer and responded to his messianic summons were one and the same as the *eklektoi* (Luke 18:7), so named from their share in both present and future salvation (Mark 13:20,22,27=Matt 24:22,24,31). In the gospel literature the whole accent falls on the contintuity, not discontinuity, obtaining between present response to Jesus and future acquittal/condemnation at the judgment (Mark 8:38; Matt 7:24-27=Luke 6:47-49; Matt 10:32-33=Luke 12:8-9; Matt 12:41-42=Luke 11: 31-32). So, though there is a difference between restored Israel in the present (whether of Jesus' ministry or of the post-Easter community) and definitive salvation in the future, it is not very helpful, in the context of efforts to retrieve what gospel texts themselves meant, to differentiate between election to the one and election to the other.

The second way of deabsolutizing the logion has been somewhat more successful. It lay in the observation that Jesus' intention had not been to satisfy curiosity about whether most human beings are saved or lost (see Luke 13:22-24). More probably, he was referring to the painfully unsatisfactory response of his contemporaries to his mission. Out of the great mass of those to whom he appealed only a few stood ready to respond to his summons. These constituted the remnant among whom Israel found eschatological restoration (see the notes appended in the *New Jerusalem Bible* to Matt 22:14; 24:22; Rom 11:1,16).

This interpretative move represented in some respects a step forward toward historical concreteness, but on reflection it does not nearly go far enough. Insofar as it represents Jesus as making an absolute statement on the "few" out of Israel who are to be saved, it stands entirely isolated. It seems at first to derive some support from Matt 7:13-14=Luke 13:23. But that paraenetic text, besides putting the accent on human behavior rather than on God's judgment, does not, in fact, allude to a positive "few."[3]

Jesus never gave up on his mission to all Israel. At the Last Supper he fasted for Israel and intended his death as expiatory for the world, but above all for Israel.[4] It seems hardly credible that at some earlier point he would have settled the matter that only a "few" out of Israel would be saved. In this matter, as in every other aspect of his disposition, attitude, and policy toward Israel at large, he seems to have adopted a view at the opposite pole to that of Qumran.[5]

The one fundamentally successful deabsolutizing of the logion, so far as I can judge, was that of Edmond Boissard, in 1952.[6] Boissard set the logion in the context of Hebrew and Aramaic idiom. Both languages lacked comparative forms of the adjective, and Hebrew lacked even such comparative adverbs as "more" and "less." Comparison, however, is basic and indispensable in thought and speech. Speakers and writers have accordingly pressed these languages in resourceful fashion to express the comparative.[7] Translation into Greek of Aramaic devices for expressing the comparative has often obscured the sense of gospel texts; repeatedly they have been cleared up only when interpreters have had recourse to the Aramaic substratum of the texts.[8]

Among the many ways in which positive forms have been made to express comparative meanings, the correlative comparative stands out. "Large" (*gādôl*) is said by relation to "small" (*qāṭōn*), the two thus signifying "larger"/"smaller." According to Gen 1:16 God made "two major [*gĕdōlîm*] lights [major by contrast with minor or smaller lights, i.e., the stars], a larger [*gādôl*] light to rule the day and a smaller [*qāṭōn*] light to rule the night." Using three adjectives, all in the positive form, this text refers to the moon as a "major light" by comparison with the stars and as a "smaller light" by comparison with the sun.

Boissard urged that such was the case for the use of "many" and "few" in Matt 22:14. He accordingly translated into Latin: *numerosiores sunt vocati, pauciores electi*, and into French: *plus nombreux les appelés, plus rares les élus;* that is, "more numerous are those called, less numerous are those chosen." The gospel saying in this version leaves totally untouched the question of whether the elect = predestined = saved are many or few. Moreover, it should be noted that the text does not focus on "the lost"; it does not, for example, say that the lost are more numerous than the saved. It simply says: *not all are chosen.* In Boissard's words this "not all" becomes: "Among the great number of the called, a certain portion (whether few or many the saying does not say) will by its own fault elude final election . . ." In Boissard's view the main teaching both of the saying and of the parable to which it is attached is "that to be chosen it does not suffice to be called."[9]

After Boissard had completed his analysis, he discovered that he had been anticipated by a note in Crampon, *La Sainte Bible*, édition revue par le Père A. Piffard, S.J., tome VI (1904) p. 79, on Matt 20:16, which reads as follows: "We should first of all note that in accord with the manner of expression of the Hebrews, who do not have comparatives, this saying simply means that there will be fewer elect than called."[10]

*Theology Digest* drew attention to Boissard's article in 1955, presenting a summary of it in English.[11] Why is it that his view has nevertheless had so little impact on New Testament studies? Perhaps not enough attention is paid, in general, to French Catholic scholarship among German, British, and American exegetes. But the original French Jerusalem Bible (1956) also passed over Boissard in silence. Two further observations may, then, be relevant. First, the Old Testa-

ment evidence that Boissard adduced, though both copious and relevant
to his analysis, did not include use of the terms *polloi/oligoi* and their
Hebrew equivalents *rab/mě'at*. Second, Boissard's observations on context concentrated exclusively on the placement of this saying in Matthew, leaving unexplored considerations of context in the historic drama of Jesus' mission. In what follows I would like to make good these
omissions .

There are many biblical texts in which *rab* and *mě'at* are
played off against each other (e.g., Num 13:18; 26:54, 56; 33:54; 35:8;
Deut 7:7; 1 Sam 14:6; 2 Kings 10:18; Hag 1:6,9). Here let it suffice to
adduce Num 26:52-56 (REB):

> The LORD said to Moses, "The land is to be apportioned
> among these tribes according to the number of names recorded.
> To the larger group (*lārab*) give a larger share of territory and
> to the smaller (*wělamě 'at*) a smaller; a share will be given to
> each in proportion to its size as shown in the census. The land,
> however, is to be apportioned by lot, the lots being cast for the
> territory by families in the father's line, and shares apportioned
> by lot between the larger families and the smaller (*bên rab limě
> 'at*)."[12]

Here large and small, larger and smaller, are said by relation to one another. The text does not allow us to say whether any of the smaller
tribes were "few" (*me at*). What the text does allow us to say is that the
tribes were not equal; some were larger than others. Therefore their inheritance ought not to be equal. Rather, it was to be divided proportion-
ately, whether among tribes or families. Both *rab* and *me at* are positive
in form, comparative in sense.

LXX Num 26:56 underscores the specifically comparative use
of *rab* and *mě'at* (REV "between the larger [families] and the smaller")
by *anameson pollōn kai oligōn* ("between the many and the few," i.e.,
between the more numerous and the less numerous). This quite clearly
exemplifies the correlative comparative use of *polloi* and *oligoi* and, I
would say, clinches Boissard's case for the existence of this semitizing
idiom.

Some further indicative instances: *rab* and *mě'at* are correlative comparatives in Num 35:8. Forty-eight cities were to be taken from
the tribes and given to the Levites in accord with due proportion: "you

should allot more (*hărab*) from a larger tribe and less (*hamĕ'aṭ*) from a smaller" (REB). According to LXX Num 35:8, "Many (=more) [cities] from the tribes that have many (=more) (*apo tōn ta polla, polla*), less from the lesser (*apo tōn elattonōn, elattō*)."

Again, when Israel was starving in the wilderness, the Lord provided "bread." Each head of family was to gather one omer for each family member. According to LXX Exod 16:17-18, they did as they were told, gathering "some much (=more), some less (*ho to polu kai ho to elatton*); and when they measured it out by the omer, those who had gathered much (=more=*ho to polu*) had not gathered too much, and those who had gathered less (*ho to elatton*) had not gathered too little. Each had gathered according to the need of those who belonged to him." Given the use in both these texts of forms of the comparative *elatton*, it seems highly probable that the correlative positive forms (*polla* in Num 35 and *polu* in Exod 16) bear comparative senses.

It should be added that in Paul's citation of Exod 16:18 *elatton* is replaced by *oligon*. Despite the failure of translators of the New Testament to notice, *to polu* and *to oligon* in 2 Cor 8:15 are correlative comparatives: "they who had more had no excess, and they who had less, no lack." The surplus (*perisseuma*) of the Corinthian community is strictly correlative to the deficiency (*husterēma*) of the saints in Jerusalem. The Corinthians did not have "much," but they did have "more" than the poverty-stricken Jerusalem Christians.

It will not be amiss now to distinguish the substantival uses of *polloi* in the New Testament. First, (*hoi*) *polloi* means "many" (e.g., Mark 6:2). Second, *hoi polloi* (literally, "the many") is sometimes used relatively to mean "most, the majority" (e.g., Matt 24:12). Third, *hoi polloi* is used, under the influence of Heb. (*ha*) *rabbîm*/Aram. *saggî'în*, to refer to a numerous totality, sometimes inclusive of all (within a given set). There is no exact Hebrew or Aramaic equivalent of "all." Though Heb. *kol*/Aram. *kollā'* designates "the totality," this totality neither is nor allows a plural. Of itself it leaves open whether the totality is one unit or a sum of units. (*Hā*) *rabbim*/*saggî'în*, on the other hand, implies a sum of units, but of itself leaves open whether the sum is total, i.e., all-inclusive. When the intended referent is inclusive in this sense, the expression becomes the functional equivalent of "all" (e.g., *polloi* in Matt 8:11).[13] Fourth and finally, I am arguing that, as in LXX Num 26:56, *polloi* and *oligoi* are used in Matt 22:14 as correlative comparatives to mean "more numerous" and "less numerous."[14]

Indeed, Matt 22:14 illustrates both the third and the fourth categories. This ascertainment resolves an age-old *crux interpretum*. On the one hand, *polloi gar eisin klētoi* in Matt 22:14 is inclusive (=all), for, as Joachim Jeremias observed, otherwise there would be "a selection in both clauses," yielding a gratuitously clouded sense.[15] (Jeremias invoked the parallel of 4 Ezra 8:3, *multi quidem creati sunt, pauci autem salvabuntur*. Here *multi* was clearly inclusive, for there were no human beings that had not been created.) On the other hand, *oligoi de eklektoi* does not mean that the chosen are "few," but that they are fewer than those called. But "fewer than all" means "not all." In short, whereas *polloi* and *oligoi* in Matt 22:14 retain their correlative comparative sense of "more/fewer," their consciously intended respective referents are "all/not all."[16]

Jeremias grasped half of this. "The call is unlimited," he rightly observed.[17] But, not having considered the possibility of positive forms correlated to yield a comparative sense, he found himself forced to conclude that the saying reduced the *eklektoi* to "few." To mitigate the harshness of this sense, he urged that the thrust of *eklektoi* was limited (it was not "predestinarian," but just a "fixed technical term for the messianic community")[18] and that "Jesus is not to blame if only a few reach the goal (Matt 22:14)."[19] Such mitigating and limiting considerations lose their point, once *polloi* and *oligoi* are correctly understood as correlative comparatives.

This conclusion, it seems to me, holds also for the *multi* and *pauci* of 4 Ezra 8:3. Many (=more=all) were created, but few (=fewer=not all) will be saved. Just as the saying of Matt 22:14 accords perfectly with the sense of the imagery of the parable to which it is attached, so 4 Ezra 8:3, in the version proposed here, accords perfectly with the sense and imagery of 4 Ezra 8:41:

> For just as the farmer sows many seeds upon the ground and plants a multitude of seedlings, and yet *not all* that have been sown will come up in due season, and *not all* that were planted will take root; so *not all* those who have been sown in the world will be saved.[20]

At this point the semantic parallel between Matt 22:14 and 4 Ezra 8:3 is striking.

We should insist that this reading of the Matthean text disposes of the entire nest of problems respecting how the saying that caps the
two-part parable of Matt 22:1-13 is meant to illuminate it. There is no
longer any need for exegetical gymnastics, e.g., the common but inher-
ently improbable view that this "generalizing conclusion" attached to
part two of the parable relates only to part one. Given the interpretation
offered here, the saying is relevant to both parts.

Finally, there is a further issue of context. Is this word, as is
sometimes proposed,[21] a product of Matthean composition? Or, if it is
pre-Matthean and, indeed, a word of the historical Jesus, what will have
been its original context and originally intended sense?

The fact that we have here a semitizing idiom—the correlative
comparative use of positive forms, and *polloi* with all-inclusive referent—suggests that the saying (cf. 4 Ezra 8:3) was coined not in Greek
but in Aramaic.[22] That it was a Jewish proverb[23] is possible but unlikely, insofar as the saying contradicts the common soteriological views of
the time (cf. Sanh. 10.1, "all Israel has a share in the age to come"). The
index of originality[24] would favor the attribution of the saying to Jesus
himself rather than to the Aramaic-speaking post-Easter community.
Judaism said: all Israel is called (Isa 48:12) and chosen (Isa 49:7). Jesus
said: called, yes; chosen, that depends!

This refusal to take the election of all Israel for granted was
anything but isolated among Jesus' words. Like the Baptist, he did indeed direct his proclamation and summons to all Israel. Like the Baptist
(Luke 3:8=Matt 3:9), he consistently affirmed that the maintenance of
election in the sight of God hinged on response to the final call of God.
That the sanction of this claim would be the coming judgment is a
theme copiously attested by the Synoptic tradition (e.g., [a] Mark
6:11=Matt 10:4=Luke 9:5=10:10-11; [b] Mark 8:38=Matt 16:27=Luke
9:26; [c] Matt 7:22-23=Luke 13:26-27; [d] Matt 7:24-27=Luke 5:47-
49; [e] Matt 10:32-33=Luke 12:8-9; [f] Matt 12:41-42=Luke 11:31-32).
Response to Jesus' eschatological and election-historical mission was
not optional, but absolutely requisite. To the righteous who rejected it,
he issued a warning: "Publicans and prostitutes [who had responded
positively to his call] will enter the reign of God, and you [the right-
eous] will not" (Matt 21:31).[25] In more general terms, with the accent
falling on the second clause, "many (=more=all) are called, but few
(=fewer=not all) are chosen (Matt 22 :14).

# NOTES

1. See, e.g., E. F. Sutcliffe, "Many Are Called But Few Are Chosen," *Irish Theological Quarterly* 28 (1961) 126-131.

2. Meyer, *Aims*, 171-173.

3. See below, note 14.

4. Jeremias, *Eucharistic*, 207-218, 225-231.

5. In the view of the Qumran community the "sons of darkness" to be defeated in the eschatological war (1QM 1:1,7,10,16,; 3:6,9, etc.) were already represented in contemporary Israel (1QS 1:10). Whereas the ultimate future of empirical Israel was obscure and for the most part inglorious, the Qumran brethren "were the faithful 'remnant' of their time, and indeed the final 'remnant' of all time." Geza Vermes, *The Dead Sea Scrolls in English* (Harmondsworth: Penguin, 1975) 35.

6. Edmond Boissard, "Note sur l'interprétation du texte 'Multi sunt vocati, pauci vero electi'," *Revue Thomiste* 52 (1952) 569-585.

7. See Paul Joüon, *Grammaire de l'hébreu biblique* (Rome: Biblical Institute Press, 1947) 436. Modern Hebrew uses *yôtēr* (cf. Qoh 12:12) and *pāḥût*. Also: Blass-Debrunner-Funk, *A Greek Grammar of the New Testament* (Cambridge: University Press; Chicago: University of Chicago Press, 1961) 127-128; Blass-Debrunner-Rehkopf, *Grammatik des neutestamentlichen Griechisch* (Göttingen: Vandenhoeck & Ruprecht, fifteenth edition, 1979) 194-197.

8. This is especially the case when "comparative *min*" has been used in the Aramaic substratum in an exclusive sense (e.g., Luke 18:14). A survey of the Greek renderings of this Semitic phenomenon is offered by J. Jeremias, *Unknown Sayings of Jesus* (London: SPCK, 1957) 78, note 1 (not included in the second edition of 1964). See also Blass-Debrunner-Funk, 128.

9. See Boissard "Note," 581 for both citations.

10. Boissard, "Note," 573, note 1.

11. Edmond Boissard, "Many Are Called, Few Are Chosen," *Theology Digest* 3 (1955) 46-50.

12. In *The Holy Scriptures* (Philadelphia: The Jewish Publication Society of America, 1955) the final phrase in Num 26:56 is rendered "between the more and the fewer"—in exactly literal accord with the LXX Num 26:56, as we shall see.

13. J. Jeremias, *"polloi,"* TDNT VI, 536-545, at 541-542.

14. The following New Testament passages exhibit forms of *polus* and *oligos* played off against one another: Matt 7:13-14 (cf. Luke 13:23-24); Matt 9:37=Luke 10:2; Matt 22:14 (v.l. 20:16); Matt 25:21-23 (cf. Luke 19:17); Luke 7:47; 2 Cor 8:15. Of them I take the following five texts to exhibit the correlative comparative and hence to call for new translations: Matt 7:13-14 (the greater part—the lesser part; or, the more numerous—the less numerous); Matt 22:14 (many=more= all—few=fewer=not all; see below); Matt 24:21,23 (a lesser charge—a greater charge); Luke 7:47c (one who is forgiven less loves less [is less grateful]); 2 Cor 8:15 (more—less) .

15. "*polloi,* " 542.

16. Jeremias, "*polloi,*" put it this way: "Formally there is an antithesis between a great and a small number, but materially the many represent the totality." I would make one change in this sentence: not "great" and "small," but "greater" and "smaller."

17. Jeremias, *Theology*, 131.

18. Jeremias, *Theology*, 130-131.

19. Jeremias, *Theology*, 177.

20. We translate "not all" rather than "all . . . not" in the recognition that, whereas it is a trait of Semitic syntax not to negate the pronoun, English requires it. Cf. Matt 5:18,36; 24:22; Mark 13:20; Luke 1:37; 11:46. Cf. Jeremias, *Parables*, 219, note 53.

21. Among recent studies, Otto Knoch, *Wer Ohren hat, der höre* (Stuttgart: Katholisches Bibelwerk, 1983) 143, 147.

22. Aramaic reconstruction proposed by Dalman, JJ, 227, and accepted by Jeremias, *Theology*, 25: ssaggᵊᵓîn dĕᵓ innûn zᵉmînîn

wᵉṣibḥad dĕᵓ innûn bᵉḥîrîn.

There are not enough data available to offer confirmatory evidence on the correlative comparative use of *saggî/ṣibḥād*.

23. R. Bultmann, *The History of the Synoptic Tradition* (Oxford: Blackwell, second edition 1968 ) 105, with reference to "parallels in Dalman, " (Dalman, *JJ* 228, cites Midr. Sam. 8: "There are elect who are rejected and again brought near; but there are also elect who, once rejected, are never brought near again") entertains the possibility, no more, that it was "a traditional saying of Jewish apocalyptic." That this cannot be apodictically excluded is clear from what is said above about 4 Ezra 8:3. But this by no means rules out the probability that the words were spoken by Jesus—a point clearer to Dalman than to Bultmann. Otherwise, in Bultmann's view, the saying would belong to the authentic words of Jesus as "teacher of wisdom."

24. Meyer, *Aims*, 86.

25 Jeremias, *Theology*, 117.

## 6

## HOW JESUS CHARGED LANGUAGE WITH MEANING: A STUDY IN RHETORIC

Beginning with the clash between Socrates and the Sophists, "rhetoric" has often seemed to the *conoscenti* to be a dangerous business, best kept strictly in its place. Philosophers blamed rhetoric for undermining the pure desire to know and turning seekers after truth into seekers after prizes (Plato). Poets blamed rhetoric, first, for pretending to be subtler and finer than poetry (Milton); second, for wrecking poetry by artifice (Verlaine, Pound, Eliot). Theologians of our time blame their predecessors for allowing such logical and rhetorical ideals as clarity, coherence, and rigour to dress up static abstractions in the guise of eternal truths (Lonergan).

But if the word "rhetoric" comes to us trailing connotations of pretention and artificiality, of language trying too hard to do too much, it remains that in the present context and for present purposes rhetoric is the study of style. Cicero, moreover, did have a point when (in the *De Oratore*, III, 32) he deplored the Socratic split between the wise and the eloquent or, as he put it, between the heart and the tongue. For heart and tongue belong together, heart setting tongue in motion, tongue making heart understood.

In biblical tradition "heart" signified the whole of human intentionality, which showed itself in bodily and facial expression, but above all in words. Authentic speech revealed the pure heart, skilled speech the wise heart. The "understanding" or "hearing" heart (*lēb šōmēʿa*) that Solomon prayed for (1 Kings 3:9) and that the Lord immediately conferred on him, was to set the speech of Solomon apart, "so that none like you has been before you and none like you shall arise after you" (1 Kings 3:12). But we are about to take up the speech of one who spoke in the consciousness that the mission coming to expression in his words meant that his words outstripped Solomon's (Matt 12:42=Luke 11:31). Yet the same speaker spoke out of a consciousness of being "'meek and lowly of heart" (Matt 11:29); as a poor man among the poor he thanked his Father (Matt 11:25-26=Luke 10:21) for reserving revelation for the "simple" *(nēpioi/šabrîn)*. To advert from the start to this paradoxical consciousness—an abyss of riches, an abyss of poverty—is to offer a foretaste of the antitheses, paradoxes, and reversals that are the *ipsissima vox Jesu*. Here was one who without training, without writing, so charged language with meaning as to elicit, generation after generation, the disarming protest, "Lord, to whom shall we go? You have the words of eternal life" (John 6:68).

Ezra Pound specified three ways of charging language with meaning: by *phanopoeia* (or the presentation of sharp and evocative visual images), by *melopoeia* (or the orchestration of sound), and by *logopoeia* (or the exploitation of resonances latent in the listener's memory).[1] We shall act on this clue, inquiring into the practice of Jesus as phanopoeist, as melopoeist, and as logopoeist. Though the parables of Jesus exhibit his rhetorical art at its finest, and though we intend to take account of the visual imagery of the parables, we shall limit our treatment of texts to short sayings: proclamation of the reign of God; a macarism thematically parallel to the proclamation; epigrams given point in virtue of a distinctive coign of vantage and distinctive set of referents (both definable by the present setting-in-motion of the eschatological future); aphoristic challenges to his disciples, to steel them for the impending eschatological ordeal; and, finally, a prophetic word offering a glimpse of his scenario of the future.

## Phanopoeia

We shall begin by surveying the repertory of visual images to be found in the words of the historical Jesus. These images first of all reflect the fields and villages among which he was nurtured: they are images of alternating sun and rain (Matt 5:45); of the hot sun scorching the tender shoot (Matt 13:6=Mark 4:6; cf. Luke 8:6); of evening rain-cloud alternating with south wind blowing (Luke 12:54; cf. Matt 16:2-3); of the sky and its ravens (Matt 6:26; Luke 12:23); fields of wild grass (Matt 6:30=Luke 12:28) and wild lilies (Matt 6:28=Luke 12:27);

the freshly ploughed field being sown, an image played off against the same field ready for harvest (Matt 13:1-9=Mark 4:1-9=Luke 8:4-8); the image of the tiniest seed (say) cupped in the hand, played off against that of the great bush that will have grown out of it (Matt 13:3-4=Mark 4:31-32=Luke 13:18-19). There is also the imagery of foxes and their lairs, birds and their nests (Matt 8:20=Luke 9:58); the unwitting bird about to be snared (Luke 21:34); plentiful sparrows (Matt 10:29=Luke 12:6); birds of prey circling over a carcass (Matt 24:28=Luke 17:37). Other countryside images are the fruit tree and its fruit (Matt 7:16-19=Luke 6:43-44; Matt 12:33); the fig tree as its leaves return (Matt 24:32=Mark 13:28=Luke 21:29); sowers and reapers (Matt 9:37=Luke 10:2); sheep and wolves (Matt 10:16; Luke 10:3); dogs and swine (Matt 7:6).

The defining imagery, however, is that of village life: children playing "Wedding" with mimicry of flute music, or "Funeral" with breast-beating; grown-up weddings with proper bridesmaids (Matt 25:1-13) and real funerals with their mourners and flute-players (Luke 7:11-13; Matt 8:22=Luke 9:60; cf. Matt 9:23). The village is made up mainly of single-roomed houses barred at night (Luke 11:7), a small oil-lamp flickering (Matt 5.15=Luke 11:33). It is a village of rich and poor, farmers and fishermen, women and children, widows and judges.

There is also Jerusalem: the city set on a hill (Matt 5:14); the courts and buildings of the temple (Matt 24:1-2=Mark 13:1-2=Luke 21:5); ceremony at the altar of holocausts (Matt 5:23). The city has a varied population: side by side, the very rich and the utterly destitute (Luke 16:19-21); notorious sinners and the famously pious praying in public places (Matt 6:5) and conspicuously fasting (Matt 6:16); a hereditary aristocracy and a meritocracy of scribes; tax-collectors and publicans; an underclass of thieves and beggars. In Jesus' speech villagers and city-folk alike come alive engaged in routine transactions or caught at critical moments of reward or punishment, sudden good fortune or catastrophic reversal.

The immediate world of Jesus was greatly expanded by popular and especially biblical lore. In the former we meet an imagery of great wealth: great houses administered by a numerous retinue; great transactions involving large sums of money; and festive parties. This world is gentile. Now and again we meet commonsense conceptions shared by Jews and gentiles but foreign to us (the extramission theory of vision—if your eye is good, it shows that your body is full of light

[Matt 6:22=Luke 11:24], or the physical anthropology that attributes hunger to the soul [Matt 6:25]).

The biblical world sometimes seems remote, but in fact it is omnipresent in Jesus' speech. Again and again his words betray an acute awareness of biblical promise. Where, however, the classic biblical imagery of salvation recurs in Jesus' words, it is shorn of its stately expression. Such charged images as the new wine (symbol of salvation) or the new cloak (renewal of the cosmos) occur with artless ease in the most ordinary figurative idiom (Matt 9:16-17=Mark 2:21-22=Luke 5:36-38), which nevertheless designates the present as fulfillment. This kind of fulfillment likewise draws on the imagery of wedding (Matt 9:15=Mark 2:19=Luke 5:34), banquet (Matt 22:1-14=Luke 14:16-24), and harvest (Matt 9:37=Luke 10.2).

The deliberately toned down exploitation of biblical symbol goes hand in hand with a generic trait: a pronounced simplicity and sobriety in the use of visual imagery. There seems not to be a single image dwelt on for its own sake, i.e., for even fleeting aesthetic effect. True, one might detect in Jesus' imagery of field and sky, bird and flower, a spontaneous affectivity towards nature; still, this affectivity is radically and pervasively theocentric (Matt 6.28-30=Luke 12:26-28; Matt 10:29-30=Luke 12:67). Deft use of the evocative visual image, which is what Pound meant by phanopoeia, does characterize the words of Jesus; but always the point was to turn a line memorable not for disinterested beauty but for didactic truth. And if the visual images that we have just surveyed do indeed belong to memorable parables and short sayings, they have all been made memorable for their suprapoetic message.

## Melopoeia

Melopoeia, or the orchestration of sound, is the stylistic factor least likely to survive translation. But *parallelismus membrorum*, which is found in 80% of the Synoptic units of Jesus' sayings material,[2] does survive translation, and in the Greek form of Jesus' sayings it is often an index to the original rhythm. This is among the lessons taught by two accomplished philologians, Gustaf Dalman (1855-1941) and Charles Fox Burney (1868-1925), both of whom have given us retroversions into Aramaic of the words of Jesus. Dalman, the founder of modern Aramaic studies, was the severest critic of the retroversions proposed by late-nineteenth century scholars. Burney allied himself with Dalman in identifying the linguistic wellsprings on which Jesus drew. The study of Aramaic has meantime progressed; Qumran Aramaic, for example, has been specified as a currently highly appropriate, if not the most appropriate, linguistic control for reconstructing the Aramaic of Jesus. Purists, ranging from the delicate to the fanatic, will find fault with the retroversions of Dalman and Burney even in their variously corrected forms; and it is true that these retroversions will always be subject to incidental correction. For my part, I expect such incidental correction and am unintimidated by the prospect of it.

The principal sound-factors are rhythm, particularly as measured by the number of accents per line, and tone-color: rime, assonance, consonance, alliteration, and onomatopoeia. Synoptic sayings material exhibits lines of two beats, of three beats, of four beats, and combinations, especially that in which a three-beat line is followed by a two-beat line (*qînâ* or dirge rhythm). The same material is rich in tone-color, especially rime, but with copious assonance and consonance, and not infrequent alliteration.

The two-beat line, though by no means commonplace, is well attested: "Bless your cursers/pray for your persecutors" (Luke 6:28),

*barĕkûn lĕlātêkôn / ṣallôn ʿal radĕpêkôn.*[3]

Again, in the Our Father, "Let your name be hallowed!/Let your reign come!" (Matt 6:9b-10=Luke 11:2b).

*yitqaddaš šĕmāk / tēʾtēʾ malkûtāk.*[4]

Tone-coloring in the first of these two texts derives especially from rimes (*-kôn, -lôn, -kôn*) and consonance in k-sounds (*-kûn, - kôn, - kôn*). The second text displays end-rimes (*-māk* and *-tāk*) and assonance in a-sounds (*-qaddāš, -māk, mal- tāk*). The terse two-beat line suggests urgency.

The three-beat line is far commoner. Here is a distich in three-beat rhythm: "'Blessed are the poor/for the reign of God is for them'" (based on Matt 5:3=Luke 6:20), *tûbêhôn miskĕnayyā᾽ / dĕdilĕhôn malkûtā᾽ dĕ᾽lāhā᾽.*[5]

First of all, we have riming here: *-hôn, -hôn / -yā᾽ -tā᾽, -lāhā᾽*. Consonantal sound-texture is established by m-sounds: *mis-, mal-*; by h-sounds: *hôn, -hôn, -ha᾽*); and if, in our retroversion, we were simply to adopt the Lukan text ("Blessed are you poor, for the reign of God is for you"), we would have consonance with four k-sounds: *tûbêkôn mis-kĕnayyā᾽ / dĕdilĕkôn malkûtā᾽ dĕ᾽lāhā᾽*.

Dalman gave us two retroversions of the aphorism "Many are called, but few are chosen" (Matt 22:14). First, a distich in two-beat rhythm:

*saggī᾽in zĕmînîn / zĕ῾ênîn bĕḥîrîn.*[6]

Here all four words rime. Some years later Dalman gave us a more likely retroversion, a distich in three-beat rhythm, the usual rhythm of aphorisms:

*saggī᾽in dĕ᾽innûn zĕmînîn / wĕṣibḥad dĕ᾽innûn bĕḥîrîn.*[7]

The riming is somewhat less prominent; there is also, perhaps by chance, what we would call an anapestic accent pattern.

Another, quite different, three-beat distich: a lightly revised form of the last word of Jesus to the high priest, according to Luke: "Soon the Son of man/will be seated at the right hand of Power" (Luke 22:69):

*ûmin kaddûn bar ᾽ĕnāšā᾽ / yātēb min yammînā᾽ digĕbûrĕtā᾽.*[8]

Some examples of four-beat rhythm: first, in the Greek text of "from the fullness of the heart the mouth speaks" (Matt 12:34=Luke 6.45)—*ek perisseumatos tēs kardias to stoma lalei*—liquid consonants roll trippingly from the tongue. Likewise in the Aramaic retroversion:

*min môtĕrēh dĕlibbā᾽ pummā᾽ mĕmallêl.*[9]

The proclamation formula, the reign of God is at hand, may be disputed. For Paul Joüon the formula is a three-beat line: *qĕrabat malkûtā᾽*

*dišĕmayyā⁾*; for Dalman, a four-beat line: *qarîbâ malkûtā⁾ dišĕmayyā⁾ lĕmêtê.* More likely than either would be the three-beat *mĕṭā⁾ malkûtā⁾ dĕ⁾lāhā⁾*; or, still more likely, in view of Greek *ēggiken,*

qĕrabat malkûtā⁾ dĕ⁾lāhā⁾.[10]

From among the instructions of disciples we have a distich in four beats followed by a half-line: "If anyone wishes to follow me, let him deny himself and take up his cross and (so) follow me" Matt 16:24=Mark 8:34=Luke 9:23):

kol man dibá⁽ê mĕhallākāh bātĕray
yikpōr bĕgarmēh wĕyiṭ⁽an ṣĕlîbēh
wĕyêtê bātĕray.[11]

We have here two sets of rimes: *rime riche* in the repetition "after me," *bātĕray/bātĕray,* and *rime suffisant* in lines two and three: *bĕgarmēh/ṣĕlîbēh/wĕyêtê.*

*Qînâ* rhythm (three beats/two beats) in Aramaic may be illustrated by the text addressed to followers: "Whoever wishes to save his life will lose it, and whoever loses his life for my sake will save it":

man dibĕ⁽a⁾ lĕhayyā⁾ â napšēh / môbēd yātah
ûman dĕmôbēd napšēh bĕginnî / mĕhayyê yātah.[12]

This saying comes to us in four forms, of which the first appears in two variants. I have cited the variant in Mark 8:35 and Luke 9:24, where the chiasmus runs: save / lose // lose / save. The variant form in Luke 17:33 reads: preserve / lose // lose / preserve. A second form, in Matt 10:39, reads: find / lose // lose / find; and there are mixed forms in Matt 16:25 and John 12:25.

This retroversion most obviously features assonance in a-sounds. As for consonance, there is the m-sound: *man, mô-, -man, -mô, me*; an n-sound: *man, nap-, man, nap-, ginnî*; a soft b-sound (v): *-bĕ-, -bēd, -bēd*; and a d-sound: *dib-, bēd, dĕmôbēd.*

## Four Contextual Factors

Before considering some typical instances of logopoeia in the words of Jesus, it may be in order to interject a clarification on charging words with meaning. Ezra Pound's analysis took the rudiments of discourse for granted. Phanopoeia, melopoeia, and logopoeia provide, not the substance of meaning, but its heightening or enhancement. Before considering how logopoeia heightens or enhances Jesus' words, we should recall four factors that define the situations out of which he spoke.

First, the origins of his public career lay in the movement of John the Baptist, who summoned all Israel to repentance, the confession of sins, and a rite of washing in the face of God's impending judgment. Second, Jesus, like John, addressed his message to all Israel; it was epitomized in the word, "the reign of God is at hand!" Third, Jesus, like John, conceived his mission and message in election-historical terms; that is, those who answered with yes were destined for acquittal and restoration; those who answered with no were destined for condemnation and ruin.[13]

This third point has two corollaries, sometimes overlooked or otherwise rendered harmless. Corollary one: Inasmuch as Jesus, like John, understood his mission to derive from the God of Israel and to have an eschatological (climactic and definitive) bearing on Israel's election/salvation, he can hardly have conceived his mission either in terms of political revolution or in terms of mere religious reform. This partly *a priori* observation is solidly confirmed by examination of the relevant data, which are copious and interlocking. Jesus understood himself as *fulfiller*: the agent chosen to announce and bring about the final restoration of Israel promised in the scriptures.[14]

Corollary two: since the election-historical terms in which he conceived his mission meant that on it hinged the standing of Israel before God, Jesus was necessarily aware of an enormous risk. Refusal by Israel would convert a ministry of acquittal and restoration and life into a ministry of condemnation and ruin and death. In any such situation of refusal, what could be done for the refuser? Jesus' answer, his response to the prospect of refusal, was the resolve to offer his life not only to seal the new covenant but as ransom and expiatory sacrifice for Israel and the world.[15]

Fourth and last point: Jesus' prophetic scenario projected a drama in two acts. Act one was the eschatological ordeal. His own death would launch it. It would engulf his disciples and, indeed, the whole nation, its capital and temple. Act two was the resolution of the ordeal by the glorification of the Son of man, the pilgrimage of the world to Zion, the judgment, and the banquet of the saved.[16]

These four points, here given necessarily swift and jejune formulation, allow us to hear Jesus' words in dramatic context and to attend to their diversity of tone and diverse exploitation of biblical resonance.

## Logopoeia

To return, then, to sayings we have already seen and heard, but now looking for instances of language charged by implicit allusion: "The reign of God is at hand!" To many, at least, who first heard it, *qĕrabat malkûtâ³ dĕ³lāhā³* could hardly have failed to recall the news of salvation capsulized in the cry, *mālak ³ĕlōhàik*, your God reigns! (Isa 52.7). John Gray may well be right in urging a cultic origin for this word and its proclamation: the great Autumn festival remembered by Deutero-Isaiah (Isa 52:7) and attested for pre-Exilic Israel by Nahum (Nahum 2:1)[17] But Jesus' evocation of *mālak ³ĕlōhàik* struck the apocalypticizing note that the word *mĕlak* had already acquired in the Synagogue. The voice of the Isaian *mĕbaśśēr/euaggelizomenos* (Isa 52:7; cf. 61:1), anointed (Isa 61:1) to break news of salvation to Israel, declared God's definitive triumph: the end of the old world, the birth of the new. The heart of the news was the advent of restoration, the day Israel had prayed for every Sabbath in the *Qaddiš*.[18] Jesus was summoning the children of Abraham to welcome God's climactic saving act, summoning them to the banquet with the patriarchs (see *kalesai* in Matt 9:13=Mark 2:17b=Luke 5:32; cf. Luke 14:16-17 and Matt 8:11-12= Luke 13:28-29).

Paul Joüon long ago established the probability, confirmed by synonymous parallelism in Mark 1:15 and by such parallels as Luke 4:17-21, that the proclamation of Jesus announced the *presence* of the reign of God.[19] Salvation was now. God was already comforting his people, already redeeming Jerusalem (cf. Isa 52:9b).

Just as Isa 61:1-3 takes up and carries forward themes from Isa 52:7-10 (the texts, it is worth noting, are brought together in 11QMelch), so too the Synoptic tradition—especially the Lukan account of Jesus at Nazareth (Luke 4:17-21), the Lukan form of the beatitudes (Luke 6:20-21; cf. Matt 5:1-3) and the account of himself that Jesus sent to John (Matt 11:5=Luke 7:22)—join together the motifs of Isa 52 and Isa 61, namely, the reign of God (Isa 52:7), the news of salvation (Isa 52:7; 61:1), and the poor, the mourners, and the captives as its beneficiaries (Isa 61:1-3). The latter parts of Isaiah resonate equally in Jesus' proclamation (*qĕrabat malkûtā' dē'lāhā'*), in his "Happy the poor" (*tûbêkôn miskĕnayyā', dĕdilĕhôn malkûtā' dē'lāhā'*), and in the lyric staccato of his answer to John (Matt 11:5=Luke 7:22).[20] But Jesus' *malkûtā' dē'lāhā'* for the poor appealed to more than the isolated text of Isa 61; it evoked the entire *'ănāwîm* tradition that got underway with Jeremiah, Zephaniah, and the Psalms and lived on even when classical prophecy died out. In Jesus' words and acts in favor of the simple, the afflicted, and the outcast[21] global logopoeia of this kind was recurrent.

We go now to the called and the chosen: *saggî'în dē' innûn zĕmînîn / wĕṣibḥad dĕ'innûn beḥîrîn*. This, of course, has long been a *crux interpretum*. In 1952 a French Benedictine, Edmond Boissard, offered a solution to the scandal that Jesus seemed to say that only a few would be saved.[22] The positive forms "many" and "few," he argued, were played off against one another precisely so as to yield a comparative sense: "many" became "more" and "few" became "'fewer." This semantic particularity may be illustrated by Gen 1:16, where the two "great lights," the sun and the moon, were "great" by comparison with the stars: they were the *major* lights, or "*greater* lights." Moreover, the text went on to specify "the great light to rule the day" and "the small light to rule the night." Again, great and small were positive in form, comparative in sense: greater and smaller, or lesser. This semantic usage may be named the correlative comparative. If it is true that *polloi* and *oligoi* in Matt 22:14 represent this idiom, the hitherto baffling scandal of the text is dissipated. The "chosen," and hence saved, are simply "fewer" than the "called." As Boissard put it, "to be chosen, it does not suffice to be called," or again, "not all are chosen."[23]

If Boissard's solution has not been widely adopted, it must be because he failed to illustrate the correlative comparative by the precise words "many" and "few" (*rab* and *mĕ'aṭ* in Hebrew, *polus* and *oligos* in

Greek). But since we do in fact have instances of this usage in Hebrew and in Greek translation (e.g., Num 26:52-56; LXX Num 26:54-56; see also Exod 16:17-18 in MT and LXX),[24] Boissard's solution is probably correct. Only one addition to it must be made: Joachim Jeremias's observation that here the referent of *polloi* is inclusive.[25] Accordingly, the sense of Jesus' saying is: "all are called, but not all are chosen." And now what becomes clear is that we have to do with quite a different scandal. In Isa 48:12 Israel is "my called one" (*mĕqōrā̕î*); in Isa 49:7 the phrase "who has chosen you" is almost an epithet of the LORD. Judaism, selectively echoing the Law and the prophets, was entirely at home with: all Israel is called and chosen. By logopoeia with reverse English, Jesus said: called, yes; chosen, that depends. That depends on whether the response to this eschatological, i.e., climactic and definitive, mission is yes or no.

The tone is not sorrowful but severe. The word is a warning that recalls the Baptist's sharp admonition to Israel (Matt 3:9=Luke 3:8); and it is richly paralleled, filled as the Synoptic tradition is with sharp warnings against the reigning soteriological optimism. See the "this generation" texts (e.g., Mark 8:12,38; 9:19; Matt 11:16; 12:39; Luke 11:30,50; 17:25); add thereto the words addressed to scoffers (Luke 17:26-27=Matt 24:37-39); the image of the unwitting bird about to be snared (Luke 21:34), the salt that has lost its savor (Matt 5:13=Luke 14.34), the barren fig tree (Luke 13:6-9).

An eschatological mission, heavy with consequence, to be accepted or rejected, defined Jesus' dramatic role: "that of mediator of God's final controversy with his people."[26] The prospect of rejection, the theme in which the Caesarea Philippi pericopes climax, entailed numerous consequences. One of the most deadly of them—potential desertion by his followers—prompted a new call to discipleship: "If anyone wishes to follow me, let him deny himself and take up his cross, and (so) follow me" (Matt 16:24=Mark 8:34=Luke 9:23).

First, we may take up line one: *kol man dibaᶜê mĕhallākāh bātĕray* . . . To walk behind or follow after is a biblicism (*hālak ̕ăhĕr*) denoting allegiance. But perhaps we should recall here that the Palestinian shepherd walked before his flock when taking the sheep out to pasture.[27] "Come after" in the phrase "if anyone would come after me" might accordingly suggest the correlation of this text with those in which Jesus, drawing on the tradition of the messianic shepherd in Ezekiel and Zecharaiah (Ezek 34:23-24; 37:24; Zech 13:7-9; cf. 12:10; 13:1-6), explicitly presented himself in the shepherd image: "I was sent only to the lost sheep that are the house of Israel" (Matt 15:24); or, I have "come to seek and save the lost [sheep]" (Luke 19:10); or "You will all fall away, for it is written, 'I will strike the shepherd and the sheep will be scattered'" and, most significant parallel of all, complementary to the preceding text and so evoking the shepherd leading the previously scattered flock: "I will go before you into Galilee" (Matt 26:32=Mark 14:28; cf. John 10:4,5,27).[28] If there is a submerged shepherd imagery here, its effect is simply to invest the motif of the following of Jesus with messianic connotations.

     Now consider lines two and three: the point of the present saying is to name a new condition of discipleship in the face of the impending ordeal: heroic willingness to accept expulsion from society as the cost of discipleship. Such expulsion—a prospect for disciples of a rejected Messiah—was caught perfectly in the image of the condemned man at the moment when, taking the crossbar on his shoulder to carry it to the place of execution, he turns to face the contemptuous throng that has disowned him. The tone is one of challenge. Are you ready for this? The second and third lines of the saying,

| | |
|---|---|
| *yikpōr bĕgarmēh* | (let him deny himself |
| *wĕyiṭ'an sĕlîbēh* | and take up his cross |
| *wĕyêtê bātĕray* | and [so] follow me) |

are unparalleled in biblical tradition.

     The same generic situation—the prospect of the impending ordeal—is reflected in the *qînâ*-quatrain:

*man dibĕ'a' lĕhayyā'â napšeh / môbēd yātah*
*ûman dĕmôbēd napšeh bĕginnî / mĕhayyê yātah;*
whoever is set on saving his life / will lose it
and whoever loses his life for my sake / will save it.

This eschatological riddle (Mark 8:35=Luke 9:24; cf. Luke 17:33; Matt 10:39; 16:25; John 12:25), heard in context, is a mystagogy: Jesus invites his disciples into the messianic mystery of his own death and life. The first half warns the disciples against apostasy under pressure. It is without parallel in biblical tradition. And though, for that matter, there is no truly close parallel to the lapidary antithesis of the second half, its major premise—the blessing of life for the faithful—pervades the Law and the prophets. It is grounded in the theme of the living God (*ʾĕlōhîm ḥayyîm*), Deut 5:26; Josh 3:10; 1 Sam 17:26,36; 2 Kings 19:4,10; Isa 37:4; Jer 10:10; 23:36; Ps 84:3) who has life in himself and lives forever; from whom all life comes; who gives life to his people; and who is himself this life (Jer 2:13; 17:13; Ps 36:9).

In the gospels the imposing theme of the Lord of life (Job 34:14-15; Ps 104:29-30), who made to live and who made to die (Deut 32:39), remained in the background (Matt 10:28=Luke 12:5). But the field of meaning that implicitly, unthematically, defined and energized the mission of Jesus could only be made thematic by themes of life. Outside the ambit of his saving mission there was only death and the dead (Matt 8:22=Luke 9:60). Themes of life were subjacent to the gospels' language of "saving"[29] and would find adequate expression in Johannine theology as well as in the early community's description of Jesus as "prince (of life)" (Acts 3:15; 5:31) and "savior" (Luke 2:11; Acts 5:31; 13:23).

Jesus' word on saving one's life and losing it, losing it on his account and saving it, affirmed (in the new context of this age and the age to come) the age-old orthodoxy of life as God's blessing on the faithful. This held, said Jesus, even for the dreadful situation that would be produced by his death.[30] Those who persevered in their allegience to him would not escape death—and still they would live! Here logopoeia in a broad sense lay in the act of setting the imminent ordeal under the sign of a great scriptural theme.

Finally, in words spoken by Jesus in the last week of his earthly life his distinctive scenario of the future came to expression on several occasions. These words drew on a wide range of biblical resources. I shall cite only one of them: the warning word of Jesus to the high priest, in its Lukan form, lightly revised:

*ûmin kaddûn barʾĕnāšā / yātēb min yammînāʾ digĕbûrĕtāʾ*,[31]
and soon the Son of man / will be seated at the right hand of
                                                                    Power.

The word evoked judgment. Through *bar ʾĕnāšā* and the motif of judgment there shone the scene of Dan 7. But in Luke 22:69 (contrast the parallels in Matt 26:64 and Mark 14:62) only the words *ho hui-*

*os tou anthrōpou*/*bar ʾĕnāšāʾ* reflect the wording of Dan 7. Having two facets, the saying strikes two notes: one of assurance, one of warning. Here Jesus affirmed that *bar ʾĕnāšā* would vindicate his messianic mission; by the same words he warned that *bar ʾĕnāšāʾ* would confront his judges as judge. This would happen *mikkʾān* or *min kaddûn*—a word that the Lukan text renders by *apo tou nun*, but the most obvious sense of which is "soon." Jesus would be vindicated soon; his judges would meet judgment soon.

This "soon" appears to be unfulfilled prophecy;[32] for that very reason it savors strongly of historical authenticity. The word yields a glimpse of how Jesus saw the promise of Dan 7: the triumph of God would subsume and sublate the triumph of justice.

## Conclusion

As rhetorician, Jesus was a moderate. He was a skilled but sober phanopoeist. He was equally proficient and equally restrained as melopoeist. Visual imagery and the orchestration of sound were kept rigorously functional to a unique mission, covertly sublime, delicate and dangerous. It was the mission of a prince sent to his people in the guise of a commoner commissioned to fire their allegiances against the day when he would be revealed and enthroned as their rightful king.

The going-awry of this scenario was itself hidden piecemeal in the scriptures. The originality of Jesus as logopoeist lay less in implicit allusion as a technique than in the vision of things fashioned by his choice and articulation of biblical themes. True, the technique belongs to rhetoric; the vision does not. But rhetoric does give access to the vision. Only the Son knows the Father; and he has taken great pains, including rhetorical pains, to reveal him.

## NOTES

1. Ezra Pound, *The ABC of Reading* (London: Routledge, and New Haven: Yale University Press, 1934).

2. Rainer Riesner, "Der Ursprung der Jesus-Uberlieferung," *Theologische Zeitschrift* 38 (1982) 493-513, at 507.

3. Burney, *Poetry*, 169.

4. Jeremias, *Theology*, 196.

5. Revised from Burney, *Poetry*, 166. With Burney here and with Jeremias, *Theology*, 24, we are positing two accents in *miskĕnayyā'*, namely on the first and on the last syllables.

6. Dalman, *Words*, 119.

7. Dalman, *JJ*, 228.

8. Revised from Dalman, *Words*, 311. With Burney, *Poetry*, 132, 142, and Jeremias, *Theology*, 23 (cf. 282), I would find one or two beats in *bar ʾĕnāśāʾ*, depending on what seems to be required by the rhythmic pattern of the text in which the words stand.

9. Jeremias, *Theology*, 22.

10. Jeremias, *Theology*, 97, points out that "kingdom of heaven" appears for the first time in Jewish literature half a century after Jesus' ministry'; this rules out *malkûtāʾ dišĕmayyāʾ* proposed by both Joüon, "Notes philologiques sur les Évangiles," *Recherches de science religieuse* 17 (1927) 537-540 at 538, and Dalman, *Words*, 106. I am inferring from the synonymous parallelism of Mark 1:15 and sense of *ēggisen* in Matt 21:34 that the verb *qārēb/qĕrêb* could signify "has arrived" and the adjective *qārîbāʾ* could signify "'present, here," (Joüon, 538, adduces Hebrew examples of *qārēb*=has arrived.) But however one settles the most likely retroversion of this text, it is clear that in Jesus' teaching generally the *malkût* of God was *formaliter* future (e.g., Matt 10:23) and *virtualiter* present (e.g., Matt 12:28=Luke 11:20).

11. Dalman, *JJ*, 191.

12. Jeremias, *Theology*, 26.

13. See Joachim Jeremias, *Jesus' Promise to the Nations* (London: SCM, 1958; Philadelphia: Fortress, 1982) 50-51.

14. The hallmark of this restoration was a set of reversals having both a pragmatic and a symbolic dimension. God was on the point of enriching the poor, consoling the mourners, giving the hungry their fill. Already Jesus was giving sight to the blind, mobility to the crippled, release to the possessed. These effective reversals, together with his startling initiatives towards notorious sinners, were all charged with symbolic meaning: all depressed classes—the poor and the ill, the sinners and the ostracized, women and children, the unimportant, unpowerful, and unpromising—imaged the situation of Israel vis-à-vis God. Salvation, in a word, was to show, not that Israel was good, but that God was good.

15. See Rudolf Pesch, *Das Abendmahl und Jesu Todesverständnis* (Freiburg: Herder, 1978) 103-109.

16. See Meyer, *Aims*, 202-206.

17. John Gray, *The Biblical Doctrine of the Reign of God* (Edinburgh: Clark, 1979) 6, 11.

18. Meyer, *Aims*, 134, 138.

19. See the reference above, note 11.

20. Jeremias, *Theology*, 197-198. See also the good observations on Isa 61 in Matthew and Luke by D. C. Allison, Jr. in "Jesus and the Covenant," *Journal for the Study of the New Testament* 29 (1987) 57-78 at 77, note 29.

21. See Meyer, *Aims*, 171-172.

22. Edmond Boissard, "Note sur l'interprétation du texte 'Multi sunt vocati, pauci vero electi.' " *Revue Thomiste* 52 (1952) 569-585.

23. "Note," 581.

24. See "'Many (=All) are Called, but Few (=Not All) are Chosen" (Chapter Five).

25. J. Jeremias, "polloi," *Theological Dictionary of the New Testament*, vol. VI, ed. G. Kittel, G. Friedrich (Grand Rapids: Eerdmans, 1965-74) 536-545, at 542.

26. Amos N. Wilder, "Eschatology and the Speech-Modes of the Gospel," in *Zeit und Geschichte* [Bultmann Festschrift] (Tübingen: Mohr-Siebeck, 1964) 19-30, at 29.

27. Gustaf Dalman, "Arbeit und Sitte in Palästina VI," *Beiträge zur Förderung christlicher Theologie*, series 2, 41 (1939) 249-250, 253-255.

28. Jeremias, *Theology*, 297-298.

29. On the Aramaic substratum of gospel texts using the language of "saving, salvation,," see Joüon, "Quelques aramaïsmes sous-jacents au grec des Évangiles," *Recherches de science religieuse* 17 (1927) 210-229, at 225-227.

30. Jeremias, *Theology*, 127-128 with reference especially to Luke 22:53; 23:28-31; also 241 with reference especially to Luke 22:35-38.

31. If *min yammînâ⁾* is a deliberate allusion to Ps 110:1, this text would offer a base from which to reconsider the historicity of Matt 22:41-46=Mark 12:35-37a=Luke 20:41-44.

32. On the issue of historicity in such cases, see Jeremias, *Theology*, 2; 139-140. But, while acknowledging the evidential value for historicity of "non-fulfillment," I would set the entire matter of seeming non-fulfillment in the context of the traits of prophetic knowledge generally and of the prophetic knowledge of Jesus in particular. See Meyer, *Aims*, 245-249.

## 7

## JESUS AND HIS MISSION:
## FINDING THE *GESTALT*

### In Search of Form

    The most demanding challenge of historical-Jesus research has to do with a grasp of the whole. The classical hermeneutic circle ("I understand the whole in function of understanding the parts; I understand the parts in function of understanding the whole") says why the challenge is not only demanding but indispensable. No matter how enlightening the insights that deal with facets or parts, the lack of an equally enlightening hold on the whole keeps such insights in the category of unfinished business. Moreover, the issue of "seeing Jesus whole" and grasping the whole form of his mission provides an opportunity for reconsidering the approach to the historical-Jesus project as a whole. How much of the legacy of recent scholarship remains valuable or even indispensable? What new proposals should be heard?

    In the column of "valuable" and even "indispensable" we should first of all range environmental and social-scientific studies. They admittedly are limited to the understanding of aspects or parts. A vast, more or less continuous effort of research from the 1940s to the present has illuminated not only Palestinian philology, fauna, and flora (à la Dalman), but has taken up the investigation of the social, economic, political, and cultural systems. The three most intensely cultivated areas of inquiry have been: the impact of Hellenistic culture on the life, including the intimate religious life, of Palestinian Judaism;[1] the Essenes of Qumran;[2] functional and dysfunctional factors in the economic, political, and social systems of Palestinian Jews, including the social forces that led to the revolt of 66-73.[3]

    Second, historical analysis of the parables still appears to belong in the "indispensable" column. Indeed, the work that is most indispensable dates from early in the history of research, the 1930s and 1940s. It played a key role (dissembled and underrated) in the rise of the so-called "new quest" by the post-Bultmannian existentialists from the 1950s to the 1970s. (Most parables-analysis since then has shifted the emphasis from historical to literary purposes; some claims have been made that this contributes to history, but they are doubtful.) The work of the first wave by A. T. Cadoux, B. T. D. Smith, C. H. Dodd, and Joachim Jeremias,[4] capitalizing on the preservatory power of the parable-form (the form preserves the originally controlling image) and on the common functions of the parable (explanation and debate), asked what concrete issue was being addressed and illuminated by each parable of Jesus. An ongoing process of trial and error, guided by philological, environmental, and social research, slowly but surely brought to light recurrent themes of Jesus' teaching. Thus, it emerged that the repentance he called for was not Torah-oriented, but reign-of-God-oriented; that Jesus and his mission were time and again an underlying issue of debate; that, for example, pressed repeatedly to defend his initiative towards notorious sinners, he showed how perfectly this cohered with a proclamation of salvation made operative simply by the vital act of acceptance.[5] Such results have remained a critical countercontrol vis-à-vis more recent proposals respecting the core of Jesus' interests.

Opinions reasonably differ on the claim to the "valuable" and "indispensable" column of (a) form critical studies of the gospels since the Second World War, (b) studies of the Synoptic question, (c) of miracles in the ancient world and of the miracles of Jesus, (d) of christological aspects of the Synoptic tradition, e.g., the Son of man question, and other topics. Despite efforts to make form criticism a positively productive factor, little has found general acceptance. Proposals of the form "sentences of holy law," of oracles of early Christian prophets, and the like have had indifferent success. A few dissertations on form-critical study of gospel stories, less original, fared somewhat better.[6] By contrast, the form-critical account of the origins of the Synoptic tradition has come to seem less and less plausible, although competing proposals still win only lukewarm support.[7] Reconsiderations of the Synoptic question have tended to end indecisively, their one solid result a greater willingness of the majority to acknowledge the hypothetical nature of the Two-Source Theory.[8] Studies of the miracles have thus far still left the individual accounts in the question-mark column. To move to christology: notwithstanding intense discussion, the Son-of-man question resists consensus. But a fully articulated view must now take account of data on nontitular uses of the phrase *bar ʾĕnāšāʾ*;[9] it must reckon with the fact of many parallels to Son-of-man sayings, which, howeover, do without the Son-of-man title;[10] it must take account of the suffering-motif of the saints in Daniel, of the non-use of the suffering Son-of-man motif in Q,[11] and of the quite plausible reconstruction of the Aramaic antecedent to Mark 9:31 with its numerous parallels.[12] Again, though "the Son of man" may be the only title or quasi-title that stamped Jesus' own idiom, studies of soteriology and christology continue to point to the pre-Easter roots of the Church's redemptive christology in Jesus' own consciousness.[13]

There have been numerous proposals for the reorientation of historical-Jesus research, some taking their point of departure from social-scientific work, others from literary criticism. None of the efforts from the latter category seem to have succeeded. From the social-scientific side, however, there have been a number of helpful contributions. Richard Horsley proposed in 1986[14] that Jesus' ministry be studied comparatively with Josephus's data on popular messianic figures and their movements. Theudas and "the Egyptian" were, like Jesus, leaders of movements of some consequence. Since then Horsley has given us a fuller notion of what he had in mind.[15] The proposal turns out to have been good but quite limited. What it, perhaps predictably, does not do is to penetrate to what R. G. Collingwood called "the inside of the event." This turns on such intensely personal correlative factors as horizons, perspectives, purposes. These, however, cannot be grasped without drawing on just those massive resources in the religious tradition (e.g., the scriptures) that Horsley found artificial and sterile.

Among monographs incorporating new proposals on the methodological front, Sean Freyne's *Galilee, Jesus and the Gospels*[16] urged attention to the Galilean background, to recent social-scientific work, and recent literary criticism. The monograph showed these emphases to be helpful, probably because they were adopted in so moderate a fashion, without extravagant expectations or claims. (Freyne's neglect of eschatological perspectives—a move insistently promoted by M. J. Borg and others[17]—proved not to be a forward step.)

The following are a few items on which the present writer considers work to have been more than ordinarily helpful. Dale C. Allison's dissertation, *The End of the Ages Has Come*, aimed at showing why the phenomenon of "realized eschatology" imposed itself in the early Christian community. This inquiry could build on work that had been guided by another question: how to understand the eschatological sense or consciousness exhibited by the words and acts of Jesus in the gospels. Dodd in 1935 had dealt with this issue in *The Parables of the Kingdom*. According to the scenario that he recovered (and that Joachim Jeremias amended in 1941)[18] Jesus foresaw a future in two acts: first, the ordeal of the end-time, to be opened by his own arrest, repudiation, passion, and death, followed by a fierce, if brief, time of affliction/ordeal/tribulation engulfing his disciples and all Israel; second, "the day of the [Son of] Man," or the day when "the [Son of] Man is revealed" (Luke 17:30), which would bring the ordeal to an end with the vindication of Jesus and with the judgment and reign of God.

Such was the scenario. What actually happened? "The Easter experience of the disciples" took place, but did not bring with it the consummation of history (=the reign of God). This revelation-event was neither offered nor open to an undifferentiated public; hence, it could not be flatly identified with the conspicuously public "Day of the [Son of] Man." Rather, it marked the beginning of an interim which that Day would bring to an end. The scenario of Jesus was accordingly differentiated *ex eventu*. No early Christian can be credited with having fashioned from whole cloth the new scenario of resurrection, mission, ordeal of the end-time, and parousia. *This was simply Jesus' own scenario as modified by the actuality of events* and specifically by the fact of an interim between resurrection and parousia. With variations appropriate to the distinct vantage points of the writers, this scenario found acknowledgement in Paul (e.g., 1 Cor 15; Rom 9-11), Luke (e.g., Luke 24:26-27,46-49; Acts 1:3-11; 3:13-26 etc.) and other early witnesses.

Allison hardly considered this scheme as a whole. He did consider the discrete parts, noting that (in isolation) they failed to explain the emergence of post-Easter realized eschatology. Thus, Jesus' proclamation of the reign of God did not suffice of itself, nor did the interpretation of the reign of God as having in some sense (i.e., operationally or virtually) already come in the cures and exorcisms of Jesus. What brought into being the early Church's realized eschatology was the disciples' pre-Easter grasp of Jesus' death as belonging to the tribulation of the end-time and of his vindication as belonging with, grounding, initiating the resurrection of the dead.[19] The force of the book lies in the thoroughness of both its discussion and its documentation.

Excellent as this study is, it would have been improved by a consideration of the Dodd-Jeremias proposal as a whole, for two reasons. First, from the vantage point of the disciples, the tradition was an experiential continuum. That is, it held together as a single, cumulative experience: Jesus' proclamation (they repeatedly shared personally in making it); the miracles (if, as is probable, there was a pre-Easter formation of gospel materials,[20] they themselves shaped stories of cures and exorcisms, rehearsed Jesus' interpretative words on them, and moreover shared in working these wonders, Mark 9:18=Matt 17:16= Luke 9:40; Mark 9:28=Matt 17:19); harsh warnings of the coming ordeal, which they too issued to the public; and the esoteric tradition of private instruction (including, as we shall see, words and acts of the Last Supper). It is surely this total experience that explains the community's post-Easter conviction of "realized eschatology." In the charged experience of the diciples, shaped by Jesus, the fulfillment of the scriptures began with the appearance of the Baptist in the desert, continued with Jesus' proclamation and prophetic career, and reached a climax in the master's repudiation and vindication. They were aware of how he understood these matters. They found what they learned from him vindicated by the Easter experience.

The second reason for preferring not to isolate the pre-Easter understanding of Jesus' death as belonging to the tribulation and of his vindication as belonging to the coming "resurrection of the dead," relates to the limits of our own knowledge, i.e., to the futility of nice analytic efforts on our part to differentiate between necessary and unnecessary, and between "necessary but insufficient" and "sufficient by itself" to effect the result in question.[21] Jesus' words and acts, his initiatives and reactions, made up a patterned whole. Very much the product of one man, this whole—words, acts, interpreted events—anticipated the post-Easter eschatology of the Church and stands as its fully adequate historical explanation.

Among other contributions to a grasp of the whole of Jesus' public career, I would list Gerd Theissen's trenchant article on the charismatic values-revolution effected in and by Jesus and the earliest Jesus movement.[22] Theissen is explicit in not classifying Jesus as a revolutionary in the proper sense. He nevertheless penetrates to crucial features of Jesus' impact on his world by drawing on points of contact between revolutions and Jesus' eschatological program. Revolutions exhibit two moments: first, the delegitimizing of one system and the legitimizing of another; second, the actual redistribution of goods (power, property, culture) that follows. Jesus' proclamation and teaching corresponds to the first; the advent of the reign of God he announced corresponds to the second.

Such proposals carry conviction to the extent that they illuminate the subject (here, the careers of John the Baptist and of Jesus) in concrete detail. In this instance the proposal has a certain undeniable relevance and utility. For example, the "redistribution" in question in revolutions is a matter of altering relations among classes. The new meanings and values that emerge from the words of John and especially of Jesus—all of them are charged with eschatological themes—conspicuously include the extension of "aristocratic" or royal values to ordinary people. Jesus and the Jesus movement bring within the ken of "little people" values and modes of behavior traditionally bound up with the upper classes: wisdom, peacemaking, the reconciliation of enemies, clemency and generosity. They promise, moreover, that the adoption of these values will be validated and recompensed at the advent of the reign of God. *This* is the Jesus revolution—a stunning reversal of Nietzsche's steamy theorizing on Jesus and his values.

The analogy with revolution is, to be sure, imperfect. First, the eschatological proclamation of Jesus stands in contrast not merely to some current regime or state of affairs but to the entire situation and time of anticipation, i.e., to the whole past, of Israel. Second, the proclamation presents itself implicitly and explicitly as the fulfillment of God's word throughout this time of anticipation: the fulfillment of divine promises, prophecies, and types. Third, the Jesus revolution far transcends changes in the distribution of goods. It is a change of *destiny*. It thus corresponds to the great prophetic theme of *šûb šĕbût*, the divinely effected reversal and restoration of Israel's fortunes. With reference to all this "revolution" is a weak metaphor indeed, and "revolutionary" a very partial denomination of Jesus' mission and message.

In accord with the above critique, I would list, among other helpful proposals in current research, the proposal of *the restoration of Israel* as the appropriate context and appeal of revolutionary movements, reform movements, and preparationist movements (such as those of the Baptist and Jesus) alike. E. L. Dietrich's slim philological monograph of 1925 showed that the phrase *sûb sebût*, common in the prophets, expressed precisely this potent theme.[23] Biblical and intertestamental texts converged on its pervasive contribution to post-Exilic expectations.[24] It made up one among the countless threads that bound Jesus to the national mainstream. Here it is appropriate to recall a corollary, not new, but more significant than is commonly thought. Inasmuch as "reign of God" and "restoration of Israel" positively correlate, another set of thematic correlates accrues to the reign of God theme, not by any absolute necessity, but by a kind of connatural association: "new covenant," "new temple," and "new cult."[25]

Respecting "new cult," we should recall developments on Last Supper research since Rudolf Pesch's 1978 study of the eucharistic words.[26] The context of Pesch's work had been one of contradictory movements in German New Testament scholarship: a sharpening of the issue of Jesus' interpretation of his coming death together with a growing scepticism about the eucharistic words. Pesch's main literary purpose was to establish the reliability of the Last Supper tradition in Mark; his main historical purpose was to reconstruct Jesus' interpretation of his coming death. His first move was to define (probably more emphatically and cogently than ever before) the genre of the eucharistic text in 1 Cor 11:23-25 as "cultic aetiology" and that of Mark 14:22-24 as "historical report." He paid particular attention to the role played by the eucharistic words in the transition from the eve of Jesus' death to the preaching of the apostles in Jerusalem a short time later.

C. K. Barrett's contribution to the 1984 volume celebrating the hundredth anniversary of Bultmann's birth was an effort to answer the question of how the proclaimer became the proclaimed.[27] In this context Barrett called attention to the peculiarity of what the Church was doing in taking in and repeating, from a post-Easter coign of vantage, words spoken by Jesus on the eve of his death.

This was a most adroit suggestion. Yet something important was missing from it. The force of liturgical performance (1 Cor 11:26-29) is derivative: it derives from Jesus' death as expiatory offering and covenant sacrifice. But the real character of Jesus' death hinges in turn on his historic intention—an issue that Barrett neither poses nor supposes. Hence, whereas the essay retains its formal elegance, it leaves a crucial point unmade.

If in this limited sense the essay falls short, liturgical celebration itself did not. For, as Hans-Josef Klauck and Otfried Hofius have recently and rightly insisted,[28] the distinctive note of the cultic aetiology of 1 Cor 11:23-25 was the complexity of its reference. It intended both a liturgical action and a historical event: "The Lord Jesus, on the night that he was delivered up" did such and such. . . (1 Cor 11:23). So, this aetiology, unlike most Hellenistic parallels, functions not only as a liturgical libretto but also as an index both to how a given community's consciousness developed (e.g., the proclaimer becoming the proclaimed), and to *the authenticity of that development* in terms of its point of departure, the deliberate act, or historic intention, of Jesus.

The liturgical text, then, is fully sufficient as it stands. It is meant to provide an index to the intention of Jesus and to realize that same intention. The community *believes* that its liturgical action comes *apo tou Kuriou*, "from the Lord" as its author or originator. Below we shall follow this up with further reasons for thinking that they were right in this belief.

We wish to know how to interpret Jesus, and especially how to describe the patterned whole that was his conscious mission. We have elsewhere recalled the debate in the 1970s on whether the intentions expressed in the eucharistic words can be made to cohere with those of the proclamation of the reign of God.[29] Here the issue is how to work out an account, not exhaustive but comprehensive in principle, of Jesus' mission. If we take as point of departure the proclamation of the reign of God, the categories of "preparation" (Isa 40; Elijah traditions; the Baptist) and of "promise and fulfillment" (*Qaddiš*, Luke 24; Matthean fulfillment citations) immediately suggest themselves. If, however, we take into account the eucharistic words, the category of "problem and solution" straightway suggests itself.

There is no real reason why these categories should not cohere and reciprocally reinforce each other. The promises of God in the prophets envisage the solution of the human problem: substitution of a heart of flesh for man's heart of stone (Ezekiel), a new heart and a new spirit (Jeremiah and Ezekiel), a new creation (Deutero- and Trito-Isaiah), making possible the restoration of Israel; moreover, as the Isaian tradition in particular conceived it, this restoration entailed the salvation of the nations, as well.

Before finally focusing on how to define the Jesus mission as a whole, we should settle how good a claim to historicity the theme of his death for the many makes. This involves the events that led up to

Jesus' death.

## Conspiracy, Last Supper, Death

The cleansing of the temple was the most charged symbolic act of the public life of Jesus. Persistent efforts in recent scholarship to unpack its meaning have at least won acceptance of the symbolic dimension of the event.[30] But what did it symbolize?

The gospels accounts as they stand have registered the influence of a number of factors, notably, the writers' resolute will to keep Jesus from being falsely construed as a revolutionary. The cleansing was a dangerous memory, toned down by shortening the account of it (Matthew and Luke each devote two verses to the event) and obscuring its relationship to the plot that issued in Jesus' death (neither Matthew nor Luke acknowledges the causal nexus expressed in Mark 11:18, and John has altogether removed the cleansing from the passion story). We detect here a deliberate rounding of the sharp edges of the event, a softening of the harshness of the clash it provoked.

The most primitive account is that of Mark, which differs from its parallels (a) by the detail (Mark 11:16) that Jesus would not allow anybody to carry anything through the temple grounds, i.e., to use the temple as shortcut for commerce between Ophel and the eastern suburbs (cf. *m. Ber.* 9:5); (b) by the explicit connection of the cleansing of the temple with the last (and successful) plot against Jesus (Mark 11:18); and (c) by a remnant from the positive symbolism of the event: that the temple was destined finally to be a house of prayer "for all nations" (Mark 11:17).

As they stand, the Markan and other redactions predominantly accent the negative symbolism of the event. If we take our cue from them, the event might be thought to have mainly foreshadowed the coming destruction of the temple. (If and however this figured in the original event, the accent on it alone certainly represents a foreshortening of the full intended meaning of the event.) In the eschatological scenario of Jesus the destruction of the temple belonged to the ordeal/tribulation; the new sanctuary that Jesus would build "after three days"[31] belonged, in Jesus' intended meaning, to the triumphant resolution of the ordeal. But Jesus' followers—the embattled *ekklēsia*/(messianic) congregation (Matt 16:18), the remnant whose restoration was already inaugurated and in process of realization—had a life to live in the interim between these two moments. Its life, that is, was to be lived through the ordeal itself.

Consider both aspects of this. First, the Last Supper becomes the positive counterpart to the cleansing of the temple. In the intention of Jesus, revealed successively, in fragmentary fashion and riddling form, partly to the public, partly to his immediate disciples, the whole sacrificial system of Israel was to yield to a simple cultic act (a) of re-membering/renewing Jesus' own self-dedication to death (as expiatory offering and covenant-sealing sacrifice) as well as the death itself, and (b) of calling on God to bring an end to the ordeal with the vindication, exaltation, and triumph of Jesus. Second, this shows how dominantly the ordeal looms as the context of this future cultic act. The ʾabbāʾ prayer which Jesus gave his followers similarly envisioned the ordeal and prayed not to fall victim to it (Matt 6:13=Luke 11:4c). Here the new cultic act which Jesus bequeathed them on the night before he suf-fered and died becomes their resource for survival of the ordeal.

This reconstruction builds on the historicity of the Last Sup-per, of the eucharistic words, and of the accompanying remembrance mandate (the last-mentioned admittedly enjoying less probability than the rest).[32] It presents the sense of the words in the scenario not of the Easter Church but of Jesus himself at the Last Supper.

Recovery of the credibility of the eucharistic words should take into account the datum of testimony intending Jesus as author of the eucharistic words, as mentioned above apropos of 1 Cor 11: 23, *apo tou Kuriou*=from the Lord [as originator]). We cannot retrieve the at-tendant particulars that in Corinth made this witness concretely compel-ling; on the other hand, we have resources that they did not.

Among them are linguistic data that allow us to differentiate strata in the tradition of the eucharistic words. The form of the eucharis-tic words in Matthew, with its explanatory gloss (Matt 26:28c), meticu-lous concern for sequence (Matt 26:27b) and syntactical improvements (Matt 26:26a,27c,29a) is surely—failing compelling counter-evidence —secondary vis-à-vis Mark. Whereas (a) the "for (the) many" of the Markan word on the cup is underivable from the "for you" of the Pau-line word on the bread (as well as of both the word on the bread and that on the cup in Luke), and whereas, (b) on the contrary, the "for you" is easily derivable from Markan "for (the) many"; and whereas (c) the

Markan word-order to *ekchunnomenon huper pollōn*="poured out for
(the) many" corresponds to Aramaic word-order and the Lukan form
(="given for you"/"poured out for you"=*to huper humōn dedomenon/to
huper humōn ekchunnomenon*) does not,[33] it seems to follow with reasonable probability that the eucharistic words in Mark are primitive vis-
à-vis their parallels.[34]

The minute and convergent observations of Dalman and Jeremias respecting the probability that the words derived from the Passover meal, were based in significant part on the head-of-the-household's
appointed task of speaking words interpreting the elements of the meal
(though Jesus' interpretative words at the grace before the main meal
over the unleavened loaves=*maṣṣôt/paṭṭîrayyā²*, and his second word
over the third of the four cups, "the cup of blessing" =*kôs šel bĕrākāh/
kassā² dĕbirkĕtā²*, were not required, and so were somewhat unusual
and must have come to those present as something of a surprise). The
cumulative force of all the above observations grounds the accuracy of
Paul's *apo tou Kuriou* from the Lord (1 Cor 11:23). In an atmosphere
redolent of the biblical and cultic tradition of past and future redemption—a tradition that his own mission was climaxing—Jesus, as he
broke the *maṣṣôt*, defined the bread and the breaking of it: it was his
flesh/body and the violent death for which that flesh/body was destined.
Then, having spoken the blessing after the Passover meal, he defined
the wine: it was his blood soon to be shed to seal a covenant of forgiveness and life. Just as, by the totality of his words over the bread and
over the cup, Jesus specified himself in advance as going to his death
for the life of the world, so the disciples invited to eat this bread and
drink this wine specified themselves, by their eating and drinking, as
sharers in the saving power of that death.

Now, what immediately follows bears on our question of the
mission of Jesus indirectly but significantly. It deals directly with the
impact of events on the community; thence we shall return to our own
controlling question. Jesus died; and, on the testimony of those who
met the risen Christ, his death was in turn followed by eschatological
resurrection. A new set of factors immediately impinged on the fibre
and tone of the community of his followers, giving it a distinctive elan,
a now fully thematic awareness of the expiatory character of Jesus'
death and its divine acceptance, a celebration of his messianic/
kyriological exaltation, a new pledge of identity as the messianic com-

munity, nucleus of restored Israel.

Their liturgical action did not, then, implore the vindication and triumph of Jesus (the original sense of the remembrance mandate); it celebrated Jesus already vindicated and implored his return in triumph. What effected the change of scenario? A fulfillment event that took place "on the third day."

How else did that "third day" impinge on the life of the community? Among the acute observations offered by Rudolf Pesch on the significance of the eucharistic words for a satisfactory account of developments in the earliest life of the Easter Church, the renewal of the mission to Israel merits first mention. This renewal becomes fully intelligible in the light of (a) God's acceptance of the sacrifice of Jesus, and (b) the need now to appropriate by a positive human act of acceptance, the saving power of the death of Christ.

Just as atoning efficacy required intention and not merely a physical act, so the appropriation of atonement equally required a conscious act of acceptance (=faith). If Jesus himself placed the positive act of *going to his death for all*, the community conscious of this intention must have found itself positively *obliged* to devise a kerygmatic appeal to Israel, first heir of salvation. Given the faith of the Easter community, it was quite impossible that Jesus should not have become "the proclaimed." Intrinsically and of itself this faith (and this, of course, by no means rules out or conflicts with an explicit missionary mandate of the risen Jesus) was apt and open to and called for addressing a new summons to Israel. This faith, which we find repeatedly defined by pre-Pauline formulas in the Pauline letters (1 Cor 11:23-25; 15:3-5; Rom 3:25-26; 4:25; 8:34; 10:9, etc.), accordingly contributes to an accounting for both the fact and the content of the kerygma.

A second consideration represents Pesch's argument lightly revised in the light of the change of scenario prompted by the Easter experience. Both the expiatory death of Jesus and his resurrection from the dead illuminate the Easter adoption of the baptismal rite of initiation and its specifically expiatory and redemptive sense. Despite my strictures above against hoping to differentiate exactly what brought into being the realized eschatology of the early Church, I am willing to entertain the following fundamental speculation. Had the resurrection been held off (in literal accord with the symbolic scenario of Jesus) till the advent of the reign of God, the soteriological center of gravity in the messianic community would have been future, and future-oriented symbols (like John's baptism) might have sufficed. But the resurrection was not held off; and once given, in the destiny of Jesus, the advance realization of eschatological resurrection, the soteriological center of gravity shifted to the realized element of an "eschatology inaugurated and in process of realization." Hence the felt need on the part of the community leaders for baptism *lĕšēm yešû al en tǭ onomati* or *eis to onoma Iēsou*—in English, "the Jesus baptism."[35] The point to be made here is that the eucharistic words of Jesus, which register his intending of his coming death as expiatory for the world, became the defining principle of this rite. From the start, as Pesch has insisted, the Jesus baptism—the rite of entree into the messianic community—was charged with the sense of participation in the atonement and new life later attested in Romans 6:3-5.[36]

We return to the quest of seeing Jesus whole and defining the patterned whole of his mission. But we approach the issue armed with a new insight. The eucharistic words of Jesus show—and nothing more incisively shows—that he understood the human problem to be the state of impotent immersion in sin. With respect to this problem he understood himself and his mission to be the divinely chosen and wholly adequate solution. The impact of the eucharist words on the earliest Church backs up this conclusion. In any case Jesus' mission bore on the solution of the human problem. In the actual final form of his mission, that solution would lie in his death as expiatory and covenantal sacrifice.

Under no hypothesis was the restoration of Israel optional. Israel as a whole had not known its own need. No halaka could meet it. Israel as a whole had not recognized in Jesus the meeting of its need. Jesus, by contrast, evinced the consciousness of one chosen by God to invite Israel's acceptance of a climactic offer: *God's long promised, long hoped for, act of definitively restoring his people.* He offered the saving restoration for which the Synagogue prayed weekly in the *Qaddiš* but rejected when offered. The offer was accepted by a "little flock" (Luke 12:32), the simple (*nēpioi, mikroi/elachistoi*=little ones, the socially insignificant, women and children included), the afflicted (*ptōchoi*=the poor, *peinōntes*=the hungry, *daimonizomenoi*=the possessed, *kakōs echontes*= the ill), and the outcast (*hamartōloi*, notorious sinners for whom the initiatives of Jesus were irresistible). *The messianic restoration of Israel would find fulfillment only in this open remnant.*

Therefore, through no antecedent necessity, but in accord with the historical situation as it took shape, the mission of Jesus included his death for "the many," i.e., for the world, and cannot be defined without reference to that. If the messianic secret bore on the messianic presence of the reign of God in the person of Jesus, the messianic mystery lay in Jesus' willingness to go to his death for the life of the world. In the perspective of the disciples' Easter experience, the mission was vindicated, sublated, transformed by God's raising Jesus from the dead—so, while the world would still await the advent of the reign of God, resurrection inaugurated the reign of his messianic Son.

The form of Jesus' mission cannot, then, be grasped without reference to the esoteric tradition of the gospels—a neglected but basic issue. The era of Rudolf Bultmann's great influence is gone, leaving, however, a residue of inhibitions. His cavalier dismissal of the esoteric tradition (private instruction of disciples and events shared only with them) hangs on, its toleration attendant on the general lack of exigent argument respecting evidence for historicity. When discontinuity between Jesus and Church does not obtain, the quite mistaken tendency has been to overlook supplementary indices to historicity and simply to assume nonhistoricity.[37] Among other negative effects, this makes an exact account of the mission of Jesus impossible.

Jesus himself often defined his purposes. They included some seeming contradictions: on the one hand, his task is to save all, the righteous and the sinners alike (Matt 20:1-16); on the other, he summons to the banquet not the righteous but the sinners (Mark 2:17=Matt 9:13=Luke 5:32), warning that sinners will be saved and the righteous lost! (Matt 21:28-31). He has come for the scattered flock of Israel (Matt 10:6; 15:24), but warns that gentiles will be saved and sons of the reign lost! (Matt 8:11-12=Luke 13:28-29). He speaks of the straying sheep that must be restored to the flock (Luke 15:4-6=Matt 18:12-14), but he treats the whole flock, all Israel, as "lost sheep" (Mark 6:34; Matt 9:36; Matt 10:6; 15:24). And in contrast to all he says and does in the service of reconciliation, he has come to kindle fire on earth (Luke 12:49) and to bring not peace but a sword (Matt 10:34=Luke 12:51).

It is true that these sayings cease to seem incoherent, once their perspectives are more exactly specified and ordered. The fact remains that Jesus did not recoil from division. His mission was not a straightforward benefaction, like a check drawn on oil revenues and presented to all citizens of a state. He called for a response of the heart, for acceptance, trust, belief; and he was dismayed, bewildered, angered, and sorrowed at refusal. He knew that division was not to be avoided. His task included launching the ordeal (this was the fire he was to kindle; it would comprehend the sword of division and the heartbreak of families broken over him). He did not share the soteriological optimism of the time, but, like the Baptist, harkened back to the prophets. His task was to renew all things, but restoration was a drama that divided individuals, families, villages, the nation (Matt 10:12-15).

We might, moreover, take the mission of Jesus as a wider question than the aims of Jesus. It includes the significant whole of his personal performance. Illuminated by types and titles, that performance is nevertheless not exhausted by them. The types and titles recall scriptural traditions, but also supersede and define them anew. Like John, Jesus was "more than a prophet" (Matt 11:9=Luke 7:26). Like John, his whole effort was to prepare Israel for the consummation. But his own distinctive mission was to bring all scriptural types, promises, and prophecies to fulfillment, thus to usher in the judgment of the world that would rectify all things, to restore and renew the people of God, to give it a new heart and a new spirit, to renew temple and cult in the most transcendent fashion, to bring to pass the climactic and definitive reign of God, caught in the image of the banquet with the patriarchs.

Even if we were to correlate the spectrum of scriptural images and themes with the surprising range of antitypes and other forms of fulfillment as they appear in the words and symbolic acts of Jesus, basic aspects of his historic mission would still be left untouched. To express his personal destiny he called on extraordinary scriptural themes: the suffering servant (Isa 52:13-53:12) and the Son of man (Dan 7:13-14).[38] Whereas his task was conceived in harmony with biblical tradition, it involved a revolution of values, and some of this revolution must have emerged less from ideas and the work of intelligence than from the personal selfhood peculiar to Jesus.

New people, new heart and spirit, new code: a salient aspect of this newness is a new view of enemies. It is very hard to take seriously the claim that Jesus was a pacifist on principle, political or personal. It is nonetheless clear that he rejected every zealot-like appeal. He pressed the theme of love for (personal) adversaries.[39] He impressed on his disciples the principle of returning good for evil. He commanded repeated forgiveness, and (at a certain point)[40] he fully accepted the role of the Isaian Servant for himself. This stand set a newly potent force

free in the world, deflating the prestige of violence and inspiring heroic
rejection of it. This was of a piece with the repudiation of vengeance in
a cultural world that at its best merely hoped to moderate the implaca-
ble blood-feud and the standing animosities of Mediterranean and
Near-Eastern life.

Some aspects of Jesus and his work had never previously been
objectified, not in the Law and the prophets, not in the halaka of the
scribes. They derived from his personal being and had to do with his
personal wholeness. Nowhere in the scriptures is to be found the policy
toward "sinners" that was so fundamental a factor in the conflicts of Jesus with the best and the brightest.[41] This violation of values, which
outdid even the rejection of Sabbath halaka in engendering religious
hostility, exhibited a boldness that far exceeded that of the Easter community.[42] The same may be said of his facile transcending of the cultural prohibitions and inhibitions in dealing with women, which Hanna
Wolff traced to the psychosexual integration and consequent freedom
and independence of Jesus' personality.[43]

These considerations invite us to consider his mission in terms
of *realized personal authenticity.* There has never been a human culture
unoffended by conspicuous, dramatic instances of such authenticity.
The death of Socrates, like that of Jesus, remains of inexhaustible interest to mankind. Our historically conscious age has witnessed a recovery
of the classic Greek (as distinguished from the late medieval, Renaissance, and Enlightenment) conception of "reason." As Josef Pieper
found in Socrates' long, articulate battle with the sophists the foundations of Socratic-Platonic thought,[44] as Eric Voegelin found existential
tension toward the divine ground of being in the "pull" and "counter-
pull" thematized by Plato,[45] so in our search for the whole figure of Jesus and the whole form of his mission, we might look for light in the
conflicts between Jesus and the religious elite, and in the gap between
him and his disciples.

From the start Jesus understood his task in terms irreducible to
those familiar to and cherished by the learned and pious. This elite
found fault with miraculous cures—if they were worked on the Sabbath
(e.g., Mark 3:1-6=Matt 12:9-14=Luke 6:6-11). They found fault with
stunning conversions—if they involved irregular behavior towards as
yet unconverted "sinners" (e.g., Luke 19:7-8). What an outrage: he acted as if free to commit what tradition branded "an abomination to the
LORD" (Prov 17:15), namely, stamping out the line between the good

and the wicked. It was seemingly irrelevant to these critics that this strange comportment broke down the defenses of the reprobates. The learned and pious were so busy protecting "the system" that they ended by blinding themselves to epiphanies of love.

His own disciples, moreover, could not make head nor tail of what he had to say about possessions, divorce, and sex (Mark 10:23-27; Matt 19: 23-26=Luke 18:24-27; Matt 19:10-12). They recoiled from his combining Messianic identity with a destiny of repudiation and suffering (Mark 8:32-33=Matt 16:22-23). Even at the end of his career their eye-witness observation of extraordinary incidents failed to shatter the habitual and conventional judgments in which they had been bred (Mark 14:6-8=Matt 26:10-12).[46]

The national restoration that Jesus proposed he first of all incarnated in himself. His was a selfhood independent of routine. He purified the tradition he inherited and bequeathed it—bettered, made whole (Matt 5:20)—to his followers. He expressed the major aspects of this restoration in words—many many words, charged with feeling, skillfully fashioned, unforgettable—but in acts as well as in words. His proclamation said: salvation, free, now. Besides the beatitude-form, this took the form of gestures, initiatives, blessings, cures and exorcisms, offers of table fellowship. The beneficiaries of these actions included the likely and unlikely, the rich and the poor. It included the wise and the bright, the hale and the flourishing, the pillars and the just, but, above all, *their opposite numbers, the simple, the afflicted, and the outcast.* His task was to prepare Israel for the consummation, so fulfilling all promises, prophecies and types. It was to prepare the nation for judgment by winning the remission of sins for all who wanted it. It was to bring the nations into salvation along with Israel. It was, finally, to create the conditions in which human bonds of affection could flourish without hindrance; in which the Father, his name hallowed by the nations, would reign supreme; and in which, restored to his friends, Jesus himself would end his abstinence, drinking wine "new" on "that day" (Mark 14:25=Matt 27:29) when his work would be wholly done.

# NOTES

1. Saul Liebermann, *Greek in Jewish Palestine* (New York: Jewish Theological Seminary, 1942) and *Hellenism in Jewish Palestine* (New York: Jewish Theological Seminary, 1950). Victor Tcherikover, *Hellenistic Civilization and the Jews* (Philadelphia: Jewish Publication Society of America, 1959); Martin Hengel, *Judaism and Hellenism: Studies in Their Encounter in Palestine during the Early Hellenistic Period* 2 vols. (London: SCM; Philadelphia: Fortress, 1974). Emil Schürer, *The History of the Jewish People in the Age of Jesus Christ* 3 vols. (in four books); Revised and edited by Geza Vermes, Fergus Millar, and Martin Goodman (Edinburgh: Clark, 1973-1986); *Compendia Rerum Iudaicarum ad Novum Testamentum*. Section I: *The Jewish People in the First Century* 2 vols. (eds.) Shmuel Safrai and M. Stern (Assen: Van Gorcum; Philadelphia: Fortress, vol. 1, 1974; vol. 2, 1976); Section II: *The Literature of the Jewish People in the Period of the Second Temple and the Talmud* 3 vols: vol. 1, 1990; vol. 2, 1984; vol. 3 forthcoming. Section III: *Jewish Traditions in Early Christian Literature*, vol. 1, 1990. Elias J. Bickerman, *The Jews in the Greek Age* (Cambridge: Harvard University Press, 1988).

2. See Joseph A. Fitzmyer, *The Dead Sea Scrolls: Major Publications and Tools for Study* (Missoula: Scholars, 1975; 2nd edition, 1990). For a brief up-to-date account, see Jerome Murphy-O'Connor, "Recent Discoveries: The Judean Desert" in *Early Judaism and its Modern Interpreters* (eds.) R. A. Kraft, G. W. E. Nickelsburg (Atlanta: Scholars, 1986) 119-156.

3. Gerd Theissen, *Sociology of Early Palestinian Christianity* (London: SCM; Philadelphia: Fortress, 1977). R. A. Horsley and J. S. Hanson, *Bandits, Prophets, and Messiahs: Popular Movements at the Time of Jesus* (Minneapolis: Winston, 1985). R. A. Horsley, *Jesus and the Spiral of Violence* (San Francisco: Harper, 1987); idem, *Sociology and the Jesus Movement* (New York: Crossroad, 1989); Sean Freyne, *Galilee, Jesus and the Gospels* (Philadelphia: Fortress, 1988) 135-272.

4. C. H. Dodd, *Parables of the Kingdom* (London: Nisbet, 1935; repr. London-Glasgow [Fontana] 1961). Joachim Jeremias, "Eine neue Schau der Zukunftsaussagen Jesu," *Theologische Blätter* (1941) col. 216-222. A. T. Cadoux, *The Parables of Jesus. Their Art and Use* (London: Clarke, 1930; New York: Macmillan, 1931); B. T. D. Smith, *The Parables of the Synoptic Gospels* (Cambridge: Cambridge University Press, 1937); for Dodd, see preceding note; J. Jeremias, *The Parables of Jesus* (London: SCM; New York: Scribner, 1963).

5. Jesus' initiative towards notorious sinners did not, of course, signify his not requiring repentance at all; rather, it dramatically demonstrated his break with Torah-oriented in favor of reign-of-God-oriented repentance. To see how Jesus himself conceived the matter, one need only press the parables that defended his initiative and that everywhere suppose the relevance of conversion (e.g., the Two Sons, Matt 21:28-31; the Two Debtors, Luke 7:41-43; the Prodigal Son, Luke 15:11-32; the Lost Sheep, Luke 15:4-7=Matt 18:12-14; the Good Employer, Matt 20:1-15, the Pharisee and the Publican, Luke 18:9-14). See also the Zacchaeus paradigm (Luke 19:1-10).

6. Ernst Käsemann, "Sentences of Holy Law" in *New Testament Questions of Today* (London: SCM, 1969) 66-81. See also Klaus Berger, "Die sogenannten 'Sätze heiligen Rechts'" *New Testament Studies* 17 (1970) 10-40. Whether or not we can specify a distinctive form is unclear; in any case the issue of historicity is not settled by that of form, as numerous participants in this discussion have observed. Despite beguiling parallels in nongospel literature (Revelation, the Odes of Solomon) there is still no solid evidence that Synoptic sayings represent words of early Christian prophets adopted as words of Jesus. Form-critical works alluded to: A. J. Hultgren, *Jesus and his Adversaries* (Minneapolis: Augsburg, 1979); Gerd Theissen, *The Miracle Stories of the Early Gospel Tradition* (Philadelphia: Fortress, 1983).

7. On what is lacking in the form-critical account of gospel origins, see Riesner, *Lehrer*, 6-96. Variations on the views of Birger Gerhardsson are increasingly accepted, but with apparently little enthusiasm for Gerhardsson's own proposals, possibly a hangover from the harsh criticism that they met on their first appearance.

8. On the current state of the debate: *The Interrelations of the Gospels* (ed.) David L. Dungan (Leuven: Peeters, 1990).

9. On non-titular uses of *bar ᵓĕnāšaᵓ* see Jeremias, *Theology*, "The philological position," 260-262. A review of the debate between Geza Vermes and Joseph A. Fitzmyer on whether in the time of Jesus *bar ᵓĕnāšaᵓ* was used as a straightforward surrogate for "I/me," see J. R. Donahue, "Recent Studies on the Origin of the 'Son of Man' in the Gospels," *Catholic Biblical Quarterly* 48 (1986) 484-498 .

10. J. Jeremias, "Die älteste Schicht der Menschensohn-logien in den Evangelien," *Zeitschrift für die neutestamentliche Wissenschaft* 58 (1967) 159-172

11. In Daniel the persecution of the saints is the leading motif (Dan 7: 21, 25). On Q see Athanasius Polag, "Die theologische Mitte der Logienquelle," in *Das Evangelium und die Evangelien* (ed.) Peter Stuhlmacher (Tübingen: Mohr-Siebeck, 1983) 103-111.

12. Jeremias, *Theology*, 295-297; Allison, *Ages* 137-140 (with resurrection prediction).

13. Even the Christian affirmation of the divinity of Christ lay, not, as had mistakenly been repeated for a hundred years, in a late phase of apostolic history (good treatment by L. W. Hurtado, *One God, One Lord* [London: SCM, 1988]), but (in my opinion) in its very earliest phase, the Easter experience. What took time was conceptual and linguistic articulation, which proceeded step by step through the whole New Testament era, from the first to the last texts.

14. *Journal for the Study of the New Testament* 26 ( 1986 ) 23.

15. Richard A. Horsley, *Jesus and the Spiral of Violence* (San Francisco: Harper & Row, 1987).

16. Sean Freyne, *Galilee, Jesus and the Gospels* (Philadelphia: Fortress, 1988 ).

17 . See above, 77, notes 15, 16, 17.

18. C. H. Dodd, *Parables* (see above, note 4) ch. 3; Jeremias, "Eine neue Schau der Zukunktsaussage Jesu" *Theologische Blätter* 20 (1941) 216-222.

19. On the death of Jesus as belonging to the tribulation, see Jeremias, *Parables*, 220; TDNT VI, 493 and often elsewhere.

20. See H. Schürmann, "Die vorösterlichen Anfänge der Logientradition," in *Der historische Jesus and der kerygmatische Christus* (ed.) H. Ristow and K. Matthiae (Berlin: Evangelische Verlagsanstalt, 1960) 342-370. Polag, "Logienquelle," 108; Riesner, *Lehrer*, 73-74 (who, note 26, cites well over a dozen scholars who have assented to Schürmann's proposal).

21. The only analytic proposal that seems plausible to me is the specifying of the conditions of possibility: "that without which X would not be possible"—leaving aside all guesswork on actual sufficiency. Another point: Allison is of the opinion that Jesus considered the eschatological tribulation to run all through his public mission. If, as seems positively probable, Luke 12:49-50 is an authentic word of Jesus and refers to this ordeal, it is rather a future event, signaled and opened by the suffering of Jesus. Nothing in the gospels, so far as I can see, contradicts this. It coheres positively with the relevant texts. Allison himself is quite right to distinguish between "the trials or temptations of everyday life" and "the final time of trouble which precedes the renewal" (140).

22. Gerd Theissen, "Jesusbewegung als charismatische Wertrevolution," *New Testament Studies* 35 (1989) 343-360.

23. Ernst Ludwig Dietrich, *SWB SBWT. Die endzeitliche Wiederherstellung der Propheten* (Giessen: Töpelmann, 1925).

24. Meyer, *Aims*, 120-123, 132-137; Gerhard Lohfink, *Jesus and Community* (Philadelphia: Fortress; New York/Ramsey: Paulist, 1984) 7-29 passim; E. P. Sanders, *Jesus and Judaism* (London: SCM; Philadelphia: Fortress, 1985) 77-119.

25. Jeremias, *Eucharistic*, 226; Sanders, *Jesus and Judaism*, 77.

26. Rudolf Pesch, *Das Abendmahl and Jesu Todesverständnis* (Freiburg: Herder, 1978).

27. C. K. Barrett, "Jesus and the Word," in *Rudolf Bultmanns Werk und Wirkung* (ed.) Bernd Jaspert (Darmstadt: Wissenschaftliche Buchgesellschaft, 1984) 81-91.

28. Hans-Josef Klauck, Präsenz im Herrenmahl. 1 Kor 11,23-26 im Kontext hellenistischer Religionsgeschichte," in Klauck, *Gemeinde—Amt—Sakrament* (Würzburg: Echter, 1989) 313-330. Otfried Hofius, "Herrenmahl und Herrenmahlsparadosis. Erwägungen zu 1 Kor 11, 23b-25," *Zeitschrift für Theologie und Kirche* 86 (1989) 371-408; reprinted in Hofius, *Paulusstudien* (Tübingen: Mohr-Siebeck, 1989) 203-240.

29. See above 38, notes 17 and 18.

30. See, for example, Maria Trautmann, *Zeichenhafte Handlungen Jesu* (Würzburg: Echter, 1980) 78-131, with critique of earlier treatments. Among others: Borg, *Conflict*, 170-199 (attack on the "holiness-paradigm"). Sanders, *Jesus and Judaism*, 61-76; B. F. Meyer, *Gregorianum* 69 (1988) 481-486.

31. Aramaic *litĕlātā' yômîn* can be, and in the gospel tradition was, rendered variously into Greek: *dia triōn hēmerōn* (Mark 14:58=Matt 26:61), *en trisin hēmerais* (Mark 15:29=Matt 27:40; John 2:19), *meta treis hēmeras* (Mark 8:31; 9:31; 10:34). It may equally stand behind [*en de*] *tē̦ tritē̦* [*hēmera̦*] (e.g., Luke 13:32; cf. 9: 22). In the riddle on destroying/building the sanctuary, the accent falls on the contrast between old and new—the sanctuary in ruins and the sudden appearance of its greater successor. The time notice denotes the mere lapse of time (not the period during which the sanctuary is being raised or built). The connotation of shortness serves to accent the miraculous character of the contrast. Hence, in the originally intended sense of this word of Jesus, *litĕl-ātā' yômîn* probably meant "after three days": *meta treis hēmeras*.

32. One condition of the historicity of the anamnesis-mandate is that it accord with the historical Jesus' scenario of the future. Since inattention to this has been all but universal, it is not surprising that few have approved (or even understood in its implications) the analysis of Joachim Jeremias, *Eucharistic*, 237-255, which still remains the most deft and probable account. (The sense of the mandate, to be sure, was changed after Easter, as we can see from the Pauline anamnesis.)

33. Jeremias, *Eucharistic Words*, 167.

34. Peter Stuhlmacher, *Jesus von Nazareth* (Stuttgart: Calwer, 1988) 68-69, defines a principle by which to judge relative priority among competing versions: "In the quest of the original wording of the words of institution (as also in text criticism) that version should be preferred which most easily makes historically understandable how the other versions arose." On this reasonably formulated principle and on the basis of its clear applicability to the eucharistic

words, he concludes as we do to the priority of the Markan form.

35. See Lars Hartman, "'Into the Name of Jesus,'" *New Testament Studies* 20 (1974) 432-440. Cf. *idem*, "Baptism 'Into the Name of Jesus' and Early Christology. Some Tentative Considerations," *Studia Theologica* 28 (1974) 21-48.

36. Pesch, *Abendmahlsworte*, 115-122.

37. "One might as well attribute to Jesus the doctrine of the Trinity or of the Incarnation" as acknowledge the historicity of the eucharistic words. Sanders, *Jesus and Judaism*, 332.

38. Peter Stuhlmacher, "Vicariously Giving His Life for Many, Mark 10:45 (Matt 20:28)," in *Reconciliation. Law and Righteousness* (Philadelphia: Fortress, 1986) 16-29.

39. Recent writers (e.g., Borg) looking for political advice in Jesus have found in the *echthros* of Matt 5:43f. national enemies of Israel (rather than a personal adversary of the individual). Perhaps. On the other hand, if the text has an Aramaic substratum, it may be read, "but thou needst not love thy (personal) adversary" (Joüon, *L'Évangile de Notre-Seigneur Jesus-Christ* [Paris: Beauchesne, 1930] 26; similarly, Jeremias, *Theology*, 213, note 3; Horsley, *Sociology*, 129, n. 25. The political context is in a sense ever-present in the Israel of Jesus' time, and Jesus urged against the hatred of all enemies of all kinds, but to insist on the political note in this text and its parallel (Luke 6:27-28) seems artificial.

40. Thomas Aquinas so understood the Sermon on the Mount on turning the other cheek: it envisaged the situation in which, resistance no longer being effective, the disciple assumed the role of servant-martyr. Commentary on John 18, lect. 4, 2.

41. Jeremias's "scale of rejection," the negative reactions toward Jesus found in the Synoptic data (*Theology*, 118), goes back *in toto* (except for the charge of "blasphemy") to Jesus' dining with sinners. C. F. D. Moule," The Gravamen Against Jesus" (see above, 22, note 3) has provided an impressive synthesis of factors at the root of Jesus' "authority" and affecting his rejection by his critics.

42. Still, it is noteworthy that according to Acts 10:6 Peter is said to be "lodging with Simon, a tanner," for this was among the professions with whose members Israel's religious elite were to have no contact.

43. Hanna Wolff, *Jesus the Therapist* (Oak Park, IL: Meyer-Stone, 1987).

44. See Josef Pieper, *Enthusiasm and Divine Madness* (New York: Harcourt, 1964).

45. See Eric Voegelin, "The Gospel and Culture," in *Jesus and Man's Hope* II (eds.) D. G. Miller and D. Y. Hadidian (Pittsburgh: Pittsburgh Theological Seminary, 1971) 59-101. Earlier, A. D. Nock had written: "It was the

emergence of Jesus and of the belief that he was a supernatural being who had appeared on earth which precipitated elements elements previously suspended in solution." "Gnosticism," in *Essays on Religion and the Ancient World*, (ed.) Zeph Stewart (Oxford: Clarendon, 1972) II, 940-959, at 958.

46. The sense of Mark 14:6-8=Matt 26:10-12 supposes the distinction between good works (alms) and works of love. The second rank higher. Whereas the first can always (*pantote*, v. 7) be performed, the second are timely and call for personal intervention. Correcting the disciples, Jesus says that the woman has not placed an act of waste that might better have been an act of alms; rather, she has placed an act of love—(advance) anointing for burial!

## 8

# THE EASTER EXPERIENCE INTERPRETED
# AND SECURED

Easter came as a matchless surprise. It might well be appropriate, then, to begin our account of the Easter experience with the factor of surprise. Next, we shall try to understand the character of "the Easter experience" in general, and the limited sense in which it might be shared. Finally, we shall take up the transition from the earthly Jesus to the Easter and post-Easter life of the Church.

Since this is an essay rather than a full-fledged, massive inquiry, we shall limit ourselves to a few watchwords: "surprise," "experience," and "integrity." The last refers to the way in which the integrity of the Easter experience has been made to impinge permanently on living Christian faith. Poets and thinkers, said Aquinas, have a common object in "the marvellous" (Commentary on Aristotle's *De metaphysica* 1,3; #55). Here we are concerned not with one marvel/*mirandum* but two: the resurrection of Jesus and the entry into history of "a new creation."

## Easter as Surprise

Here was a strange state of affairs: in the last period of his life Jesus had made what lay ahead a main theme of the instruction of his closest circle of disciples. Yet Easter seems to have come to them as a total surprise.

We cannot reasonably suppose that surprise was added late. It is an entirely believable element of the tradition. Though the Easter traditions, beginning with the tradition of the empty tomb, have been reworked more thoroughly than most parts of the gospel tradition (so making any exact differentiation of strata peculiarly difficult), some facets of the tradition retain their freshness and immediacy. The surprise motif, which is recurrent without being objectified for itself, is one such facet. It occurs in the stories of Mary Magdalene (John 20:13-17), of the reaction of the disciples to the tale of the women (Luke 24:12), of Cleopas and his companion (Luke 24:17-24), and elsewhere (John 20:24-29; cf. Matt 28:17). Yet there are excellent reasons for affirming the pre-Easter origin of Jesus' esoteric instructions on the coming eschatological crisis and its resolution, which included his vindication by resurrection.

The paradox finds a solution by specifying those aspects of esoteric instruction that were formulated *after the fact*. Jesus had indeed forewarned his disciples of the looming prospect of repudiation. He had come (=his intention/mission was) to kindle a fire on earth (Luke 12:49), to bring not peace but a sword (Matt 10:34=Luke 12:51).[1] He intended, in a word, to launch the "time of affliction" (ʿēt ṣārāh, Jer 30:5,7; Dan 12:1). This element of his mission (the eschatological test/ Ordeal), he promised, would be brief; God had already decided to shorten it for the sake of the chosen, Jesus' followers (Mark 13:20b=Matt 24:22b).[2]

One of the ways of saying "brief" or "soon" was, as we shall see, through the idiom of three days: in three days it will all be over. In the first Markan prediction text, that following the profession of faith ("You are the Messiah!") made by Simon in the region of Caesarea Philippi, there is a formulation of the coming events of repudiation, suffering, death, and resurrection that so exactly reflects the gospel account of what happened that it must have been formulated after the fact.[3] Except, possibly, for two fragments. The first "fragment" is the *māšāl* found in the text parallel to "the first prediction"; it is the second prediction of the passion, in Mark 9: 31c,d.[4] The second fragment is the time notice *meta treis hēmeras*, which appears in all three Markan forms of the prediction.

"Days" is a semantic device that makes up for the lack of Semitic abstract expressions for time, the durative aspect of which might be qualified by "long" and "short." One Semitic solution is circumlocution. "Many days" (Deut 1:46) is a long time. "Three days" is a short time.[5] The notions "short" and "long" are, of course, necessarily relative to some context.

In the Markan prediction the Son of man was to be raised "af-

ter three days" (Mark 8:31). Now, this has about it much the same sort
of initial, possibly trivial, problem as clings to the Matthean form of the
Jonah saying (Matt 12:40). Jesus' body did not, in any account, spend
three consecutive days and nights in the tomb, as Jonah had in the belly
of the sea-monster. No narrative tradition on the event uses the Greek
expression "after three days" to say when Jesus was raised. Even supposing that the Markan phrase "after three days" might be saved, namely, as belonging to a system of counting that took any part of each day
as a full, distinct unit,[6] we should still note that Matthew and Luke offer an expression that would puzzle no one: "on the third day" (Matt
16:21=Luke 9:22; cf. Matt 17:23 in contrast to Mark 9:31; and Matt
20:19d=Luke 18: 33b in contrast to Mark 10:34e).

Aramaic *litĕlātā' yômîn* can be rendered by Greek *en trisin
hēmerais*/in three days, *dia triōn hēmerōn*/through three days, *meta
treis hēmeras*/after three days and, in view of the principle of counting
mentioned above, *tę̄ tritę̄ hēmerą*/on the third day.[7] Now, we do not
know for certain whether Jesus told his disciples that his vindication
would come "in/after three days" or "on the third day," for this time-
notice may be as much of the nature of a secondary post-factum element as the precisely specified details of the "passion story in predic-
tion-form" in which it is embedded. But if, in fact, this time-notice did
derive from Jesus (a possibility favored more by the Markan than the
other forms), it is maximally probable that it had the exact same *metaphorical* sense as did its use in other contexts: (a) in the riddle of the
new sanctuary (Mark 14:58= Matt 26:61) and (b) in two words presented by Luke as belonging to the answer of Jesus to Antipas (Luke 13:32-
33). Outside the texts that we are discussing now, which predict the
passion and resurrection, and which (in large part, at least) are secondary, *the expression is never used to refer to three literal days.* In each
instance the use is metaphorical and the meaning indeterminate.

The phrase on the three days between the ruin of the sanctuary
and the building of a new sanctuary is meant to accent the shortness of
time, but we are not told what the short time in question might literally
amount to. If, as is positively and indeed highly probable, the three
days refer to the duration of the ordeal,[8] the time might be literally
counted in weeks, months, or even a year or so. We have some idea of
the duration of Jesus' public life; the three days referring to it (Luke
13:33) or the two days to be followed by the third day on which he ar-

rives at/achieves his goal (Luke 13:32) would be measured in *a few years*. The expression means "short time," but in any given instance of its use context must be called on to indicate two things, namely, whether the accent falls on shortness or not, and what the shortness of time would amount to in concrete context.

It should be noticed that the three-day sayings in the gospels fit easily into Jesus' scenario. The days of the Law and the prophets came to an end with the advent of John. The days of John were the opening act of fulfillment and salvation. After the days of John came the days of Jesus' own public activity (described with the use of the three-days schema in Luke 13:32-33). Jesus expected the end to come soon, e.g., immediately following "this present moment" (*ton de kairon touton*, Luke 12:56). And the repudiation of God's ultimate or messianic envoy would be followed by what? The post-paschal predictions we have been considering, which were at least largely retrojected into the story of Jesus, say: by Jesus' resurrection three days later. *All other indications of what Jesus expected say*: the rejection will unleash the tide of affliction breaking over Israel, its capital and temple, as well as over the disciples of the rejected Messiah.

As we learn from a few texts (such as Matt 10:23), the Master commanded his disciples to carry on their mission to Israel during this period, even against all odds.[9] But this period would be mercifully brief. If the riddle on the sanctuary of the temple (Mark 14:58=Matt 26:61; John 2:19; cf. Mark 15:29=Matt 27:40; Acts 6:14) epitomized the ordeal by reference to the destruction of the old sanctuary, it also promised that the time of the ordeal would be *short*: "after three days" Jesus himself would build the new sanctuary!

Apart from "the reign of God," no theme of Jesus' public preaching was as prominent as the warning of the coming crisis/ordeal. For most it would come utterly without warning, overtaking them in the midst of the ordinary business of life. It would be ferocious, bringing death and destruction on a generation of the blandly indifferent. The crisis/ordeal would be brought to an end by divine act, variously presented to various audiences. One veiled expression was "the sign" for which the religious elite had pressed Jesus in vain (Luke 11:29). Yes, there would be a sign, the Jonah sign: i.e., the triumph of one returning from the belly of death and defeat (Luke 11:30).[10] In words spoken to his disciples we find, rather, the imagery of "the (Son of) Man" (Luke

17:24). The data on prediction make up a rich fund—but apart from a few formulations which, as we have seen, are transparently *ex eventu* (Matt 16:21=Luke 9:22; Matt 17:23; 20:19d=Luke 18:33b), none of it was specific on the "when" of Jesus' vindication. Like the outbreak of the crisis/ordeal, this great "day" would suddenly, unexpectedly, be there. Since in authentic material the scenario invariably called for the great ordeal to engulf all Israel before the vindication would come, Easter was necessarily a surprise. The disciples had been told nothing of a vindication of Jesus that would cut right through the ordeal, cut it off before it got underway, so to speak. *They knew of no resurrection to take place on the literally "third day" following Jesus' death.* Even had they not been paralyzed, as they were, by the death of Jesus, they had in any case been forewarned of something different. This provides part, at least, of the relevant background to why the disciples, first over-whelmed by the execution of Jesus, then by the joy of Easter, moved, quite variously, toward reinterpretations of Jesus' prophecy of the ordeal.[11]

The Easter Church of Jerusalem had been transformed. From the start they were, and through the decades to follow they remained, liable to the hatred of the Sadducean temple clergy. Otherwise, they did their best to live in harmony with Israel, winning the good opinion of many by their public piety. They regularly frequented the temple for teaching and prayer. (This certainly was the tack adopted by James, who was careful to live as closely as possible in accord with the model of the Jewish holy man.)[12] Unlike the Greek-speaking Christians—whose harsh (if penetrating) assessment of how the resurrection of Jesus should orient the life of the messianic community drew an immediate, fiercely hostile response from the orthodox (e.g., Paul)—the Aramaic-speaking Christian community was intent on winning over all Israel to prepare for the Messiah's imminent return in glory. Despite the obstacles, all was buoyant optimism.

So much for the motif of "surprise." We move now to the motif of "experience." By way of introduction, however, we should recover the sense that Jews of the time of Jesus attached to the term "resurrection."

## The Meaning of Resurrection

In the faith of Israel "resurrection" signified far more than the resuscitation of the dead. According to Dan 12:2-3, which was the first in a series of creative rereadings/*relectures* of the great Servant text of Isa 52:13-53:12,[13] the risen would shine "like the stars for ever and ever" (cf. the use of "stars" for angels in Dan 8:10). Similarly, Jesus corrected the Sadducees: "when they rise from the dead, they neither marry nor are given in marriage, but are like angels in heaven" (Mark 12:25=Matt 22:30=Luke 20:35); Luke adds: "for they cannot die any more. . . " (Luke 20:36).

Paul cited what was probably a Christian distich from the community of Antioch in 1 Cor 15:50.

> Flesh and blood cannot inherit the reign of God
> neither does decay inherit immunity from decay.

As Joachim Jeremias pointed out, following Adolf Schlatter,[14] the two lines are not in perfectly synonymous parallelism, for the subject of the first is "the living" and the subject of the second, "the dead." The point of this theological distich is that neither the living nor the dead can enter into the risen life of the age to come *as they are*. If this is a problem, the solution (for the dead) lies in the kind of transformative resurrection affirmed by Judaism and Jewish Christianity and as outlined by Paul in 1 Cor 15:42b-44a.

> The sowing takes place in decay,
> the raising in immunity to decay;
> the sowing in humiliation, the raising in glory;
> the sowing in weakness, the raising in power;
> a natural body is sown, a spiritual body is raised.

What Paul calls "a secret" (1 Cor 15:51) contains the solution for those still living at the consummation of time: at the very moment that the dead are raised, the living shall be transformed. The two events together would constitute God's victory over the last enemy, death.[15] The life of the age to come would accordingly differ *toto caelo* from the conditions of present life. Such was the teaching of the rabbis; such the teaching of Jesus and of Paul. Those who shared "the Easter experience" (cf. 1 Cor 15:3-8) offer a testimony that accords well with this understanding.

All this, however, we are taking for granted. We are fortunate in having the work of Rodolphe Morissette on how Jews and Christians, notably Paul, understood "resurrection."[16] We are equally fortunate in having a number of helpful literary studies of the resurrection texts in the gospels, for example, the study of John 20, which the late Pierre Benoit gave us nearly forty years ago.[17] This provides an outstanding example of how the earliest account of a given event (in this instance, the first moment of the Easter experience) appears in the last of the gospels.

Our main interest centers on two further issues, irreducible to literary categories. The first asks: what was the element of "experience" in the "Easter experience"? How did the subjects of this experience construe it? What followed from their construal? The second asks: between "the Easter experience" and "the doctrine of Easter," is there an unbridgeable chasm? Or is there an unbreakable bond?

## "Experience" in "the Easter Experience"

We shall take the element of "experience" in the phrase "Easter experience" in a narrow sense. It was the combination of "data" and "consciousness" that is typical of any human meeting.

Two friends meet; each is aware of the other, and (whether one should happen to advert to it or not) each is "present" to himself in the act of registering the presence of the other. We classify as "data" all that I am aware of in the presence of my friend to me. And we classify as "consciousness" the element of my presence to myself in the act of registering the presence of my friend.[18]

A meeting is an instance of co-subjectivity in which "I" am the subject and my friend, the co-subject, is present to me as an object. (We should immediately note that while this is a perfectly legitimate sense of "object," it is obviously not "object" in the merely etymological or Kantian sense [something sensible that "lies opposite"] or in a personalist sense [a thing as distinguished from a person]. In a personalist sense, my friend is co-subject; but in terms of human intentionality, he/she is an object—namely, of my awareness.)

Now, we have had numerous efforts to deal reductively with

the Easter experience. James M. Robinson has proposed that it was essentially an experience of light.[19] The model for this theory is the appearance to Paul—not as recounted by Paul himself, however; rather, in a considerably later source, i.e., as recounted by Acts. In Robinson's reconstruction, the *original* experience, one of blinding light, was at some early point thought to lend itself all too readily to the development that would end finally with the gnosticism of Valentinus; so it was altered along the lines that the New Testament texts ultimately came to exhibit.

We have here something akin to the situation that David Friedrich Strauss found in the treatment of the miracles: the Rationalists, he said, dismantled the texts, saving this, dropping that. But Strauss urged that the texts are our one and only source of information. To dismantle them, preserving their "natural" parts and dropping (or explaining "naturally") the "supernatural" parts is to abandon our sole lead whether to the sense of the text or to its intended referents. What Robinson does in the appearance narratives (save the light, drop the personal appearance) is not dissimilar.

There was indeed an Easter experience, Robinson holds, but it did not originally exhibit the "meeting" dimension. That had been added to it after the fact. Strauss's question to the Rationalists was: why keep anything at all? (He invited his own readership, in any case, to solve the Rationalists' problem by judging the whole text of the miracle-account to be unhistorical.) Picking and choosing, on no basis other than the Rationalist critic's finding the supernatural indigestible, was, Strauss argued, an arbitrary tack to take. How is keeping "light" from the appearance texts any less arbitrary than the Rationalists' keeping the furniture, so to speak, of the miracle accounts? This solved the problem of the Rationalist, but at the cost of failing to confront the text, its intention, character, and challenge. In the course of the nineteenth century the conviction grew that Strauss had been right. The Rationalist flagship of the Enlightenment sank, and the so-called "mythological interpretation" took its turn in history.

We are dealing with "experience." It is not so much the particularity of concrete points dropped from the text that should fix our attention. The critic's purposes are one thing, those intrinsic to the text are another. What should fix our attention is the question whether, once stripped of the "meeting" motif, the text still has enough reason for its existence to make sense. There are numerous discrete points at which the tack taken by Robinson might well be considered less liable to critique than that taken by the Rationalists when dealing with miracle accounts. First, "resurrection" and evidences of resurrection have a uniqueness that places appearance accounts in a category apart. If there were not the whole tradition of Israel to lend intelligibility and credibility to the story of John the Baptist and Jesus, and if there were not the whole story of John and Jesus to lend intelligibility and credibility to the early Christian theme "'The Lord is risen indeed and has appeared to Simon!'" (Luke 24:34), we would be hard put to give serious thought to any appearance narratives. Miraculous phenomena, on the other hand, are far commoner and intrinsically more credible than claims to resurrection from the dead. Second, there is a genuine critical probability that the appearance narratives, as mentioned above, had a complex development. There is nothing intrinsically unreasonable about raising the question of what might have been initially given data (light motifs?) and what might have been added to the texts in the course of time. But we must not allow ourselves to think that any kind of text we might imagine is a genuine candidate for actual historical existence at the springs of the gospel tradition. We have no basis for positing as probable that there ever existed a resurrection text celebrating a "light experience," just as we have little basis, virtually none, for positing as probable that there ever existed a vital tradition focused on Jesus that did not depend on the affirmation "the Lord is risen indeed . . . " (Luke 24:34). Remove appearance from the appearance texts, and no plausibly imaginable tradition is left on which to build a hypothesis (such as that "the *original* tradition began with the play of light motifs . . . ").

## Securing the Meaning and Integrity of the Easter Experience

There is a sense in which the Easter experience could not be and was not secured, but was unique and intransmissible. The Easter experience in its empirical actuality was an unrepeatable grace, or *charis*, a gracious gift bestowed on particular persons and groups. The experience itself could not be extended to others. The *truth* of this experiential blessing could nevertheless be shared. In fact, the will to share that truth is what generated the apostolic witness. This was an act that only they could place who had been graced by the Easter experience. When

those witnesses died—the women, like Mary Magdalene, Cephas and
the twelve, the five hundred brethren, Paul, James and others—the act
that was the apostolic testimony ceased with them. But the truth of their
testimony, which might also have died, did not. In that sense the Christian *koinōnia*/communion/fellowship somehow did secure the Easter
experience. Our question is how?

In general, by the act of fixing this witness in formulas to be
believed and confessed:

> Christ died for our sins according to the scriptures,
> and he was buried,
> and he was raised on the third day according
> to the scriptures,
> and he appeared to Cephas, and then to the twelve
> (1 Cor 15:3-5).

We have here a formula which, by common consent dating
from early in the life of the Church, makes thematic a double mode of
witness: that of Cephas and the twelve, and that of the scriptures that
they invoked.

There is no need to survey the whole range of apostolic witness. Our point is narrower. We are asking how the early Church
shared the unique Easter experience; we have answered that *the experience* was indeed not shared, but that the truth of the experience, the *that*
of Jesus' resurrection, was mediated by a process of formulaic conden-
sation. We have little assured knowledge of the literary origin of the
faith-formula in 1 Cor 15:3-5; we can nonetheless safely say that Cephas and the twelve authored it in the sense that they sponsored the tradition that it defined and stabilized.

We have here a formulaic fixation of the experience of appearance and meeting. One may entertain as many hypotheses as one pleas-
es about the Easter experience; the only hypothesis that has found formulaic fixation was that the experience had an encounter- or meeting-
character: "Christ . . . appeared to Cephas, and then to the twelve" (relative to this precise point see also 1 Cor 15:6,7,8).

To appreciate the force and the functions of formulation, we
must go further. Among the key resurrection texts of the gospel literature is the story of Thomas in John 20. If ever there was a scene of
which the climax is charged, eloquent, memorable, this is it: "My Lord

and my God!" Our question is: what does Thomas's confession ("My Lord and my God") gain by translation into the forms of formulaic confession ("Jesus is Lord," etc.)?

First and last, there is the essential legitimacy of the translation, *for if the risen Christ were not the Lord and God of every human being, neither would he be the Lord and God of Thomas*. To affirm the fullness, the integrity, the truth of the experience of Thomas (in the presence of the twelve) is implicitly to affirm that "Jesus is Lord," or "Jesus is Lord and God." Religious experience is peculiarly liable to the risk of illusion. On the other hand, texts such as this one challenge us to measure up at least to their intended sense. This transcends the sphere of merely subjective convictions (however firm or fierce they might be).

Second, the doctrinal form (if, in view of the *inclusio* binding John 1:1, "and the Word was God," with the confession of Thomas in John 20:28, we may take the Prologue as foremost among the doctrinal forms of Thomas's confession) is designed to *safeguard the integrity of the original experience*. It functions to keep us from diminishing or watering down the experience. It allows us to grasp the experience of Thomas in its density and context, that of the Church. This was not a private, isolated experience. It would be far more plausible to propose that the text climaxing in the confession of Thomas was an ideal scene representing the faith of the early Church than to propose that the seed of the text was some unidentifiable experience of Thomas, that with time was built up into the scene as it exists at present in the text. Our point here, however, is not to list the factors that might tell for or against historicity; it is to invite an insight into the relation between the Easter experience of the followers of Jesus and the ongoing faith of the Church. The insight is a grasp of the correlation between "experience" and "doctrine." The doctrine depends on the experience; the experience would be lost without the doctrine that secures its integrity and truth.

## The Transition Signified by "Easter"

Among the many aspects of the transition there is, first, its simply historical aspect. Events that took place once and once only were succeeded by equally unique events at a further point in time, with the usual traits of continuity and discontinuity both in evidence. As there was a time before the death of Jesus, so there was a time after it; the time after it was specified by the charged Easter experience of the disciples (namely, meetings through which they came to understood him as *risen*). The disciples carried over much from their time with Jesus, as we shall see in a moment, and Easter transformed this heritage.

Second, there are the schemes of thought in accord with which the disciples came to understand both their encounters with the risen Jesus and with the world as they saw it, new, in the light of the risen "Messiah and Lord." These schemes of thought prominently include the motif of *fulfillment*.

> Did not our hearts burn within us as he talked to us
> on the road, while he opened to us the scriptures?
> (Luke 24:32).
> . . . and he was raised on the third day in accordance
> with the scripture (1 Cor 15:4).

Third, with particular reference to the promises and prophecies of Jesus himself, the Easter transition is from symbol to referent. A common misconception has had to do with "fulfillment." (Has this been the result of conceiving fulfillment in more or less rationalist terms, e.g., in a context of rationalist apologetics?) The misconception has lain in equating the transition from promise to fulfillment with the transition from faith to vision. (There is indeed an authentic bond between "faith" and "vision," but the vision in question is unavailable in this life. It is not ordinary empirical knowledge, whether in the post-Easter period or any other time. In the language of Philip the Chancellor, it is that "supernatural" vision, or beatific vision, that corresponds to, while transcending, an equally "supernatural" faith.)

If fulfillment were conceived apart from the mediation of faith, the transition would be open to all and sundry. But it is not. Fulfillment was revealed "not to all the people, but to us who were chosen by God as witnesses" (Acts 10:41). Where do we find the contrary attested? And why should we suppose that fulfillment is any less addressed to faith than the promise or prophecy that comes to fulfillment?

In large part the promise and prophecy of Jesus remained, for the early Church as for us, reserved for the future. There are, to be sure, instances of realized eschatology. In the language of symbol the gentiles were to come into the legacy of salvation in and through the eschatological pilgrimage of the nations to Zion. Actually, it was through an energetic mission first launched by the "Hellenists" (*hellēnistai*) that gentiles found salvation in Christ. And if to the eye of faith there is indeed a bond between Jesus' word on the pilgrimage of the nations and the event of the world mission, still to the cold eye of the unbeliever the connection between these two is imaginary.

A fourth aspect takes account of all the above: transition in simply historical terms, "fulfillment" as lead category, symbol and its "translation" into non-symbolic referent. But this fourth aspect has to do with "thought." What did thought make of the first three aspects of the resurrection?

To begin with, the disciples of Jesus carried over into their Jerusalem life a decisive legacy from their life in the company of Jesus. "The Easter experience" illuminated and transformed it. (The primary evidence of this legacy is, as Luke 1:1-4 attests, *the substance of the Synoptic tradition.*) This legacy included the modes of thought and thematic motifs of Jesus' absolute or apocalyptic eschatology: (a) antitypes corresponding to biblical types: the Servant whose role had at last been realized in flesh and blood; the (new) covenant celebrated in the eucharist; "the (Son of) Man" still to come; (b) fulfillment of the promises of the prophets ("blind men see, cripples walk . . . "; "the reign of God has overtaken you"); (c) the perfecting of the provisional, especially of the Law (Matt 5:17);[20] and (d) the filling up to their appointed fullness of all the eschatological measures (Matt 5:21-22,33-34, etc.; 23:32; Mark 4:29; 13:20; cf. Luke 14:22-24; Mark 1:15).

The Easter experience transformed this legacy in numerous ways: for the subjects of this experience it *vindicated* the legacy of Jesus. Again, very slowly the life of the Jerusalem community and of the other communities of the Levant and, still later, of the Mediterranean world translated some of the symbolic prophecy of Jesus into historic fulfillment-events: salvation for the gentiles in the world mission, death by martyrdom for many disciples, failure of the forces of death to prevail over rock and the temple (="Church") built on it.

Thought, the fourth aspect of post-Easter life, was a new way of taking hold of what had happened, not necessarily (nor even possibly) in the mode of "system," but in the mode of consciously elaborated reflection, coherently drawing on whatever conceptual resources were available. The most immediately accessible evidence of this kind of development is a performance recoverable from the Pauline letters, namely, Paul's performance or achievement as a missionary thinker. It is Pauline thought on the coherence of the Christ event with the scriptures of Israel; on God, his saving act as culmination of a divine plan; on Christ, on the Spirit, on the Church. It is difficult to deny Paul the name of "theologian." It is equally difficult to deny the epithet "theological" to pre-Pauline, para-Pauline, and post-Pauline lyrical and other compositions: the Philippians hymn (Phil 2:6-11), the Colossians hymn (Col 1:15-20), the letter to the Hebrews . . . . The efforts of minute critical exegesis have revealed a harvest of schemes of thought in early Christianity which, for all their conceptual diversity, are remarkable for their non-contradictory character.

What the combination of "non-contradictory" thinking with "unharmonizable" conceptual diversity means may be illustrated by two views of baptism: that in Rom 6:3-11 and that in Eph 2:1-7. In the first passage the baptized share in the death of Christ; they also share in his newness of life. But Paul is careful not to attribute to the baptized an already realized resurrection together with the risen Christ. In the second passage the Pauline (if also post-Pauline) author affirms that God "made us alive together with Christ . . . and raised us up with him, and made us sit with him in the heavenly places in Christ Jesus" (Eph 2:5-6). Here are two ways of thinking about the effects of baptism. They are *verbally* contradictory on resurrection, but the contradiction, though irresolvable into a single seamless conceptuality, is resolved into a unity of analogous conceptions. They are not plausibly harmonizable, though one might plausibly, even probably, hypothesize that the second way was a *development* that, like many aspects of the theology of Colossians and Ephesians, took its point of departure precisely from Paul.[21] It would certainly be a mistake to think that the view in Ephesians stands in unqualified (rather than "verbal" and "conceptual") contradiction to that in Romans, as if either one of these conceptions dispensed with the future eschatology of the parousia and the resurrection of the dead. The difference between the two is in fact confined to the sphere of baptismal or sacramental reflection. Early in Ephesians there is the distinction between having already been "sealed with the promised Holy Spirit" and the future that this guarantees: "the guarantee of our inheritance *until we acquire possession of it*, to the praise of his glory" (Eph 1:13-14). Colossians is very like Ephesians in its distinctively post-Pauline realized eschatology (Col 3:1), and it similarly maintains a future eschatology and future hope (3:3-4), including the full reality of resurrection.

This fourth development may be said to have been inevitable. Nevertheless, the non-contradictory trait of the first Christian efforts of reflection, their non-contradictory character even when diverse efforts of reflection are conceptually diverse and nonharmonizable, ought not to be taken for granted, as if it were commonplace and richly paralleled. The phenomena of gnosis and gnosticism that came to full flower along with New Testament and early patristic Christianity found an exceedingly rich and diverse expression, but it altogether lacked the non-contradictory character of New Testament thought. (The one way in which it could be treated as a single phenomenon was pioneered by Hans Jonas, who grasped gnosis and gnosticism, not in their endlessly complex and contradictory symbolizations, but in their common psychic root: a despairing revolt against the cosmos.) The individually coherent reflective efforts by which early Christians attempted to make clear to themselves, to each other, and to outsiders just what had happened among them, what had happened to them, where they stood in the world and where they and the world were headed, were quite indispensable to early Christianity. We cannot imagine Paul, in the absence of Pauline theology, being able to solve (as he did) the unending mass of practical problems complicating the life of his young missionary churches.

Moreover, in retrospect we must regard all these efforts of early Christian reflection as charged with the direction of the Christian future. This was the kind of meaning that Hilary Armstrong saw in the Church's second-century decision against gnosticism.[22] But Christianity's positive orientation to human intelligence is already alive and productive in the main writings of the New Testament.

We do not find in earliest Christianity anything akin to a programmatic humanism. What we do find, however, is a creationist theology inherited from Judaism: the world God made is good, the human race is good, the body is good, life is good. Jesus did not fear or despise the world. The whole of it had come from the hand of God and remained in every detail under God's conserving, loving surveillance (Matt 10:29=Luke 12:6). His love for nature was theocentric (Matt 6:28-30=Luke 12:26-28). His affirmations took the goodness of the or-

dinary structures of life—personal, sexual, social, familial, occupational—for granted (e.g., Matt 19:1-12=Mark 10:1-10; Mark 10:14=Matt
19:14=Luke 18:16; Matt 7:ll=Luke 11:13; Mark 12:17=Matt 22:21b-
22=Luke 20:25). This held for the ordinary customs (Luke 11:5-8; Matt
25:1-12) and daily occupations of his surrounding world (agricultural in
Mark 4 and Matt 13, in Matt 20:1-16, etc.). Recent efforts to convert
the evidences of his political awareness into evidence of passionate political purpose have been misleading. He was aware of political oppres-
sion but not absorbed by it (Mark 12:16-17=Matt 22:15-22=Luke
20:20-26). This altogether Jewish set of suppositions and attitudes provided a remote but significant orientation to Christian openness to the
world and life in the world.

　　　　Furthermore, the roots of what later would become the view of
Christians as the "third race" (*gens tertia*) alongside or (in their own
view) transcendent alike of "Jew and Greek," are given in the drive of
Paul and his missionary allies to de-Judaize Christianity in selective
fashion. But the *positive* counterpart of this drive was not to Hellenize
Christianity. It was rather, in Gregory Dix's phrase, to allow Christianity "to be itself—Christianity."[23]

　　　　This implies, of course, that from the outset the followers of
Jesus made up an ecclesial reality transcending both the Jewish "congregation of the Lord" and the self-consciously superior culture (*pai-
deia*) of the Greeks. It would take a Paul to formulate it: "If anyone (is)
in Christ/new creation!" Or, in equivalent terms, "To be in Christ is
new creation!" (2 Cor 5:17). The "divine glory" (Rom 3:23), the human
reflection of God (Gen 1:26-27) that sin had defaced and lost, was now
returned. With it came into being the seed of a radically new humanism. "Know thyself" would no longer warn us to remember our limits;
it would encourge us to recognize our possibilities.

# NOTES

　　　　1. On the relation of the "I-have-come" word of Luke 12:49 to the eschatological ordeal, see Meyer, *Aims*, 213; *ibid.* on the peace/sword word.
　　　　2. On the distinctive way in which the category of "eschatological

measure" is deployed in Mark 13:20b (=Matt 24:22b), see Jeremias, *Theology*, 140-141.

    3. On formulation after the fact: Jeremias, *Theology*, 277-278.

    4. See Jeremias, *Theology*, 281-282.

    5. See Billerbeck I, 649 on the principle of early Rabbinic practice: "part of a day is reckoned as a whole day." Hence, *tẽ tritẽ hēmerą* must be included among the possible renderings of *litĕlātā'* *yômîn*.

    6. See J. Jeremias, "Die Drei-Tage-Worte der Evangelien," in *Tradition und Glaube. Das frühe Christentum in seiner Umwelt* [K. G. Kuhn Festschrift] (ed.) G. Jeremias, H.-W. Kuhn, H. Stegemann (Göttingen: Vandenhoeck & Ruprecht, 1971) 221-229, at 226-227.

    7. "Drei-Tage-Worte," 221-222. é

    8. "Drei-Tage-Worte," 222.

    9. See above, 38f., note 32.

    10. Jeremias, "Ionas," *TDNT* III, 406-410, at 409-410.

    11. Meyer, *Early Christians*, 75-78.

    12. On James, see F. C. Burkitt, *Christian Beginnings* (London: University of London Press, 1924) 54-65.

    13. H. L. Ginsburg, "The Oldest Interpretation of the Suffering Servant," *Vetus Testamentum* 3 (1953) 400-404.

    14. Jeremias, " 'Flesh and Blood Cannot Inherit the Kingdom Of God' (1 Cor. XV. 50)," in *Abba: Studien zur neutestamentlichen Theologie und Zeitgeschichte* (Göttingen: Vandenhoeck & Ruprecht, 1966) 298-307. Adolf Schlatter, *Paulus der Bote Jesu* (Stuttgart: Calwer, 1934) 441. Earlier than either: A. Robertson and A. Plummer, *A Critical and Exegetical Commentary on the First Epistle of St Paul to the Corinthians* (Edinburgh: Clark, second edition, 1914) 375-376.

    15. See Meyer, "Did Paul's View of the Resurrection of the Dead Undergo Development?" in *Critical Realism*, 99-128, at 112-114.

    16. See especially R. Morissette, "La condition de resusscité, 1 Corinthiens 15,35-49: structure littéraire de la pericope," *Biblica* 53 (1972) 208-228.

    17. Pierre Benoit, "Marie-Madelaine et les disciples au tombeau selon Joh 20,1-18," in *Judentum, Urchristentum, Kirche* (ed.) Walter Eltester (Berlin: Töpelmann, 1964) 141-152.

    18. See B. Lonergan, "Christ as Subject," in *Collection* (ed.) F. E. Crowe (New York: Herder & Herder, 1967) 164-197, esp. 173-178, but the whole essay is pertinent. Also Lonergan, *Method*, 8.

    19. James M. Robinson, "Jesus from Easter to Valentinus (or to the Apostles' Creed)," *Journal of Biblical Literature* 101 (1982) 5-37.

    20. Jeremias, *Theology*, 83-85.

    21. Meyer, *Early Christians*, 204-206.

22. A. Hilary Armstrong, "The Self-Definition of Christianity in Relation to Later Platonism," Vol. 1: *The Shaping of Christianity in the Second and Third Centiries* (ed.) E. P. Sanders (London: SCM; Philadelphia: Fortress, 1980) 74-99, 228-234, at 75-77; cf. 228.

23. Gregory Dix, *Jew and Greek,* 109.

9

# THE CHURCH IN EARLIEST CHRISTIANITY: IDENTITY AND SELF-DEFINITION

## I. Two Questions

It is now well over a hundred years since "the 1880 consensus" in critical biblical scholarship, according to which (a) there were no ties between "Jesus" and "Church," and (b) "Church" was an adventitious and profane reality.[1] Halfway through these hundred-odd years, Olof Linton, who described the 1880 consensus in his doctoral dissertation, *Das Problem der Urkirche in der neueren Forschung,* was already able to point to signs that the consensus had long since begun to fray and was now (1932) coming apart. Since then, to be sure, there have been efforts, especially during the Bultmannian ascendancy, but also in the post-Bultmannian era, to reestablish the consensus in a new form. First, many of those New Testament scholars who have taken up the historical-Jesus issue have so framed it as to exclude the complementary issue of the Church; others have indeed confronted this issue but, once again, have so framed it as to extinguish in advance all likelihood of finding evidence relevant to its solution.[2] Moreover, many scholars though supposedly examining the words of Jesus historically, read them—to put it in terms taught us by J. L. Austin[3]—as locutionary acts only, without inquiry into their illocutionary force (or how the words work: cajoling, threatening, etc.) and in a manner markedly incurious about their intended perlocutionary force or purpose. Bultmann was a master and model of this abstract, ahistorical way of dealing with the words of Jesus.[4] It allowed him to look for clues to Jesus' existential posture, without being distracted by the question of what purposes Jesus had conceived for himself, or just what he was attempting to do in the Israel of his time. Bultmann's followers, the pace-setting kerygma-theologians of the 1950s and 60s, regarded the historical question of Jesus and the church as marginal at best. They acknowledged the ubiquity of the church as maker and shaper of the texts, but never as intended and historically attested by the texts. So, for example, they took all Last Supper accounts to be aetiological and non-historical. Finally, the Schweitzerian notion that eschatology and Church were reciprocally repugnant tenaciously survived repeated refutation.

On the other hand, according to the most independent and comprehensive single work of historical-Jesus research to appear in our century, "it had to be [Jesus'] purpose to gather God's people of the time of salvation. . . . Indeed, we must put the point even more sharply: the only significance of the whole of Jesus' activity is to gather the eschatological people of God."[5] Such was the considered view of Joachim Jeremias, and since Jeremias's time there have been efforts to lend circumstantial support and nuance to this conviction and to secure, while reformulating, its essential truth.[6] Among the relevant historical ascertainments has been a double correlation: first, the long since well-acknowledged correlation between Jesus' intention and "the reign of God"; second, a newly affirmed correlation between the reign of God and the eschatological restoration of Israel.[7] This effectively amounted to a grasp of Jesus' central intention in eschatological and ecclesial terms: to bring to fulfillment (in those who responded positively to his proclamation and, above all, in his "following"—men and women who were gathered around him and traveled with him)[8] God's own long-promised, climactic and definitive *restoration of Israel*.[9]

A second issue respecting the Church, and a second effort to renovate the 1880 consensus, has borne above all on unity and diversity. The assertion of radical diversity among New Testament *kerygmata* and theologies and among the communities that engendered them, tended to sap and blunt the theme of the "the Church." The theses that Walter Bauer proposed in his 1934 monograph on orthodoxy and heresy in "earliest" (actually, second-century) Christianity[10] were retrojected to the New Testament era. Ernst Käsemann, for example, argued that the theological diversity of canonical texts was such as to ground and vindicate confessional pluralism, i.e., the present state of division between east (Orthodoxy) and west (Roman Catholicism) and, in the West, between Catholic and Protestant and between Roman Catholic and Anglican.[11] In Käsemann's view, early Christianity had never exhibited a stable or permanent ecclesial identity. But the basis of these far-reaching assertions was a painfully maladroit hermeneutic: Whatever elements proved not to be conceptually harmonizable were taken to be *eo ipso* contradictory. The vast middle ground between, on the one hand, consonance with a single (usually Pauline) conceptuality (*Begrifflichkeit*) and, on the other, irreducible incompatibility, was loftily overlooked.[12] Oversight of this kind together with a new, seemingly irresistible, nominalism, which reduced realities (referents, *die Sache)* to language (as *langue, Sprache,* world, game, code), contributed to the conviction that the New Testament was a syncretism charged with patent and latent contradictions. Diversity, confounded with division, became the order of the day, dominating treatments of New Testament proclamation and theology[13] as well as early Christian history.[14]

Over the past several generations there have nevertheless appeared studies running against this tide. Gregory Dix in *Jew and Greek* (1953)[15] pointed out that under the surface of a seemingly chaotic historical scholarship since the time of Ferdinand Christian Baur (d. 1860), there had been a single underlying but controlling question, a most basic and refractory question, namely: Was the church of Jews and gentiles (celebrated, for example, in the letter to the Ephesians) not merely related to, but *identical with*, the primitive apostolic community of Jerusalem?

Dix's observation appears in retrospect to have been both acute and profound. The issue of the Church—though often dodged, disguised, dismissed—has always been crucial, not only as pervasive in the texts, but by reason of the operative confessional divisions of the inquirers. (We may be perfectly at home with these divisions, but whether measured against the theologies of Matthew or of Luke or of Paul or of John, or against all of them collectively, they constitute a massive abnormality.)

The question of the Church, as we have been considering it, has two components: Did Jesus intend the Church? and: Has the Church had a distinct and lasting identity? Dix himself gave the second component, hardly less crucial than the first, its most trenchant articulation: The main issue of debate since Baur has been "the 'identity' of the historic Catholic Church with the primitive Apostolic community."[16]

We cannot take it for granted, however, that New Testament scholarship is in a position to measure up easily and adequately to Dix's question. What kind of inquiry is this question of "identity"? What does it mean to search out the "identity" of the messianic community and to inquire whether its successor communities on the shores of the Mediterranean basin shared in it? Is this question amenable to historical research?


## II. The Nature of the Second Question

In its integrity the "identity" of the Church comprehends many constitutive elements, witness the multiplicity of ecclesial images and themes. In the certainly authentic Pauline letters, we have, first, the paramount themes of baptism and the eucharist:

> . . . you have had yourselves washed,
> you have been consecrated,
> you have been made righteous
> through the name of our Lord Jesus Christ
> and through the Spirit of our God
>
> > (1 Cor 6:11).

Henceforth, the baptized were one, all their divisions transcended (Gal 3:28), and this oneness was precisely a participation in Christ.

> The cup of blessing that we bless,
> is it not a participation in the blood of Christ?
> The bread that we break,
> is it not a participation in the body of Christ?
> Because there is one loaf,
> we, though many, are one body,
> for all of us share in the one loaf
>
> > (1 Cor 10:16-17).

Second, this new, eschatological *ekklesia* was the fulfillment of the promise of the scriptures: the Israel of God (Gal 6:16), the new city (Matt 5:14) and sanctuary (Mark 14:58 par.; Matt 16:17-19) of God. As the goal intended by holy writ (e.g., 1 Cor. 10:6), it was consciously superior to all types and paradigms of salvation (cf. Jer 16:13; Hag 2:9). Hence, over and above the traditional images (flock; vine and vineyard; city and sanctuary of God; bride, family, household), there was realized in every Christian community "the body of Christ" or "one body in Christ" (e.g., Rom 12:5; 1 Cor 12:12-13) . An inference especially from the images of vinestock and branches (John 15:5), the bride (e.g., Mark 2:19-20 par.; John 3:29; Rev 22:17) and body of Christ, was the "identity" of the Church as itself a transcendent mystery to be affirmed by an act of faith.

At the same time, this same Church was an historic community the origins of which could be traced to the encounter between Jesus of Nazareth and Israel of the age of Tiberius. Since it was a fellowship or assembly defined not by blood but by meaning, it might be identified, first of all, by inquiry into that meaning. Indeed, whereas Paul unequivocally understood the Church as mystery, as communion and fellowship "in Christ," he has specified in equally unequivocal fashion the bond of meaning that defines and identifies *who is in Christ*. That bond he called "faith," and he understood faith as "yes" to "the gospel" (e.g., Rom 1:16).

There is no doubting the early Christian identification of "Church" as transcendent mystery. From this, however, it does not follow that successful historical inquiry into Christian identity is precluded from the outset. If from the start it was the gospel that made Christianity to be what it was, our immediate question must center on the meaning of "the gospel."

Among the numerous cheering convergences in Pauline exegesis and theology among Protestant and Roman Catholic scholars in our time is the definition of the gospel as the good news of God's climactic and definitive saving act on behalf of every human being in the death and resurrection of his Son, made Christ and Lord.[17] This gospel is what gave specificity to Christian identity. Christian identity, in other words, was the strict correlative of the gospel. He or she or they were "in Christ" who committed himself/herself/themselves—namely, by faith/baptism—to the gospel. And this ascertainment provides us with a first, solid clue to how to deal with the issue of Christian identity.

The gospel, or "message of reconciliation" came into being, according to Paul, in and through the Easter revelation. God, through Christ, had reconciled us to himself. The old order of existence was consequently finished. To be in Christ, he wrote (2 Cor 5:17), was to know by experience the fulfillment of the centuries-old hope for "new creation"! (Taken *ad litteram*, the text reads: "If anyone in Christ/new creation"! Since the words are formulated in gnomic fashion, they might be translated: "To be in Christ/(is) new creation." This is followed by:

> But  all  this comes from God,
>     who through Christ reconciled us to himself
>     and gave us the ministry of reconciliation;
> for God was in Christ reconciling the world to
>         himself,
>     not counting their transgressions against them,
>     and he founded in us the message of reconciliation.
> So we are envoys on Christ's behalf,
>     God himself making his appeal through us
>                                             (2 Cor  5:18-20).

In sum: The second of the two questions on the Church appears to be amenable to historical inquiry, for though the Church is a divine mystery, the gospel that defines it is intelligible and historically accessible both in itself and in its origins.

## III. Dealing Concretely with Unity and Diversity

Given the extraordinary outpouring of scholarly time, talent, and resoluteness on the issue of how "Church" is to be understood, and whether, historically, "Church" has been "one" or "many," the lack of a basic breakthrough comparable to that on "Jesus and the Church" makes one wonder what has been holding us back. It has occurred to me that the answer might have to do with the lack of adequate conceptual tools for discerning Christian identity and its survival or demise in the midst of dramatic conflict and ecclesial variation starting as early as the 30s in Jerusalem. Moreover, the launching of the world mission was a catalyst of developments, rapid and far-reaching, from the late 40s to the fall of Jerusalem (70) and thereafter to the death of Ignatius of Antioch.

By "adequate conceptual tools" I mean heuristic instruments suitable to the task of dealing with the often puzzling data of early Christian unity and diversity. What are the specifications or requisites for such conceptual tools?

First, they must be open enough to take into account the whole range of relevant historical data. These data include the unity that was so intense a concern of *hebraioi* and *hellēnistai* according to Acts, and the diversity, first of all, among all those Christian communities we know of in the Levant and on the northern shore of the Mediterranean basin.

Among the data of unity: (a) neither the *hebraioi* nor the *hellēnistai* looked with indifference on one another's views and policies, e.g., the missionary initiatives of certain *hellēnistai* toward Samaritans and gentiles, or the conviction of certain *hebraioi* that observance of the Mosaic Law was requisite to salvation; (b) crucial evidence of this positive concern was the approval, by the *hebraioi* gathered around "the pillars," James, Cephas, and John, of the Torah-free mission sponsored by the Antioch community in gentile lands; (c) the intense determination of Paul to bind together the Jerusalem Christian community and his own network of missionary communities in the Mediterranean.

Among the data of diversity: (a) Christian communities in Palestine sedulously observed as much of the Law as was compatible with their own new commitments;[18] (b) Antioch, the community that sponsored the first mission to the West, did not take Jerusalem for its model, but abandoned circumcision and much else in the Mosaic Law; (c) Pauline or non-Pauline, the new communities on the north shore of the Mediterranean were made up of Jews and gentiles; so, questions about observance of the Law long defined a practical issue, and one not settled in the same way everywhere.

Second, the needed tools of inquiry must be designed to fix attention on the most significant data. This supposes a sharply delineated *Fragestellung*; but we have already provided ourselves with its key element by correlating the identity of the Church first of all with what Paul called "the gospel."

Third, is it a requisite that our resources be the ready-made tools of the social sciences? The answer seems to be, no. Both in the United Kingdom and in the United States and Canada we can now count a considerable number of New Testament scholars absorbed in applying the resources of the social sciences to early Christian history. But whatever its achievements otherwise, this collective effort has not thus far contributed to the crucial, precisely delineated question that Gregory Dix formulated in the early 1950s and that we have just now further (if briefly) discussed. In previous publications I proposed (on the basis of intentionality analysis) a heuristic structure designed to facilitate the correlation of evidence for both unity and diversity in early Christianity.[19] This heuristic structure was epitomized in two terms: *identity* and *self-definition*. We have already begun the discussion of identity; neither of these terms, however, can be isolated from the other. Self-definition supposes identity. It is the answer to the question, How, in any given community, is Christian identity culturally incarnated?

In view of the multiplicity of cultures in which earliest Christianity took root, self-definition in this sense is an index to ecclesial diversity. The index may be broken down into three principles of culture, and hence *sources of cultural diversity:* horizons, self-understanding, and self-shaping. If it is true that the main diversities between early Christian churches were culturally rooted, these three sources of cultural diversity may well anticipate the main diversities among churches.

In the flesh-and-blood actuality of history, "identity" is realized in cultural context. Christian *hēllenistai* differed culturally from Christian *hebraioi* even in Jerusalem of the 30s. Inasmuch as Torah piety belonged part and parcel to the horizons of the Christian *hebraioi*, they assimilated the experience of salvation in a way that modified their understanding of the Torah but left allegiance to it intact. Nevertheless, the core-experience of salvation had been "the Easter experience"; and this allowed Paul at a particular moment in Antioch, to mount an argumentative appeal to the *hebraioi* (in the person of Cephas) to acknowledge the Easter break between Torah and salvation: "we [i.e., you as much as I] . . . have come to know [i.e., by our encounter with the risen Christ] that man is made righteous not by works of the Law but through faith in Christ . . . " (Gal 2:18-19). This kind of debate raises the question of whether the gospel, which is our key index to Christian identity, is one or many. Old hands in dealing with serious forms of "*de uno et multiplici*" know that the common pattern of intelligent resolution is to come down hard on both sides, followed by a swift and earnest effort to explain oneself. Nevertheless, one or the other must win out in the end.

So, first of all, the gospel is one, for there is only one "power of God for the salvation of every one who has faith" (Rom 1:16). To assert that "there is salvation in no one else" (Acts 4:11), to accept the truth of "apart from me you can do nothing," (John 15:6), "to confess with your lips that Jesus is Lord and believe in your heart that God raised him from the dead" (Rom 10:9), is to affirm this unique gospel. But since within the limits of this affirmation—namely, that salvation is transcendent, that it is a universal, normative economy, and that entry into it is through Christ and only through Christ—there are many facets, and the distinct possibility of diverse emphases, and an *a priori* probable need for diverse explanatory schemes, it follows that there must be some sense in which the gospel is many.

There is a form of the gospel which, on the testimony of Paul (1 Cor 15:1-11) was common to Jewish and gentile Christianity, common to himself and all the other missionaries in the Mediterranean basin. There are other formulations of the gospel, however, typified by additions to or omissions from the common form.

They are proper to particular churches or churchmen, and include especially two major forms: (a) the form in Luke-Acts, which even in its summary expression added to the common form an explicit reference to the public ministry of Jesus and, in both summary and explanatory elaboration, subtracted from the common form the motif of "atoning death"; (b) the form in John, which seemed to displace the soteriological center of gravity in the common gospel from the act of God in the expiatory death and resurrection of his Son to the saving revelation of God in the historic revelation of his Son: Jesus was the *Logos* made flesh; his public life was a series of great christophanies; his whole mission was in the service of saving "truth" recognizable to those foreordained to be "his own."

We may begin by observing that the Lucan and Johannine conceptions share in the affirmation of salvation in and through Christ alone. The effort (especially among Bultmannians in Germany of the 1950s and 60s) to range the Lucan form of the gospel under the (depreciatory) heading of the "theology of glory" and so to set it in contradiction to the common form of the gospel, may now be said to have failed. The failure has been due in part to the adoption of a more balanced mode of analysis, in part to a firmer hold on countervailing evidence in Luke and Acts.

First, with reference to Luke's avoidance of "atoning-death" motifs (the positive reasons for which have still to be specified, it seems to me, with full plausibility), it is worth noting that he allowed an exception. In Luke 22:20 the motif of expiation/ atonement objectified in *en tō̦ haimati to huper humōn ekchunnomenon* is retained,[20] probably in virtue of Luke's special conservatism respecting these most solemn words of Jesus.[21] Second, Luke has further relativized his avoidance of the motif by making unambiguously thematic the point of the motif, namely, the forgiveness of sins, which is recurrently celebrated as a messianic blessing (Acts 2:38; 5:31; 10:43; 13:38; 26:18).

That Luke in the discourses of Acts should have occasionally (though not consistently, cf. Acts 3:13-26; 4:8-12; 5:29-32) added to the common form of the gospel the motif of Jesus' public life (e.g., Acts 2:22; 10:38-39; 13:23-27) is worthy of notice in the purely literary context of early Christian formulaic texts, but is otherwise unexceptional. The Synoptic tradition obviously constitutes a massive parallel. There are parallels in Paul's global references to Jesus' earthly life (Gal 3:16; 4:4) and ministry (Rom 15:8) and in his implicit citations of the Jesus tradition (1 Cor 7:10 [=Mark 10:9-12=Matt 19:6-9]).[22] In all this Paul is very like other New Testament letter writers.[23] It follows that when all is said and done, Luke has at most modified a common formulation; by no stretch of imagination has he pioneered a new gospel.

The impact of such characteristic Johannine themes as the identification of Jesus as the *Logos* made flesh and of his life as a mission of "truth," i.e., as the divine revelation of himself as the way to God,[24] was to sublate the common gospel: to transform and enrich it, to keep what is transformed but to set it in a new key. John brought to the common form of the gospel both a content new in its explicitness and a new deepening of the common content—but primarily the second. His gospel was a transformative *approfondissement*. The death and resurrection of Jesus were not downplayed in the Johannine world of soteriological discourse, but enhanced. The common gospel said that Jesus

> was delivered up [to death] for our transgressions
> and raised [from the dead] for our acquittal
>                                          (Rom 4:25).

Of this mini-credo the Johannine story maintained and maximized both limbs and, in each of them, the "for us": "What am I to say?" asks the Johannine Jesus; "'Father, save me from this hour'? No! It was for this that I came to this hour!" (John 12:27). No one takes his life from him (John 10:18a); but he has received a charge from his Father (John 10:18e) and, in accord with it, lays down his life (John 10:11,15,17) as the "good shepherd" (John 10:11,14) who dies for his sheep. "The Father loves me," he says, "because I lay down my life, to receive it back again" (John 10:17; cf. 5:18). Again, as in the pre-Pauline formula of Rom 4:25, the Johannine Jesus is raised from the dead for the benefit of those he loves (apart from John 10 see John 7:37-39; 14:1-6; 16:19-24). The impact of such characteristic themes as Incarnation and Truth is to render the common gospel more dramatic: more charged, poignant, ironic. Though something of the sort might be said of all the major New Testament writers, the supreme example of such sublation is surely the gospel of John.

## IV.  Self-Definition

The most striking single aspect of the theological pluralism in the New Testament is its richness of horizons, perspectives, conceptions, and images, together with its total lack of dialectically (i.e., significantly and irreducibly) opposed horizons. Even such famous oppositions as those between Paul and James on faith and works or between Paul and Matthew on the Law have turned out, on examination, to fall far short of dialectical opposition.[25] There are numerous quite diverse theological conceptualities at work in the New Testament. As conceptually diverse but ultimately compatible, they all fall in the middle ground between conceptual harmonization and genuine contradiction. If, in the New Testament there was "one Lord, one faith, one baptism" (Eph 4:5), this is because there was one "power of salvation for all who have faith" (Rom 1:16). Though this power found concrete realization in a multiplicity of ways, the New Testament churchmen—and none more consciously and perspicaciously than Paul—knew that Jew and Greek, wise and foolish, rich and poor, freeman and slave, strong and weak, male and female were all one in Christ, bound to one gospel by one faith sealed in baptism and nourished by the eucharist.

Paul seems to have broken through the confusions that the world mission inevitably generated because he distinguished between two sets of opposites: first, unity vs. division; second, uniformity vs. diversity. There was one and only one gospel, hence one and only one Christian identity. But this did not keep Christian identity from being variously realized or incarnated in accord especially with the diversity between Jew and Greek.

And, as mentioned above, there were other diversities: Greeks and barbarians, the wise and the foolish (Rom 1:14), free man and bondman, male and female (Gal 3:28). We should add "the strong and the weak" (with diverse referents in Corinth and in Rome). To transpose Paul's data and Paul's convictions to the categories that we have chosen to put to the test, there was one identity among Christians, but many self-definitions.

Moreover, it seems clear that Paul's final achievement was to transcend even the Torah-free self-definition that he had so energetically (and victoriously) championed against all comers. For Paul made it clear as day that the primacy of "gospel" (=Christian identity=unity of the Church) was the key to his conspicuous flexibility respecting religious cultures or self-definitions. It was the gospel that counted in the end, neither circumcision nor uncircumcision having any independent importance (Gal 6:15; 1 Cor 7:19). Free of all, he made himself the slave of all: to those under the Law like one under the Law (though he was conscious of not being under the Law); to those free of law, like one free of law (though he was conscious of being bound to "the law of Christ"); to the weak like one of the weak (though he well knew that within narrow terms "the strong" were perfectly right. Cf. 1 Cor 9:19-22). To repeat: the distinctive elements of diversity were overshadowed in significance by the ultimate affirmation of unity: "For neither circumcision counts for anything nor uncircumcision, but a new creation" (Gal 6:15; cf. 1 Cor 7:19).

It seems equally clear from the way the generality of early Christians operated that they put a high premium on identity (the principle of unity), quite consciously and deliberately making room for plural self-definitions (the principle of diversity). This means that they found unity and diversity compatible—rightly so in the light of the distinctions evoked above. The contrary of unity is not diversity but division, just as the contrary of diversity is not unity but uniformity. Unity and division, like uniformity and diversity, were reciprocally exclusive, but there was nothing to prevent unity from coexisting with diversity—and in retrospect one might even say (indeed, should say) that, if unity was an imperative grounded in the gospel itself, diversity was a concrete human, existential, personal and cultural condition of this unity.

Before attempting to test the adequacy of the heuristic concepts "identity" and "self-definition" by dealing with data on the early Christian communities of Antioch, Corinth, and Rome, it might be well to recall the primary analogue, the only essence of which we have any knowledge worth mentioning: the human being. The primary analogue: Elizabeth is a human being. She is also a female; but though her femaleness qualifies, it does not define, her specific essence. The secondary analogue: Paul of Tarsus is a Christian. He is also a Jew. His Jewishness qualifies, it does not define, his being Christian. He is also a male and a freeman, but neither his maleness nor his political and social status defines his being Christian. What, then, was it that made him Christian? His yes to the gospel—in his case secured by a personal participation, outside Damascus, in "the Easter experience of the disciples."

In the light of these rudimentary but too often neglected or overlooked observations I have wanted—when envisaging the task of retrieving historically the life and faith of the early Church—to devise a heuristic structure allowing the inquirer to attend to "participant viewpoints," i.e., to recover, for our own purposes, the views entertained by the early Christians themselves.

If I may count on the reader's agreement respecting the issue of Christian identity (as Paul counted on Cephas' agreement on this issue at Antioch), we may move to the more contentious of the two terms, self-definition. The question is whether the heuristic concept of "self-definition"—broken down into "horizons," "self-understanding," and "self-shaping"—offers an adequate and useful set of headings under which to organize the historic data on early Christian diversity.

Let three Christian communities, Antioch, Corinth, and Rome, serve as a collective test case for the viability of "self-definition" as heuristic structure.

## V. Antioch, Corinth, and Rome

Our main sources of data on the early Christian community of Antioch are two, Paul's allusions to Antioch, and Luke's account of the Christian community there. We begin with Paul.

He explicitly mentions Antioch only in Galatians. Here the Antiochene community is represented as having adopted a style of life that has left Torah observances behind. The community itself appears unanimously to take this for granted. It was questioned from outside, namely from Jerusalem and specifically by James. Word of Cephas's eating with gentiles had reached Jerusalem and had either become a bone of contention among Jerusalem Christians or had become a theme of anti-Christian polemic, or both. Paul obviously felt no need, when writing to the churches of Galatia, to offer any explanatory information respecting the diversity of practice among the Christians of the two communities. They would have known of the practice of the mother Church of Jerusalem and would have taken for granted the coherence between their own community life and that of Antioch.

From Acts, however, we learn what made the Antioch community to be what it was. For, this community had come into being through refugees from Jerusalem, the *hellēnistai* (Greek-speaking Jewish Christians who had apparently been won over by the kerygma of the *hebraioi).* Their leader was Stephen. In so far as we can piece together their distinctive appropriation of the Christian heritage, it was remotely conditioned by Hellenistic humanism, proximately conditioned by "realized eschatology." By "Hellenistic humanism" is meant not merely the universalist ideal of post-Alexandrine pagans, but this ideal as shaped and colored among Jews by a sapiential heritage which included such eschatological themes as the coming covenant (LXX Jer 38:33-34) and the outpouring of the Spirit of God (LXX Joel 2:28-32). Their distinctive grasp of the Christian heritage was proximately conditioned by their interpretation of the paschal death of Jesus as the eschatological sublation of Jewish cult (Rom 3:25f.), of the suffering of Jesus in terms of the suffering of the obedient Servant (LXX Isa 53:2-11a), of the resurrection of Jesus as the Servant's exaltation (LXX Isa 52:13; 53:11b-12) and as the ascent and triumph of the one like a son of man (LXX Dan 7:13), which grounded his universal dominion (LXX Dan 7 14).[26]

Ferdinand Hahn's remarkable treatment of baptismal motifs in the liturgy of Christian Antioch[27] offers clues to the development of the distinctive views of the *hellēnistai:* participation in the death and risen life of Christ, recovery of the "glory" lost by Adam, conformity to the image of God's Son, sonship to God already inchoatively realized . . . Antioch may well have been a community dominantly gentile in makeup, but its leadership in the time of Paul was Jewish and probably remained Jewish, as Jacob Jervell surmised,[28] even in the wake of the fall of Jerusalem. The change to gentile leadership probably took place between A.D. 80 and 100.

Corinth, on the contrary, was a dominantly and perhaps all but exclusively gentile community. Whereas elements of the great tradition of Israel were deep-rooted in Christian Antioch, Paul had his hands full in attempting to establish such elements—religious, moral, cultural—in Corinth. Simply to recall a number of concrete items that illustrate this generalization: toleration of irregular marriage (1 Cor 5:1); the issue of food offered to idols (1 Cor 8:10); the tendency, in practice, to reduce the *deipnon kuriakon* to a standard memorial meal on the Hellenistic model (1 Cor 11). To this we should add the transposition of Jewish religious ideas to Greek and Hellenistic "wisdom" (1 Cor 1-4) and the impact of popular philosophy on "some" at least in the community, who say that there is no raising of dead men (1 Cor 15). All these issues cast Paul in the role not only of apostolic judge, but of cultural mediator and manager of cultural conflict. Most important, Paul unambiguously corrected those Corinthian errors that were incompatible with Christianity. The man living with his father's wife was to be "removed from among you" (1 Cor 5:2). As to the Corinthian style of celebrating the Lord's Supper, he flatly declared that "it is not the Lord's Supper that you eat" (1 Cor 11:20). If those who argue "there is no raising of dead men" were right, then Christ has not been raised . . . your faith is futile and you are still in your sins" (1 Cor 15:16-17). In other words, the error is apodictically repudiated as incompatible with faith. On the other hand, Paul handles the issue of eating food offered to idols with exemplary discrimination. The truth is that an idol has no real existence; but the freedom that this gives is not absolute. It might lead the weak into sin. "Therefore . . . I will never eat meat, lest I cause my brother to fall" (1 Cor 8:13).

There is nothing artificial about reducing all these mistaken ideas and practices of the Corinthians to rather standard Hellenistic horizons and self-understanding, and so to standard ethical views and practices (=self-shaping). In short, the distinctive problems that arose in the Christian community of Corinth go back to pagan Hellenistic culture.

On the contrary, the diversities between *hebraioi* and *hellēnistai* in Jerusalem, and the dialectic of Jerusalemite and Antiochene self-definitions (though they surely did have some nonreligious cultural points of departure) were substantially grounded in diverse appreciations of the present experience of salvation, which led to appropriately diverse ways of relating that experience to eschatology.

Is there, in fact, anything on the Corinthian scene that is not easily and naturally accounted for by resolution back into cultural diversity? Does the triad of "horizons, self-understanding, self-shaping" cover everything? I can think of two exceptions.

When, in 1980, I first proposed these three categories as sources of diversity within both Judaism and Christianity, I suggested that great historical events impinged on social groups in *mediated* fashion, offering the following example from second century Jewish history. With the collapse of the Bar Kochba movement, the Zealot-type of option came to an end: "The rabbis interiorized that history; their interpretation succeeded in declaring that line of Judaism bankrupt." My friend and former colleague, Edward C. Hobbs retorted: "Again, you have missed the external character of it. That line lost because the Zealots were killed. There were none left to argue about it."[29] Well, there were plenty of rabbis left to ponder the tack that Aqiba had taken, but Professor Hobbs was right: Events can impinge on persons in direct and unmediated fashion by killing them, or physically compelling them into exile, etc. Apart from the drama of such direct impact, however, even great events enter our lives by impinging on our horizons, self-understanding and self-shaping.

The second exception: Events may change our understanding of things without necessarily changing our self-understanding. This new understanding, however, is unlikely to constitute the kind of dramatic differences that really did shake and test the earliest Church. There was a real difference but no historic break, for example, between those who took a rather positive view of the Empire and those who took a harshly negative view. The same could be said of many other topics. So, the two "exceptions" evoked and acknowledged here are real, but of limited significance.

With respect to the Roman Christians: Recent scholarship has, no doubt correctly, emphasized the importance of the Jewish contingent among the Roman Christians. Unlike the mixed community of Antioch, however, where the issue of the Law had been settled early, Rome clearly displayed a variety of conflicting views and practices.

Paul's treatment of "the strong" and "the weak" in Rom 14:1-15:13 made clear the intrinsic rightness of Christian freedom from dietary prescriptions ("I know and am persuaded in the Lord Jesus [or: on the authority of the Lord Jesus] that nothing is unclean in itself" (Rom 14:14). But Paul is clear and uncompromising on the practical primacy of conscience: "It is unclean for anyone who thinks it is unclean" (Rom 14:14b). The law of love, without which the unity of the Church would not be, established a viewpoint higher than the conflicting self-definitions of Roman Christians. The "strong" were right in principle; but there was a superior principle: the law of love and the unity of the Church. The strong had a pressing duty: not to use their God-given liberty if it meant destroying the work of God (Rom 14.20f.). They were *not to please themselves* (Rom 15:1).

This magnificent mini-treatise, profoundly characteristic of Paul (cf. 1 Cor 8:1-13), was a specifically ecclesial transvaluation of values. It accorded with the peculiar virtue of the letter to the Romans, to meet the need of the moment (to defend his gospel under challenge) with an eloquence that was destined to ride out the ages.

In spirit, the Roman community was closer to Antioch than to Corinth. The threat to unity derived from the issue of the Law. Rome had a large Jewish community and numerous synagogues; the Christian community was mixed (Jewish and gentile); accordingly, the main issue was how the Law—and how much of the Law—should be observed.[30] Horizons, self-understanding, and practice (=self-shaping) appear to hit off rather well the sources of diversity and tension; and if we may take Rom 14 and 15 as our guide, the key to Christian identity/ unity was precisely the gospel (14:15; cf. 1 Cor 8:11).

## Conclusion

"The question of the Church" in the context of contemporary New Testament studies mainly comprises two issues: the intention of the historical Jesus and the continuation of the messianic community in history. The second question touches us all existentially, and says why so much hinges on how we treat "unity and diversity" or, more exactly, "'identity/unity" and "self-definitional diversity."

Above, we have dealt with the correlation between "one gospel" and "one Church." But most of our effort has been spent on diversity and its sources. Here we found the charismatic genius of Paul exemplary. He fought fiercely for the unqualified legitimacy of Torah-free self-definition (e.g., Gal 1 and 2). But he subordinated all self-definitions—that of Torah-bound Jerusalem, Torah-free Corinth, and

Torah-troubled Galatia and Rome; that of the strong and the weak in Corinth and of the strong and the weak in Rome—to the supreme law of love. This was the ultimate basis of identity/unity and the real meaning of "reign of God" and "righteousness and peace and joy in the Holy Spirit" (Rom 14:17).

Our disagreements on unity and diversity in earliest Christianity impose on us the effort to attend to all relevant data, to distinguish between truly contradictory views and those that are merely unharmonizable on the conceptual plane, to take account of the ancients' evident willingness to admit cultural diversity and at the same time affirm ecclesial unity (not only Paul, but Paul above all), and to be ready to see a difference between the situation of first-century Christianity and that of Christianity today precisely on this issue. "Identity" (defined by the gospel of God's universal saving act) and "self-definition" (comprising three moments of cultural diversity) may, it seems to me, serve as heuristic concepts useful in bringing all the relevant data to bear on the resolution of our differences on unity and diversity. The unity that counts bears on the gospel. No matter how painful the diversities in early Christianity, true dialectical oppositions (they were all authoritatively resolved) were quite few. But the early Christians had to find that out for themselves. They had to learn the difference between unity and uniformity, between diversity and division. Looking back on their history, we have to do the same.

Despite the great mass of New Testament scholarship that supposes, as uniquely informed and "critical," the view that the Church of New Testament times was never really one but always many, the actual state of the evidence commends a fundamentally different view. The dominant language of the New Testament was that of "churches," not of "Church"; still, there is always a transcendent dimension, for (as we remarked above) in every church is realized "the body of Christ." The Church of the world mission was one Church. It was threatened by division, acutely aware of the threat, and clearly committed to a deeply cherished unity. It stands as a challenge to today's cultivated culture of division, a model for thought and action in the cause of corporate Christian unity.

# NOTES

1. Olof Linton, *Das Problem der Urkirche in der neueren Forschung* (Uppsala: Almquist and Wiksells, 1932).

2. The entire group of "post-Bultmannian" Bultmannians engaged in the "new quest" of the historical Jesus (G. Bornkamm, E. Käsemann, E. Fuchs, J. M. Robinson, H. Conzelmann, H. Braun et al.), having framed the issue of the Church in more or less rigidly "institutional" terms, predictably found no traces of it in the work of Jesus. Their adoption of methodical scepticism as criterion of historicity supported the same conclusion. Today, those historians, including some with a strong interest in social-scientific aspects of the story of Jesus, who have accented the supposed strongly "political" side of Jesus' religious interests, have also failed to find the Church theme in the story of Jesus. E.g.: Gerd Theissen, Marcus Borg, Richard Horsley.

3. J. L. Austin, *How to Do Things with Words* (ed.) J. O. Urmson (Oxford: Clarendon, 1962).

4. An example of Bultmann's abstraction from the drama of Jesus' life, e.g., from consideration of his words and acts as revealing his purposes or the quest of concrete responses to his proclamation, teaching, and symbolic acts: "Die Frage nach der Echtheit von Mt 16,17-19, in *Exegetica. Aufsatze zur Erforschung des Neuen Testaments* (ed.) E. Dinkler (Tübingen: Mohr-Siebeck, 1967) 255-277.

5. Jeremias, *Theology,* 170.

6. Rudolf Pesch, *Das Markusevangelium* Vol. I (Freiburg: Herder, 1976; 2nd ed. 1977); Vol. II (Freiburg: Herder, 1977); Meyer, *Aims*; Gerhard Lohfink, *Wie hat Jesus Gemeinde gewollt?* (Freiburg: Herder, 1982) E.T. *Jesus and Community* (Philadelphia: Fortress, 1984).

7. Meyer, *Aims* 129-137; E. P. Sanders, *Jesus and Judaism* (London: SCM, 1985) 77-119.

8. Progressive realization of the restoration of Israel was coterminous with positive responses to Jesus' proclamation of the reign of God; this was not limited to Jesus' entourage, but that group made up the most conspicuous link between his public career and the nascent Jerusalem community described in Acts.

9. On the restoration of Israel as major prophetic theme, see Ernst Ludwig Dietrich, *SWB SBWT. Die endzeitliche Wiederherstellung bei den Pro-*

*pheten* (Giessen: Töpelmann, 1925).

10. Walter Bauer, *Orthodoxy and Heresy in Earliest Christianity* (Philadelphia: Fortress, 1971).

11. Ernst Käsemann, "'The Canon of the New Testament and the Unity of the Church," in *Essays on New Testament Themes* (London: SCM, 1964) 95-107.

12. See the critique of Brice L. Martin, "Some Reflections on the Unity of the New Testament," *Studies in Religion/Sciences Religieuses* 8 (1979) 143-152.

13. E.g., James D. G. Dunn, *Unity and Diversity in the New Testament* (Philadelphia: Westminster, 2nd ed., 1990).

14. E.g., Helmut Koester, *Introduction to the New Testament,* Vol. II: *History and Literature of Early Christianity* (Berlin and New York: de Gruyter; Philadelphia: Fortress, 1982).

15. Gregory Dix, *Jew and Greek* (Westminster: Dacre, 1953).

16. Dix, *Jew and Greek,* 2.

17. Even in essays reflecting *Kontroverstheologie* a common note is struck in the definition of "gospel": Heinrich Schlier, "Kerygma und Sophia," in *Die Zeit der Kirche* (Freiburg: Herder, 1956) 206-232; the same thing with variant formula: Schlier, "Die 'Liturgie' des apostolischen Evangeliums," in *Das Ende der Zeit* (Freiburg: Herder, 2nd ed. 1972) 169-183; Georg Eichholz, *Die Theologie des Paulus im Unriss* (Neukirchen-Vluyn: Neukirchener Verlag, 2nd ed. 1977); on use of "gospel" as a principle of unity in the New Testament, Peter Stuhlmacher, "The Gospel of Reconciliation in Christ—Basic Features and Issues of a Biblical Theology of the New Testament," *Horizons in Biblical Theology* 1 (1979) 161-190.

18. On James, see F. C. Burkitt, *Christian Beginnings* (London: University of London Press, 1924) 57-65 (largely based on Hegesippus, in Eusebius, *Eccl. hist.* ii). Did the earliest *hebraioi* go so far as to participate in the temple slaying of the passover lambs? Joachim Jeremias, *"pascha"* TDNT V, 902, says yes. In any case they did use the temple as a place for teaching and prayer.

19. A succinct account of the intentionality analysis in question may be found in Bernard Lonergan, "Method," in *Method* 3-25. The publications: B. F. Meyer, *Self-Definition in Early Christianity* (ed.) Irene Lawrence (Berkeley: Center for Hermeneutical Studies, 1980); *idem, Early Christians;* idem,"The World Mission and the Emergent Realization of Christian Identity" in (ed.) E. P. Sanders, *Jesus. the Gospels, and the Church* [W. R. Farmer Festschrift] (Macon: Mercer University Press, 1987) 243-263.

20. The note of expiation can be removed only at the price of separating the Lucan text from its parallels and, in Luke, of separating the conjoined motifs of 1. covenant, 2. the shedding of blood, and 3. "for you." The present text, despite its not exhibiting the expression "for many" (derived from Isa

53:11-12, in an explicitly expiatory text: see ʾāšām v. 10) correlates closely with the texts that do exhibit that phrase (Mark 14:24; Matt 26:28; cf. John 6:51).

21. Among the conclusions of Joachim Jeremias's study, *Die Sprache des Lukasevangeliums. Redaktion und Tradition im Nicht-Markus-Stoff des dritten Evangeliums* (Göttingen: Vandenhoeck & Ruprecht, 1980) was Luke's special conservatism respecting Jesus' words.

22. See David L. Dungan, *The Sayings of Jesus in the Churches of Paul* (Oxford: Blackwell, 1971).

23. C. F. D. Moule, "Jesus in New Testament Kerygma," in (eds.) O. Bocher and H. Hacker, *Verborum Veritas* [G. Stählin Festschrift] (Wuppertal: Brockhaus, 1970) 5-26, esp. 18-23. The point has since been repeated, e.g., in the volume edited by D. Wenham, *The Jesus Tradition Outside the Gospels* (Sheffield: JSOT, 1985 ) .

24. Ignace de la Potterie, " 'C'est lui qui a ouvert la voie,' La finale du prologue johannique," *Biblica* 69 (1988) 340-370.

25. On Paul and James, see the articles of Peter Bläser, "Justification" and "Law in the New Testament" in (ed.) Johannes B. Bauer, *Encyclopedia of Biblical Theology. The Complete Sacramentum Verbi* (New York: Crossroad, 1981) 449-455 and 484-495. On Paul and the Law, see Brice L. Martin, *Christ and the Law in Paul* (Leiden: Brill, 1989); there is a complementary volume on Matthew and the Law (forthcoming).

26 . These topics are treated more at length in B.F. Meyer, *Early Christians* 67-104: an account of how and why the *hellēnistai*, won over to gospel and Church by the *hebraioi*, appropriated their heritage of faith in a manner remarkably different from that of the *hebraioi*.

27. Ferdinand Hahn, "Taufe und Rechtfertigung. Ein Beitrag zur paulinischen Theologie in ihrer Vor- und Nachgeschichte," in (eds.) J. Friedrich, W. Pohlmann, P. Stuhlmacher, *Rechtfertigung* [E. Käsemann Festschrift] (Tübingen: Mohr-Siebeck and Göttingen: Vandenhoeck & Ruprecht, 1976) 95-124.

28. Jacob Jervell, "The Mighty Minority," *Studia Theologica* 34 (1980) 13-38.

29. Minutes of the Colloquy of 6 January, 1980 in *Self-Definition in Early Christianity* (see above, note 19) 25-38, at 31.

30. R. E. Brown and J. P. Meier, *Antioch and Rome* (London: Chapman, 1983) 97-103. With special reference to the situation addressed by Rom 13:1-7, James D. G. Dunn, "Romans 13:1-7—A Charter for Political Quietism?" *Ex Auditu* 2 (1986) 55-68.

# PART TWO

## INTRODUCTION TO PART II

Jesus belonged—with Socrates and the Buddha, with a handful of builders, sculptors, painters, with saints like Francis of Assisi—to the company of great life-enhancers. The prime witnesses to this were the simple, the afflicted, and the outcast, all surprised by joy. The joy of a life suddenly enhanced implies being "in tune with the world"; but Christian festivity (ours, said Jerome, is "an eternal festival"[1]) has two worlds to celebrate, this world and the next. So the kind of "being in tune with the world" that this festivity attests has its secret in adding an orientation to the future to the celebration of the present: "our bread of tomorrow" (Matt 6:11=Luke 11:3), the banquet with Abraham, Isaac, and Jacob, fathers of all the saved.

Such is the Christian fact, itself a reflection of the history of Jesus. Now, a superstructure of reflection has been founded on this fact. It came into being, slowly and inevitably, with the effort to understand what has happened in and through the figure of Jesus and to relate this to the whole scheme of human meaning and value. In the first centuries of the Christian era this superstructure of reflection partly looked to the outside world, in an effort to commend Christianity to the society and establishment of the Empire, but mostly looked to its own members so as to make Christian life more fully understandable to those already committed to it.

We leave aside, however, the long history of theology and its forms in order to concentrate on the present; and in this present we focus on how theology takes account of history. Until the rise of the historical consciousness in the era of the late seventeenth century to the present, the Christian world assumed that the normal state of affairs was permanence, that change (no matter how unstoppable it actually was) was relatively insignificant, that truth was eternal. This we may call the era of classicist culture. It supposed that the familiar was universally normative. Theology tended accordingly to cultivate an excessively ahistorical orthodoxy.

In the era of modern culture (empirical, historical-minded, aware of subject and subjectivity) the supposition is that contexts inevitably change, that individuals and groups and nations can be left behind, that we have no need to be anxious over certainty nor to appease such anxiety by abstractions. Precisely this hunger for certainty and the temptation to assuage it, however, has beset theology since the early Enlightenment. In this context Bernard Lonergan underscored the date 1680:

> For that, it seems, was the time of the great beginning. Then it was that Herbert Butterfield placed the origins of modern science, then that Paul Hazard placed the beginning of the Enlightenment, then that Yves Congar placed the beginning of dogmatic theology. When modern science began, when the Enlightenment began, then the theologians began to reassure one another about their certainties.[2]

The problem today is to do theology without *in the least* infringing on the rights and reality of history. There have been many efforts to meet this problem. Lonergan's effort variously sublated the thinking of Newman, Troeltsch, Collingwood, and others.[3]

The era of the revision of classical theology, begun in the nineteenth century and still far from over, has been a drama of insight and blindness, success and failure in discernment. The fallout from failure has been agnosticism, the repudiation of classical doctrine, reductionist philosophies and reductionist accounts of the heritage of the past, of human life, the human problem and human destiny. If the fruits of success, on the other hand, are judged exigently, they have lain, first, in disengagement from impediments: the dissolution of hostility to science and to the *Geisteswissenschaften*, including literature, history, and the arts, but also psychology, anthropology, sociology, and social criticism,[4] balanced by an authentic hermeneutic of suspicion, an effort to meet ambiguity with discernment.[5] Second, there has been the positive success of Newman's *Grammar*, Collingwood's cogent objectification of the logic of question-and-answer and his focus on "the inside of the event," Lonergan's "generalized empirical method," followed up by a critical epistemology and hermeneutics, and the elaboration of a framework for collaboration.[6]

Here we offer two essays. The first takes its point of departure from the problem of cultural decline, radicalizes the problem, and offers a solution via transcendental retrieval. This operates in function of the "search" technique that Karl Rahner worked out in *Hearers of the Word*; that, with Wilhelm Thüsing, he also applied to christology (a "searching Christology") in *A New Christology*; and used again in an effort to grasp and define the *Foundations of Christian Faith*.[7] Here, however, the movement of inquiry follows still more closely Bernard Lonergan's transcendental retrieval of "the solution"—needed by a theist and undiscoverable except by a theist—to the human problem (in chapter 20 of *Insight*).[8]

The human problem in its deepest dimension is "the problem of evil"; hence, to share in the divine solution of the human problem is to share precisely in what God has done and is doing about the fact of evil. The New Testament is a celebration of the divine triumph over evil. God was in Christ, defeating evil in the act of reconciling the world to himself. But the New Testament Church was entirely aware of the limits qualifying this victory. Christ is risen, but as "first-fruits" only (1 Cor 15:20); the reign of God is here, but only in its advance form, not in its full and final power. The decisive battle has been won, but the war is still on, how far from over we do not know. The form of the present, the state of affairs in which evil, defeated only in principle, and the problem of evil, resolved only in principle and in part, is the supernatural (i.e., transcendent) counterpart of Freud's "ordinary human unhappiness," namely, that state of faith, not vision, in which we are called on to follow in the wake of Christ, defeating evil by good. In this state the evil that remains to burden us from birth to death becomes bearable by the grace of God. Without trials, Tertullian said, no one will take hold of the *regna caelestia* (*De baptismo* 20.2). The day is still future when the Father "will wipe every tear" from our eyes (Rev 21:4; cf. 7:17).

Its central procedure guarantees that this first essay break

through the merely descriptive into the sphere of affirmation on the real
order of things. The second essay, a study in biblical theology, might
have been, but has not been, conceived in merely descriptive terms.
Still, the effort to mediate the meaning of the temple to the present is
limited. The Bultmannians of the mid-twentieth century offered to bear
the whole burden of mediating the past to the present. The present effort is a far cry from all such hermeneutical heroics. I take it that the
task of mediating ancient biblical meaning to the present will be carried
out in large part by theologians incorporating into theology and so into
the message of the Church, the biblical meaning that exegetes had discovered and made assimilable. In this way the biblical legacy can make
its way through the Church to the world in an appropriate contemporary
framework, in an accessible idiom, and in as great a variety of idioms
as is needful.

R. G. Collingwood's advice to concentrate on "the inside of
the event"[9] is here enlisted in the service of biblical theology. We wish
to concentrate not simply on the inside of the Jesus event, but on the inside of the Jesus *legacy* or *product*, the product of Christ the artisan,
*Christus faber*. The procedure is reminiscent of Giambatista Vico, who
claimed (in harmony with Thomas Aquinas) that we cannot know es-
sences (i.e., what God has made), and argued that we would accordingly be well advised to concentrate on what we ourselves have made. The
truth we have access to is that of human products: *verum et factum con-
vertuntur* (the knowable/known is what we ourselves have made, and
vice versa).

Now, the present inquiry presents the Church, the house of
God, as the product of Jesus, its messianic Master-Builder. Vico and
Collingwood may be taken to advise that we break into the circle of
builder and built, understanding each in terms of the other. This, in fact,
is our purpose. We begin as Jesus himself did, with the inheritance of
temple and sanctuary. We might come to some understanding of the eschatological antitype that is the Church by concentrating first on the
pre-eschatological type, the temple of Solomon, of Zerubbabel, of Ezekiel, of Herod.

Jesus the Messiah—the one after whom we await no other—
did not exactly specify "the Church" as his legacy. What he did was to
create from among the people of God concentric circles of wellwishers,
allies, followers, disciples, friends, who responded to him and to whom

in numerous ways *he bequeathed himself*. He made them the living sanctuary in whom he would be present "until the close of the age." This is how he created the Church. Its status as the divinely chosen, hence normative, way entirely depends on the truth of Jesus' own prior election and vocation.

With a view to those participants in historical-Jesus research who suppose that Jesus lived, moved, and had his being without any special sense of election or vocation, without any bond with the scriptures other than the bond that has bound millions of other believing readers to the biblical text, we have considered at some length the datum, deep and well-attested, of his consciousness of mission. It mediated the divinely promised act of salvation.

Those, by contrast, who confront an altogether contrary problem—namely, theologians who have found historical-Jesus research irrelevant, but are inhibited by it from using the gospels in the confident way to which their predecessors were accustomed—I hope will be persuaded to abandon this stance, and take at least this much from their Latin American colleagues: the scriptures add to the doctrinal truth about Jesus the drama of options charged with passion, pathos, irony. Brecht's "Truth is concrete" (*die Wahrheit ist konkret*) is truer and deeper than he could have guessed. John the Evangelist showed that the truth that sets us free is not only concrete but personal.

## NOTES

1. Jerome, *Epistola ad Algasiam* 121, cap. 10; Migne, *Patrologia Graeca* 22, 1031.

2. "Theology in its New Context," in Lonergan, *Second Collection*, 55-67, at 55.

3. The centrality to Lonergan of the tension between theology and history was revealed in a 1969 interview: "How do you reconcile doing theology and at the same time being accurate historically? That is the fundamental problem in *Method in Theology*." See *Curiosity at the Center of One's Life*, Thomas More Institute Papers/84, (Montreal: Thomas More, 1987) 386.

4. See "The Absence of God in Modern Culture," in Lonergan, *Second Collection*, 101-116.

5. I believe that Lonergan has tacitly restructured "the hermeneutic of suspicion" (Paul Ricoeur) by setting it in the context of dialectic and assigning

it the task of "piercing through mere plausibility to its real ground." See *A Third Collection*, 164.

6. Lonergan, *Method*, on generalized empirical method (or "transcendental method") 13-25; on epistemology, 262-265; on a productive framework for collaboration in theology, 125-145, and in the intellectual life generally, 361-367.

7. Karl Rahner, *Hörer des Wortes* (Munich: Kosel, 1963); ET, *Hearers of the Word* (New York: Herder & Herder, 1969); Karl Rahner and Wilhelm Thüsing, *A New Christology* (New York: Seabury, 1980); Karl Rahner, *Foundations of Christian Faith* (New York: Seabury, 1978).

8. Lonergan, *Insight*, 687-730.

9. R. G. Collingwood, *The Idea of History* (Oxford: Oxford University Press, 1946) 213-217.

10

JESUS AND THE CHURCH: DIVINE SOLUTION
TO THE HUMAN PROBLEM

In Gibbons's account, barbarism and religion were the key to as well as the outcome of decline and fall. Whatever the merit of the great rationalist's analysis, the world today, by something approaching common consent, stands in need of whatever healing and creative resources are available, whatever the source. In our world, too, barbarians are a factor, not at the gates but within them, an internal (if figurative) proletariat, not exclusively an underclass but a throng of the disillusioned and disaffected in every class. At the heart of this phenomenon there have been the issues, not only of "freedom," but of how to find a meaning in life that would allow freedom to flower and make a creative difference.

In a continuously more desacralized world it has been an occupational hazard of theologians to be ready to offer answers to questions no one is asking. That can hardly be the case, however, when the question is about meaning, freedom, progress. For the past two hundred years no other themes have been so consistently vital to the life of the West.

As eastern Europeans begin, under conditions of penury and social dislocation, to realize their long brutally repressed hopes of political self-determination and individual human rights, the West (it should be acknowledged) is faced with an almost contrary set of problems: not how to progress toward freedom and under freedom, but how to find the mean between wisdom and folly on the limits of freedom. The Western problem has to do with insight, the reduction of oversight, the removal of blindspots.

The following study is, in a sense, another piece of "culture criticism," deriving, however, a certain relative novelty from its radicalizing of the question of cultural progress and decline as well as from its angle of vision: the ancient faith, the resources of contemporary theology, the task of Christians. Whether finally persuasive or not, its conclusions will be in an idiom different from standard cultural criticism.

The essay is structured as challenge and response. Elements of decline in the current life of the West provide the challenge (part one). But the challenge is transposed to radical terms (part two) that call for the mobilizing of equally radical resources (part three). There follow, first, a review of Bernard Lonergan's analytic reflection on the kind of solution called for by the human dilemma (part four) and a set of considerations closing the gap between this and the original question or challenge (part five).

## I. Challenge: The Issue Of Decline

We have lived through great changes since the Depression: the Second World War, the combination of prosperity (or swift growth toward prosperity) and the anxiety that accompanied the cold war, and now the end of the cold war. Other anxieties, less dramatic and intense, still beset us. Since we of the West are easily the most self-conscious set of societies in human history, we are not lacking in analyses of the problems of Western culture (i.e., of the meanings and values that ground and animate the various ways of life typical of our, or Western, civilization). The steady stream of analytic literature, which dates from the end of the First World War and has flourished ever since, has all along been accompanied by an upbeat countercurrent. There have always been partisans of healing through autosuggestion ("every day in every way I'm getting better and better") or of broad-stroke analyses meant to sustain optimism. But despite their popularity, the promoters of this countercurrent have not had the best-seller list to themselves. From the start, i.e., from the generation of Max Weber, the market for brooding and censure, supported by war and depression, has been met by writers—Spengler, Sorokin, Alfred Weber, Toynbee—in whose works the discovery of overlooked good news was rarely to be met. There has also been a literature of moralists, whether in fiction or nonfiction, of political thinkers, social scientists, social and cultural critics, often less ready with solutions than with harshly persuasive critiques.

We begin by taking up three points of departure, beginning with the conditioned reflexes of the contemporary college freshman evoked by Allan Bloom.[1] Here, says Bloom, you will find a constant amid the diversities: a relativism that bears equally on the true and the good. Its message is that truth is inaccessible and that the difference between good and evil is illusory. Loss of truth and taste for truth, loss of the moral good as an ideal, loss of taste for the good in that sense, invite loss of the readiness to work, sacrifice, exercise restraint and perseverance out of commitment to truth and moral law. The result of these losses is a social scene in which fads do well, ideologies arise, peak, and succeed one another, cynicism thrives, cowardice is shrugged off, the cultural superstructure (writers, artists, intellectuals, educators, professionals in law and journalism) suffers bouts of fecklessness, and the popular culture heads for the slum. Fitfully, dimly, the civilization senses the pull of decline.

Bloom is longer on problems than solutions. Elements of a solution can always, perhaps, be worked out in the limited but pivotal sphere of higher education, and Bloom has urged the classic thesis that higher education's authentic vocation is precisely to keep alive the issue of the good life. Should the elements of a solution come to light in the course of this supremely educational inquiry, they might or might not prove to be seminal for the culture at large. There is some virtue, in any case, in simply speaking the truth about the present; and the assaults on Bloom that greeted his book, and were all the more intemperate in view of its great success, were a sign that his own efforts at truth-telling had hit home. The part of academia committed to the adversary culture that Bloom ridiculed sputtered, furious, at his analyses.

A second starting point: parallel experiences reported by John Stuart Mill and B. F. Skinner, and explored in searing depth by Leo Tolstoy. At the peak of his young powers, Mill experienced a sudden, disheartening insight, the recognition that even if all that he hoped for were realized, this would still not make him happy.[2] A parallel experience is reported by B. F. Skinner.[3] He was listening to an opera that he loved; he was aware of being "happily married" and "a successful man"; he was able to give all his energies to causes that he took to be of the highest social importance. And yet he was quite consciously, if inexplicably, unhappy. What is it that these bright men obscurely grasped but could not wholly articulate?

We should notice what they did grasp clearly. They thought of happiness as a real possibility, and they knew enough about it to realize that neither their instinctive hankerings nor their express ideals were up to the task of generating it. Evidently, there was some non-arbitrary something, which they could not put their finger on, that might make them happy. They obscurely recognized the gap between their deep longing and their present resources. Both were acutely aware of not knowing what might close this gap.

To this experience we add that of Tolstoy's spiritual crisis, described in *A Confession* (1882).[4] Again: health and wealth, fame and happy family, all undermined by a dreadful uncertainty: why, what for, to what end? He can not only find no answer; he cannot imagine where any answer at all might come from; for the question is not in search of new facts or better logic. It is a kind of longing for what is undetermined in advance, unempirical, even boundless. . . . Here we might append a remark, that, whether or not perfectly apposite, is still revelant to Tolstoy's experience. Truly penetrating knowledge of created things, said Thomas Aquinas, induces an abysmal, an insuperable, sadness, which cannot be lifted by any natural force of knowledge or will.[5] According to the tradition that was Aquinas's mental and spiritual environment, the object of our most indestructible and poignant longing somehow escapes, overflows, the order of material reality and, in fact, the whole created order. With respect to this strange, imperfectly explicable emptiness, sadness, and longing, we should not expect the resources of science to be anything but futile. But there is something else, to which neither Mill nor Skinner laid claim, that might have offered, and still might offer, some guiding light: a Pascalian *esprit de finesse* applied to the notion of happiness and the nagging experience of unhappiness.

A third, classically religious, starting point: Paul on the workings of the moral law. Paul's word for this was the revelation of the wrath of God. In Romans, chapter one, he depicted a harshly operative law of retribution. The society that chooses not to know God finds itself subject to a cycle of decline that ends in the incapacity to distinguish good and evil. Monocausal analysis, like this sermon of Paul's, is not sufficient for our own purposes, but Paul has settled on a basic factor. Whatever the speculations of theorists, the lesson of history, including Western history in our century, is that a price-tag comes with secularization: a jump in the indexes of disorder. Moral wreckage cannot be isolated. It prompts social and cultural deterioration. Religion and morality are two factors among many, but they are basic. Simply to name them, however, does not say how exactly they fit into the picture.

A fuller account is Bernard Lonergan's rehabilitation of the theme of "progress." In his view the moral law operates, not in accord with any single rule or truth, but in accord with human intentionality as it is actually operative in the individual and in society. To the extent that human subjects, finding themselves in an imperfect world, manage to discover that certain states of affairs betray a radical lack of intelligibility (Lonergan's "inverse insight" into "the social surd"),[6] and also manage—in the measure in which the true and the good reveal themselves to them—to cultivate truth and to sacrifice for the good, *they move forward*. They plant and they build, developing their powers and capitalizing on each successive achievement. To the extent, on the contrary, that human subjects settle on a flight from intelligence and hunker down in the preference for satisfactions over values, *they opt for sterility and routine*, summoning into operation the forces of decline. The moral law, abruptly converted from mute norm into avenging power, quickens the downward spiral. Ideologies corrupt minds. Corrupt minds instinctively seize on mistaken solutions.

> Imperceptibly the corruption spreads from the harsh sphere of material advantage and power to the mass media, the stylish journals, the literary movements, the educational process, the reigning philosophies. A civilization in decline digs its own grave with a relentless consistency.[7]

We might spend a moment on the stylish journals and the literary movements. It is extraordinary, yet hardly surprising, that for over twenty years our literary mentors, especially those in the universities, have welcomed, applied, and commended to students and the cultivated world literary theories that tear at the fabric of Western civilization, culture, and tradition. Extraordinary, because this is in principle a self-destructive tack; hardly surprising, because we have seen Western academics in the humanities and social sciences who have perversely committed themselves to one intellectual program after another, the coherence or common feature of which has been the same destructive and seemingly self-promoting but actually self-destructive impulse. Ideology—deconstructionist, Marxist, New Historicist—has lately been having a heyday.

In *Death of the Soul*,[8] William Barrett has provided a compelling account of how we slowly but surely got to this point, namely, by the flight from "consciousness" and by the blight of scientism. To this he opposes a freshly illustrated might of the mind. His study, a profoundly hopeful reaffirmation of the human spirit, shows that the human spirit is immensely alive and creative in such activities as mathematics and poetry. The long history of efforts among our cultural avantgarde to undermine the spiritual status of the human person has led to remarkable convergences among the most diverse parties to this reductionism—from the literati (Barrett is thinking especially of the deconstructionists) to "the somber partisans of the computer."[9] Both are ready and willing—positively eager—to do without the human soul. But what Barrett has shown so strikingly is that the mathematics that makes the computer possible and the poetry to which the literati owe their living are products, irreducibly creative products, of human consciousness, mind, spirit, soul.

Stagnation and bad leading to worse, that is, the main indexes to decline, derive from the lack, or the rejection, of creative solutions. But the greater the need of creative solutions to problems of stagnation or disorder, the greater the inertia and irrationality that block the needed insights and keep the needed solutions from coming within our ken or from coming to effective expression or from getting a hearing. Meeting concrete problems as efficiently as possible: that is a prime order of business, not the dream of a sudden jump in moral excellence. We need more than moral excellence, which would not—single-handedly, so to speak—repair the damage and reverse the decline. We need the work of practical excellence able to consider root problems and long-term consequences. (It is the height of airy-fairy conjecture, anyway, merely to posit moral excellence. The conditions of its coming to be on a wide scale are too numerous and too steep.)

So far we have called to mind three starting points. Each evokes at least some recognizable elements of our own situation. Our cultural world is afflicted with well-intentioned (the good intentions relate to a democratic pluralism) but poisonous relativism, noetic and moral. Despite a historically unparalleled state of prosperity, this same world is deeply, unconcealably, and self-confessedly unhappy and painfully at a loss over its unhappiness. Though it knows in its bones that progress and decline are somehow the fruit of our own alertness or heedlessness, intelligence or stupidity, responsibility or caprice, this world has hailed and cheered the reign of cheap rationalizations in every sphere, backed by too many of those it had counted on for vision and leadership, but who themselves have fallen captive to ideology.

With these starting points we are admittedly still far from even the most generically adequate account of ourselves. What do we need in order to hit off the root-idiosyncrasy of our own situation? There is, first, Camus's "fractional truth," that is, honesty. We are pushed to trace our present situation back to its conditions and causes only when honesty has led us to acknowledge whatever fragmentary insight we have into its gravity; to recognize that, for all its happy aspects (e.g., the reversal of the percentages of the materially comfortable and the painfully uncomfortable, the relative success of our leading political and social institutions), our present situation is also characterized by insoluble problems. We find it harder and harder not only to solve them but to put up with them. certain states of affairs demand reversal, for they are killing us—literally killing too many of us and figuratively killing or wounding all of us. Jacques Maritain's unvarnished observation of 1925 on our secular way of life would find more resonance today than it did then: "It is a homicidal civilization."[10]

Obviously, not everything is intolerable. Despite the pervasively ideological adversary culture of the post-liberal intelligentsia, our political system and the ideals that it incarnates are both in the positive column. Our institutions, even unsatisfactory ones, are reformable. The stream of ideologically inspired criticism—a dispiriting stew of Nietzschean-leftist critique—though destructive in the cultural superstructure and not confined to it, has nevertheless failed to prevail in the culture at large. The collapse of the Marxist claim to be the key to a superior world order, has led most, East and West, to greet with skepticism the wholesale critique of Western institutions and values. The peppery Marxist rhetoric that once lent excitement to this critique has suddenly taken on the look of a deflated balloon.

A single paragraph on what everyone agrees is intolerable: having abandoned as unworkable the theme of moral responsibility, some may be cooly and loftily tolerant of crime as such, but we all find its ravages unacceptable. We may not all be sure whether to keep the supply and demand for hard drugs in the criminal column, but we are at one in our readiness to acknowledge that our drug situation has become intolerable. Second, other crime, its rate and the rate at which an enraged and vicious violence accompanies it, have likewise grown more and more intolerable. Third, there is a common root, and it is all ours, our—the West's—drug of preference: freedom without limits, potent, heady, intoxicating. Many Western liberals are persuaded that this is just what the whole world wants and where it is headed.

There is no doubt some point in considering aspects of our situation that most find intolerable. But this is just a cut above television editorials. More dangerous are the problems that we collectively fail to recognize, that we do not see coming, that suddenly blindside us. Since ideology as a category relates to blindness, we are wise to submit our systematic preferences to suspicious review. Neither the ideologists nor their actual and prospective adherents consider their thinking to be "ideological" (that is, to pertain to the rationalization of alienation)[11] or destructive, except of what "must be destroyed." All ideologists see themselves as selfless, underappreciated benefactors of the whole human race. What we "all" take to be intolerable may be hard to cope with, but it has already lost part of its punch by having been unmasked. But a civilization in decline is as unaware of its destructive and self-destructive ways as Marx or Nietzsche were of destructive/self-destructive elements in their thinking, or as Stalin or Mao or Pol Pot were unaware of possible shortcomings in their practical politics. At the subjective level we have had nothing but pure shining virtue from Robespierre to the present.

The uneasy recognition that real danger lies in what we are blind to explains in part why our eyes glaze over as the moralists take the floor. If we think of our current state of affairs in exclusively moral terms, namely, as a *boundless abuse* of freedom, it has all the sock of an old lullaby. Of course, all generations have abused their freedom. (On the other hand, this particular story, freedom, really is our own. We were the first to write "freedom" on *all* the banners. We know that the freedom ride regularly heads for antinomian asininities. But we are cool, relaxed, indulgent: come on, lighten up.)

Antinomian passion—the great passion of Western Europe and as North-American as maple syrup and apple pie—is among the maladies at the root of what has become destructive and is acknowledged as intolerable. It is the rage of the age—a passionate prejudice against any limit on the pursuit of happiness in any form the pursuit can take, any limit on the freedom to be and to act, to grab and to throw away. This, not social-scientific studies, may be the real reason why we feel all right about putting our most violent criminals back in circulation after half a dozen or so years in prison. Again, ours is the age of

*pro choice.* The choice in question is whether or not to kill our own un-
born offspring; the body-count in the United States since Roe vs. Wade
is twenty-five million, outdoing all American wars put together. Hey,
it's a free country. You're free to be, to do, to have, to get rid of whatever you want; free to take charge of your life and do your own thing, to
follow your own interest, angle, pleasure, bent, bias, taste, individual or
group code—and let heaven fall and the earth perish, i.e., the rest of the
world can go to Hades. This is a declaration of independence, but it has
a price and the price is high.

   Finally, the ideological protection of this rage is itself destructive. The reassuring lie that we find harder and harder to swallow is the
one that says restraint is obsolete, over and done with; or that distin-
guishes restraint and restraint but on grounds no one can justify. There
is a kindred, lofty illusion that hovers or gracefully glides over the
modern scene, coolly surveying all, serenely free of panic. "'The times'
always seem bad. In most eras voices cry out against the visible deca-
dence; for every generation—and especially for the aging—the world is
going to the dogs."[12] *Plus ça change . . .* And yet, even such wise old
authoritative-sounding voices occasionally quaver:

> The tremendous endings of Greece and Rome are not
> a myth . . . Despair, indifference, the obsession with
> cruelty and death, the Samson complex of wanting to
> bring down the whole edifice on one's head and the
> heads of its retarded upholders—those passions seize
> the souls of the young generations and turn them into
> violent agents of change, or disabused skeptics and
> cynics. From both the activists and the negators come
> the new ideas and ideals which permit the march of
> civilization to continue. *But it can also happen that*
> *not enough new ideas, no vitalizing hopes, emerge,*
> *and civilization falls apart in growing disorder,*
> *mounting frustration, and brainless destruction.*[13]

## II. Transposing the Challenge to More Radical Terms

Are these the only alternatives, namely, the progress that keeps the social order alive and the decline that leads to its collapse? Is there another possibility? Some find themselves tending to converge at least at one point with those cool and sophisticated spirits who do not entertain the prospect of collapse, since they take decline itself to be an illusion. These some, however, do not share the same premise; they recoil from a decline that they find painfully real, and hardly less dreadful for leaving intact the mechanisms that allow social existence to continue. Not decline and fall, but decline and regression—regression to the point at which the West actually becomes what empiricists, positivists, and behaviorists have insisted all along that it already is: a civilization without meaning.

The issue of meaning and meaninglessness is not new. So far as the antecedents of Western civilization are concerned, the issue was first raised in the mythology of the high civilizations of the eastern Mediterranean and transposed into philosophical terms by the Greeks of the fifth and fourth centuries before Christ. Their question was whether human existence was free-floating and accidental, or somehow ultimately rooted. Deterministic systems such as those of Leucippus and Democritus neither included nor vindicated the meaningfulness of life. Socrates affirmed human values, but in "calling philosophy down from the heavens," he was fully, self-confessedly aware of being unable to offer any final justification of his views. Plato and Aristotle, on the other hand, offered diverse groundings for their respective accounts of the ultimate meaningfulness of human life (meaningfulness in this sense, that purpose was intrinsic to human life without its realization being guaranteed).

Socrates's second speech in the *Phaedrus*, for example, offered a brilliant and poignant philosophic myth which promised, obscurely and perhaps only to the best of the best, relief from human bondage to matter through the bond with absolute Being. The Ideas constituted the absolute in which finite human spirits, in their proper operations and in their destiny, participated together with the gods. Aristotle corrected and added to this vision of Being and the Good. The whole mixed world of necessity and contingency was ineluctably drawn by and to the absolute goodness that was the First Unmoved Mover. Whereas Aristotle did not pronounce on life after death, Plato affirmed the dream of immortality and the myth of punishments for evildoers in the Beyond.

How did such myths come into being? They were somehow rooted in intimations of order in all aspects of the life of the universe. Ancient man, finding himself battered by ill-fortune, did not leap to the inference that human experience was without rhyme or reason. Since he lived habitually within a firm supposition of order, he sought after the why and wherefore of misfortune, and in the process found correlations between a spontaneous sense of guilt for sin and an inference of liability to punishment. He inferred, in short, patterns of data in human experience that transcended, while remaining analogous to, patterns of physical regularity. Myth, a major source for philosophy, found order at the springs of meaning.

Leszek Kolakowski, who describes this question of ultimate meaningfulness as pervading the whole history of European civilization, mounted an effort to set Marx and the Marxist scheme in context by first setting Hegel in context—not just in the context of the German thinkers whose work he synthesized (Kant and Herder, Schiller, Fichte and Schelling) but of the long and powerful tradition of "dialectic" from "the soteriology of Plotinus" through Erigena and Eckhart to Cusa, Böhme, and Silesius; and from Fénélon through Rousseau and Hume to Kant—makes available to us a philosophical and mystical radicalization of the problem of decline.[14] Out of this Hegel and Marx, each in his own way, fashioned a vision of problem and solution. Each would define and solve the problem of evil. The issue for this long tradition of thinkers and mystics was: in what does the problem of man consist, and how does it find a solution?

From Plotinus to Hegel the tradition located the problem in the gap between the empirical human being and the ideal selfhood—changeless, immaterial and undivided, not subject to time—exhibited by the concept "man." (So, from the start, we have a platonist epistemological fixation involved in the problematizing of human life and meaning.) Plotinus drew from Plato the (clearly, but not consistently, posited) concept of the enfleshment of the soul as a kind of fall from spiritual existence. The human problem, then, was a problem of being; it related not merely to human functioning but to the make-up of man. The solution, identical with happiness, would lie in contemplation, but the subject of contemplation would be the soul after death, unhampered by body, freed from time, made absolute and finally self-identical.

Plotinus had rediscovered the world of non-accidental, non-contingent being; the problem of man was met by a human destiny of bonding with this universe of being, ceasing to be an outsider to it. To this destiny death, conceived as a liberation from body, was indispensable.

Is the human problem well defined in these platonist terms? That there is a problem bearing on the whole of human existence and involving human destiny is not in question. This is grounded in human experience and attested from time immemorial by myth, religion, and philosophy, as well as by lyric, epic, and drama. The problem cannot, however, consist in the failure of the human being to be what the human being cannot possibly be: divine, or angelic, or a living abstraction, i.e., the counterpart of a concept, a being whose life is wholly free of risk and without any shortcoming at all. Despite the long history of outcries to the contrary, there is no real scandal in finite, composite (partly material), and temporal existence.[15] Nor is there anything unjust or otherwise wrong in being incomplete and directed by nature and reason towards completion.

The record of literary remains is filled with evidences that human beings have found the human being, human society, human history and destiny, to be deeply and permanently puzzling, filled with the evidence of how we have wondered about ourselves, of how variously we translate this wonder into questions, and of how baffling the variety of answers is. Most of them surely are inaccurate or inadequate. Answers that find fault with the human mode of existence (this includes the platonist, gnostic, and idealist lines) or that are far removed from ordinary human experience, may be filed under the heading of "last resort." True, the prophets of old called for the remaking of man (Jer 31:33f.; Ezek 36:26f.), for, as Jeremiah put it (17:9), "the heart is of all things the most crooked, it is beyond remedy." But they did not conceive this new man as some sort of non-bodily substance living not in time but in a kind of eternity. Solutions that envisage our transformation into some new species not now on the horizon have, wherever adopted, led to disillusionment, usually on the heels of failure or catastrophe. We are currently witnessing the dissolution of a grandiose scheme for the remaking of mankind, the human cost of which has been exorbitant and immensely tragic.

What distinguished Marx was the ambition to solve the problem of evil not just theoretically but practically. He wanted to actualize
the myth of Prometheus, himself in the lead role. Wasn't that—taken together with passionate outrage at injustice, at the cold-blooded exploitation of the weak—the real source of Marx's appeal? Wasn't that what
made it seem, for at least two or three generations, that Socialism and
especially its scientific form might belong to the Tocquevillian category of unstoppable "providential facts"? Some such view led the noble,
independently reflective Karl Jaspers to put Socialism in that category
in his *Ursprung und Ziel der Geschichte*.[16] It was at the origin of the
long struggle between ideology and experience that never ended in the
lifetime of that hero of honesty, George Orwell, but did reach a climax
in *Animal Farm* and *Ninteen-Eighty-Four*.

Marx's account of the problem, however, was surely defective
in some respects. Pre-Hegelian tradition offered, as among the permanent factors that make for human progress and decline, the contingency
and incompletion of man, the submission of mankind to accident and
chance, the lack of rootage in eternal being. Marx dismissed this part of
the "dialectical" tradition that Hegel had drawn on as mystification; and
in this he was doubtless right in part. The platonist and mystical tradition was beset by an angelism that failed to grasp and acknowledge the
role of *body* in just those powers and activities proper to and the glory
of the human race. In that respect, the Marxist critique was realistic.
But Marx too foreshortened the human problem and its correlative solution. He reduced the fact and problem of evil to bread-and-butter terms.
Evil was rooted—as in Rousseauvian and Romantic tradition—in the
shortcomings, not of the human subject, but of the arrangements of human society.

Class war, Marx saw, would contribute to rectifying economic
imbalance. But it has long been clear that violent conflict, however inevitable at times, is likely to drive one batch of evils out of the world to
make room for another. Today, the Marxist experiment is a shambles
("Seventy-two Years on the Road to Nowhere" proclaimed a memorable dissident slogan in the May Day Parade, Moscow, 1990). The world
is increasingly aware that one must look elsewhere not only for a better
economic way, but for a better account of the deeper human issues. The
West claims to know a better economic way, but is admittedly at a loss
respecting not only the deeper economic issues, but the further and

deeper issues of good and evil, meaning and meaninglessness, fundamental human progress and decline.

The platonist dialectic failed out of irrealism: essentialism in ontology and angelism in anthropology. Except in the most generic terms, its problematizing of "evil, defect, dilemma" was itself liable to critique as defective. The Marxist counterpositions were a reverse side of the platonist coin, but, though more sober, they were hardly more realistic. From his university years Marx had been subjected to a ceaseless deluge of abstractions and illusions, and managed to ward off only four-fifths of them. By the middle 1840s, when his thought had hardened into form, there yet remained a core of dogmatic counterpositions and crippling oversights. These included the rock-solid conviction that all religion was illusory; that the single condition of the proletariat's liberator-role was its abolition as a separate class; that the worker's alienation from his own labor and its products was *the key*, unique and sufficient, to the dehumanization of man.

The specification of the human dilemma in oddly non-human terms, i.e., without reference to the human subject (as if social, economic, and political arrangements could be freed of any intrinsic connections with man) has by no means been limited to Marxism. The self has disappeared from a large part of Western thought. Barrett's account of the pattern of "desubstantialization" in Sartre and Heidegger is devastating. For the latter "I" refers to just one more "mode of being," namely *Ichsein*, "I-being."

> We are nothing but an aggregate of modes of being, and any organizing and unifying center we profess to find there is something we ourselves have forged or contrived.
> Thus, there is a gaping hole at the center of our human being—at least as Heidegger describes this being. Consequently, we have in the end to acknowledge a certain desolate and empty quality about his thought .... [17]

So it is that *die Sprache spricht*; that technology becomes a conspiracy without need of conspirators; that anonymous forces, i.e., lofty abstractions, govern our fate. The most important part of the explanation of this reign of abstractions is "the gaping hole" at the center of the anthropology that it supposes. Besides "the forgetfulness of being," as Jaspers noted, there is such a thing as the forgetfulness of *the Self*,[18] and this was among the specifically Heideggerian forms of the forgetfulness of being. This illusory cop-out has had a selective impact on leftist and new-leftist political commentary, as if the real danger to free and open societies were unsponsored. It can be convenient to be able to talk long into the night without having to consider the flesh-and-blood killers at the peak of the pyramidal human direction of slave-labor camps, psychiatric prison-hospitals, and the like.

Is it, in fact, possible to specify permanent factors that make for progress and decline, and so are universally operative in human history? The First World War had practically killed all taste for the question by the time (1920) that J. B. Bury reviewed it in his *Idea of Progress*. Nevertheless, the question challenged the ambitions of Bernard Lonergan from the late 1930s, when he assembled the elements of his thinking on progress and decline in history: an analysis worked out on a Newtonian model of successive approximations.[19]

In 1684 Halley asked Newton what the orbit of a planet would be on the assumption that it was attracted to the sun in accordance with an inverse-square law of force. Newton immediately answered, "an elipse." This implied that he could connect the inverse-square supposition with Kepler's empirical first law of planetary motion. Such were the first two approximations by which Newton arrived at his planetary theory. The first approximation was the first law of motion: bodies move in a straight line with constant velocity unless some force intervenes. The second approximation added an intervening force, namely gravity between sun and planet, which yielded an elliptical orbit for the planet. The third approximation added the influence of the gravity of the planets on one another, which yielded the perturbed elipses of Newton's final account.

This discursive procedure moves toward a complete construct through the projections of one isolated factor after another, the successive additions not cancelling but complicating the original image, and bringing it closer to the reality to be understood. Lonergan's first approximation was

> the assumption that men always do what is intelligent
> and reasonable, and its implication was an ever-
> increasing progress. The second approximation was

> the radical inverse insight that men can be biased,
> and so unintelligent and unreasonable in their choices
> and decisions. The third approximation was the re-
> demptive process resulting from God's gift of his
> grace to individuals and from the manifestation of his
> love in Christ Jesus.[20]

Two points should immediately be added. First, since we are dealing with history, we must take account of the rise of the historical consciousness, that is, the awareness that human beings live in an over-arching context of change, that by their own acts of meaning—all of them embedded in contexts subject to change, be it ever so gradual—they are the makers of themselves and of the worlds they live in. This had always been the way things went; the rise of the historical consciousness signified *the realization* that this is how things went, and the concomitant determination to take the making of human history and historical destiny into one's own hands.

Second, prominent among the roots of progress is freedom; prominent among the roots of decline is bias. Freedom names the possibility without which good ideas that are also new ideas (elements of progress) cannot be implemented. This appears to be borne out again by the Soviet bureaucracy. Perestroika floundered because bureaucrats, not famous anywhere, any time, for pumping up the flow of ideas, were called on to make it work.

Bias is of several kinds. There is the bias that hinges on a spontaneous human recoil from light and truth, the self-interest of elementary passions interfering with the emergence of questions, insight, and reflection. There is the bias that seizes on the centrality of myself to myself in consciousness and in responsibility—and converts it into a more or less ruthless drive to serve me and my interests. There is the bias of the group, which is impelled to overestimate its service to society and to seek more or less ruthlessly the interests of the group. There is, finally, the bias rooted in common sense, that regards any and all "theory" as impractical. In the modern age this last, all-too-human and so perennial, problem is particularly urgent, for common sense stands in tension with the historical consciousness. We are not adequately equipped by common sense to take our destiny in the world into our own hands and to create the kind of world that our collective life requires. The one way in which common sense may be of help here is by advertence to a threat to existence. On this basis human intelligence may be confronted with "the alternative of adopting a higher viewpoint or perishing."[21] The principle has been recently illustrated by the Soviet Union in the middle 1980s.

The issues of progress and decline, of freedom and bias, of the change of context effected for the fact of evil in the world by the affirmation of God as Lord of the world: all these will enter into the solution. Meantime, we shall swiftly survey some of the resources, classic and contemporary, that are relevant to its full expression.

## III. Resources for a Response

In pondering the paradox of a West that has successfully withstood the challenge of Bolshevism's declaration of war against the world in 1917 and yet finds itself faced by hardly less threatening, self-generated forces of decline, we are not reduced to the role of mere spectators. And "we," now meaning that limited (but not infinitesimal) number of those consciously concerned about how the world goes, are not without allies. Philosophic resources, it is true, are not currently rich. The schools dominant in the West forthrightly claim to have little or nothing to contribute to resolution of the present problem. Language analysts are unequivocal about how austerely their services are circumscribed. More classical thinkers may seize on such promising clues as the poignant longing attested by Mill and Skinner.[22] But this is not yet a full-blown response to the spiral of decline.

Some Christian philosophers have taken a more radical tack. While the ravages of the Second World War were still fresh in memory and at a time when Stalin, despite the horrendous losses of the Soviet Union and its objective relative weakness vis-à-vis the United States, was looking forward to another victorious war,[23] Josef Pieper, in *Über das Ende der Zeit*,[24] projected as a possible, and dreadful, state of affairs the whole world's bondage to a single anti-human totalitarian power. As in Orwell's *Nineteen Eighty-Four*, which had appeared a year earlier, in 1949, the power of Pieper's cautionary message hinged on the positive plausibility of its awesomely repulsive vision of the whole world in chains. He projected this, not as an ultimate, but as a penultimate, state signaling "the end of time." Pieper was not projecting a specifically Soviet domination of the world. Even less than Orwell was he limited to current political states of affairs. His primary sources, on the contrary, were the Christian scriptures.

But Pieper exploited the scriptures as a philosopher bent on dealing with philosophical aspects of history—history as a philosophical question. To those who disputed his right to philosophize on the basis of this sacred tradition, he responded with the example of the Greeks, notably Plato and Aristotle. But in accord with the strategy of his inquiry, he drew sparingly on scriptural texts. These reflections resonate with the spirit of Pieper's strikingly independent book, but, as the present strategy differs from that of Pieper, so does the following brief exploration of the scriptures.

The prophets of classical Israel appealed to the personal, mysterious, unpredictable *purpose* of Yahweh. Post-exilic Israel tended to identify his purpose with the Law. Jesus of Nazareth claimed to bring the climactic and definitive revelation of the purpose of God. It was not the Law and the prophets, but a consummation of the Law and the prophets bound up with himself and his personal destiny. Paul of Tarsus, missionary and theologian, offered a full, thoroughly and dramatically thought-out answer to the issue of the shape of the human dilemma and its divine solution.

Paul's problem, to be sure, was not framed in the terms in use above. But in persuance of the solution to a similar if distinctly contextualized problem, he worked out the lines of a soteriology which he conceived to be valid for all mankind.[25] Once won over to the Christian cause by a revelation of the risen Christ that had been thrust upon him, Paul's problem was indeed "the cross"—though to him personally it was no longer the cross as insurmountable scandal (1 Cor 1:18), that problem having been met by the revelation of the risen Christ—rather, the cross as demanding a context, full and fully intelligible, in which it—the cross—would make biblically attested salvation-historical sense. The presupposition of the words, "If righteousness were through the law, then Christ died to no purpose" (Gal 3:21), was not only a divine purpose in Christ's death, but a divine purpose defining the role of Christ's death as uniquely and indispensably mediating the salvation of mankind.

If this defines Paul's "problem," his heuristic resources for its solution were principally the sacramental liturgy, particularly the liturgical and credal formulas of Jerusalem and Antioch (e.g., 1 Cor 11:23-25; 15:3-5; Rom 3: 25f.; 4:25; 8:34; 10:9f.). To bring these formulas into play as evidence of the solution he sought, he had to radicalize them. The problem—in the formulas this was generally signified by "sins" (1 Cor 15:3; Rom 3:25) or "transgressions" (Rom 4:25)—was now made to comprehend every aspect of sin and death, and the solution was correspondingly made to comprehend every aspect of acquittal and life: forgiveness, freedom, acquisition to God in Christ, redemption, reconciliation, new life, new creation.

In short, Paul did something new. He transformed his inheritance—Christ's life, death, and resurrection from the dead—into the complete and adequate solution to the human dilemma, wholly in accord with the scriptures of Israel. Christ's life was lived out in fulfillment of the promises made to Abraham, Isaac, and Jacob (Rom 15:8). His death, out of obedience to the will of his Father, reversed Adam's transgression (Rom 5:12-21), and his resurrection from the dead reversed Adam's bringing of death into the world (1 Cor 15:21f.; Rom 5:12-21). The result was the unburdening of history—not of pain, suffering, conflict, misunderstanding, frustration, failure, physical death—but of radical meaninglessness and hopelessness, the spiral into ruin.

The conception of history in terms of problem and solution and the identification of Christ as the solution supplied the principle of discernment for the legacy of Israel. The one mighty objection to Paul's new, yet scripturally attested, scheme of problem and solution was the standard view of the Law in Judaism. Paul met this objection by incisively redefining the divinely intended role of the Law. God had never intended the Law as the solution of the human problem. On the contrary, the Law had aggravated and compounded the problem! And now that Christ had come, it altogether lost its historic role as obligation precisely in function of the Mosaic covenant, now seen to have been temporary and provisional.

In this reconstruction of the genesis and development of Pauline thinking, the controlling thrust was the need to set the death and resurrection of Christ in an intelligible, scripturally attested context. From a Christian perspective (be it of Justin or of Augustine or of Aquinas or of Newman) this trenchant movement of thought complemented, as second and climactic moment, the effort of Greek and Hellenistic philosophy to find an honest and coherent solution to the problem of human contingency versus meaningfulness. Paul's typology of Adam and Christ is formally structured as a typology *per contrarium*; but the typology is unique inasmuch as type (Adam) and antitype (Christ) correspond respectively to *problem* and *solution*.

If we inquire into the unarticulated suppositions of Paul's decisive theological achievement, we would have to assign pride of place to
his sense of "the living God," the *ʾĕlōhîm ḥayyîm* of Deut 5:26; Josh
3:10; 1 Sam 17:26,36; 2 Kings 19:4,10; Isa 37.4; Jer 10:10; 23:36; Ps
84:3, who had life in himself and lived forever, from whom all life
came, who gave life to his people, and who was himself that life. This
was the Lord of life without whose positive will the world would sink
back into its native nothingness (Job 34:14-15, Ps 104:29-30). But in
fact this Lord willed the wellbeing, first, of his people Israel and, in
conjunction with Israel's definitive restoration, the wellbeing or salvation of all the nations. Such was God's *ʿēṣāh*, his purpose and plan:

> From the beginning I reveal the end,
> from ancient times what is yet to be;
> I say "My purpose (*ʿēṣāh*) stands,
> I shall accomplish all that I please"
>
> (Isa 46:10).

This purpose and plan were benefic:

> I alone know my purpose (*maḥăšābāh*)
> for you, says YHWH;
> wellbeing and not misfortune,
> and a long line of descendants after you
>
> (Jer 29:11).

Or, projecting the plan of God beyond the settling of accounts with the
border enemies of Israel, prophecy could hear Yahweh say:

> This is the plan (*ʿēṣāh*) prepared for the whole world,
> this is the hand stretched out over all the nations
>
> (Isa 14:26).

His plan is his secret, but:

> Surely the Lord YHWH does nothing,
> without revealing his secret (*sôd*) to his servants
> the prophets
>
> (Amos 3:7).

Paul saw the climax as well as the key to this divine purpose and plan in a saving act: "God was in Christ, reconciling the world to himself, not counting their transgressions against them" (2 Cor 5:19). It was God's climactic self-revelation in Christ, an act of saving righteousness (Rom 1:17; 3:21-25) in profound accord with his own nature (Rom 3:26).

Pauline thinking, then, took account of all human history; saw it as a history of sin and death, headed for ruin; celebrated the change of fortunes in Christ (a transposition of the great prophetic theme of *šûb šĕbût*)[26] that awesomely reversed the direction of history; and so affirmed a real and accessible resolution of the human dilemma, despite the fact that, even in the present world of salvation inaugurated and in process of realization, life in general and his own life as a dramatic instance exhibited such traits as pain, sorrow, anxiety, privation, humiliation, failure and desertion.[27] What then was there to celebrate? The answer must be: the stunningly achieved reality of the solution, and the boundlessly blessed destiny of whoever would take hold of it.

## IV. Lonergan on the Heuristic Structure of the Solution

Chapters 19 and 20 of *Insight* correspond respectively to the issue of God, the affirmation of whose existence converts the mere fact of evil into a problem of evil; and to the reflective anticipation of God's solution to the problem of evil.

Chapter 19, however, treats the issue of God mainly in function of its role in completely, ultimately, grounding the otherwise still limited affirmations of "the intelligible" and "the true."

> Why should the answers that satisfy the intelligence of the subject yield anything more than a subjective satisfaction? . . . Of course, we assume that they do. We can point to the fact that our assumption is confirmed by its fruits, so implicitly we grant that the universe is intelligible and, once that is granted, there arises the question whether the universe could be intelligible without having an intelligent ground.[28]

In this way of initially framing the question of God, the issue boils down to the ultimate ground and vindication of knowledge as knowledge (critical) and of knowledge as knowledge of the real (realism). Such is the question of God, not as existential but as cognitive. But Lonergan moved from this cognition-oriented approach to the existence of God to its existentially oriented counterpart. Existential reflection begins from the discovery of values, of the moral good, and inquires after *its* grounding. It thus raises the question whether the way of the world is, not indifferent to man, not neutral, but good. The question can be answered affirmatively, if

> and only if one acknowledges God's existence, his omnipotence, and his goodness . . . Unless there is a moral agent responsible for the world's being and becoming, the world cannot be said to be good in that moral sense. . . . If still man would be good, he is alien to the rest of the universe. If on the other hand he renounces authentic living and drifts into the now seductive and now harsh rhythms of his psyche and of nature, then man is alienated from himself.[29]

This way of setting up the question of God asks whether the contingent life of man, remaining free and responsible, is connected with Being and ultimately meaningful. It also indicates in advance the transition to the second issue: the shape of the divine solution to the problem of evil.

Lonergan treats this "how" question (corresponding in Paul to soteriology) in the manner of transcendental reflection, a retrieval of God's actual solution to the problem of evil by specifying, from the side of the problem, what cannot not be given in any adequate solution. A key premise, in other words, is that the solution has to meet the problem squarely.

Lonergan's argument is best read, no doubt, at length and in his own words. Here I shall indicate the style and elements of the argument, abbreviating and drawing occasionally on texts that followed *Insight*, and then return to our original question on freedom and the reversal of cultural decline.

Since there is one God, one world order, and one (individual and social) problem of evil, the solution will be one. Since the problem is not restricted to human subjects of a particular class or a particular time, the solution will be universally accessible and permanent. Since the problem is human, the solution will be adapted to human beings, not to some as yet unknown species or genus. Since the problem is located in powers by which the human subject functions, the solution will bear on some transformation of those powers.

Since nature generates the problem, the solution must be in some sense supernatural. Common sense does not meet the long-term problems of the human race; hence, the human race cannot be counted on to meet those problems squarely, regularly, effectively, in timely fashion. Living is prior to learning; it cannot wait on learning; it cannot count on the effectiveness of learning. Life is unremitting and learning is not. The solution must meet all the problems that arise from the natural condition of man: dramatic bias (spontaneous interference of sense-life with intelligence, reason, and reasonable decision), individual and group egoism, and commonsense practicality biased in favor of its own spurious omnicompetence. It must meet the problem of the natural tendency to adopt clear, obvious, and easy, but wholly mistaken, principles (the counterpositions) in speculative thought.

The solution then is conceived as irreducible to nature, and yet as a harmonious continuation of the actual order of the universe. As that order involved the successive emergence of higher integrations, so the solution will constitute a new and higher integration, itself capable of development and adaptation. In accord with the facts of human development, it seems necessary to distinguish between the realization of the full solution and the chrysalis of the solution—the emergent trend in which the full solution becomes effectively probable.

So far, the central element of the solution appears to be the transformation of human powers. We should pause over this ascertainment. It differs from the platonist view, and from the gnostic variation on the platonist view, in that it specifies on the side of the problem the need not for a new species but for a renewal of the species that exists. It accordingly corresponds to what we have noted above on the prophets' view of the human problem. It calls, on the one hand, for a renewal of the one human race that already exists; on the other, for a genuinely creative act. The problem is rooted in "the heart . . . most crooked . . . beyond remedy" (Jer 17:9), the heart of stone that God would remove (Ezek 36:26). The new creation, which Isaian tradition celebrated (Isa 42:9; 43:19; 48:6; 65:17) and the realization of which Paul identified with "being in Christ," and therefore with faith/baptism (2 Cor 5:17), lay in the transformation of man by new, supernatural powers: faith, hope, love. These new powers constituted the bond with Being that platonist dialectic from Eckhart to Fénélon would interpret as self-annihilation, but that Paul, the later Augustine, and Aquinas interpreted as the transforming realization of the self intended in creation. Redemption, then, was aligned in the most positive fashion with creation; and the tendency of Christian tradition from Paul through Augustine to the present has been to epitomize the new creation in treatments of faith, hope, and love.

Love, because only love—self-sacrificing love—can restore the good that evil has subverted. Historical process is a compound of progress and decline. Decline derives from inattentiveness, from ignorance and folly, irresponsibility and malice, all products of individual and group egoism and of the general bias that insists it can get along without worry over long-term consequences. Hence deterioration of the good of order. Those charged with maintaining it are pushed to selective indulgence, deciding how much disorder they can live with and which injustices they will wink at. Absurd situations multiply. Antagonisms harden into hatreds. Arrogance on the part of winners is matched by the resentment of losers. An even-handed justice would only displace and perpetuate these evils and enmities. Self-sacrificing love and that alone can help.

Hope, because what is required is a decision against the presumption that puts the solution of the problem entirely in the hands of man and a decision against the despair that in the face of personal involvement in evil connives with and consents to the temptation to take oneself to be worthless.[30] This double decision is hope. Moreover, hope is called for inasmuch as even the finest and most heroic contributions to recovering the good—the good of justice to the individual, the good of order, the terminal good of values, and the originating good that is the sacredness of persons—fall far short of perfect effect; nor can they possibly measure up to that X-factor in the human dilemma, which is "my death." The hope that meets the ultimately real situation of the human subject and of human society must settle not on any good that one can have, but on being, the selfness of oneself and of all one loves, on a salvation that transcends the present life and that only God can promise and bestow.

Finally, there is a role for intelligence in the grasp of the universally accessible solution; but what is it to be? There are, in general, two ways: by knowing and by believing. There is not the slightest probability, however, that human beings on their own might seek out the sum of truths that count, discerning and dismissing the errors and surefootedly making their way to independently grasped truth. The *a priori* probability is accordingly against any such supposition. What of the alternative, belief?

The role of belief in the acquisition of knowledge as well as in the social life of man generally has been very widely overlooked and underrated—a success of Enlightenment propaganda, which set itself against religious tradition and ended in the overkill and conspicuous unrealism of undermining tradition as such. Lonergan's excursus on the notion of belief makes two principal contributions. First, it offers an analysis of the triple grounding of the assent that is belief: preliminary judgments of the value of believing in general; a specific, immanently generated judgment of the rightness of believing x; and a free decision coherent with that judgment. Second, it offers a critique of beliefs that is grounded on the preceding analysis of belief. The critique deals with the origin of mistaken beliefs and a methodical way of eliminating them, namely, by examining at least one mistaken belief for clues to one's tendencies to mistaken beliefs. This would come to be called a "hermeneutic of suspicion," but here the suspicion is turned on oneself.

The solution would include a transformation of powers for the sake of meeting the problem of error and sin. In its cognitive aspect it would consist in a new and higher human collaboration in the pursuit of truth. As exemplified in the collaboration of empirical scientists, the pursuit of truth that regards human living would be, inevitably, a compound of belief and of immanently generated knowledge. But this collaboration could not be limited to human collaborators. "If men could collaborate successfully in the pursuit of truth that regards human living, there would be no problem . . . "; but in fact there is a problem; it "follows that the new and higher collaboration is, not the work of man alone, but principally the work of God." Man's role, on the cognitive side, requires that the solution bring some form qualifying human intelligence. Let us call this form faith. Since belief and only belief is universally accessible and fits harmoniously within a continuation of the actual order of the world, this faith will be a transcendent belief. "Because it is a belief within a collaboration of man with God as initiator and principal agent, the motive of faith will be the omniscience, goodness, and omnipotence of God originating and preserving the collaboration."[30]

The act of faith will include affirmations on man and on God: of man's spiritual nature, freedom, responsibility, and sinfulness, of God's existence and nature, and of the transcendent solution that God provides for man's problem of evil. It will include an announcement and an account of the solution.

Man will be intelligent, reasonable, and responsible in acknowledging the solution inasmuch as

(1) he grasps the existence of the problem of evil and, in particular, of man's inability to cope with it,

(2) he infers that divine wisdom must know many possible solutions, that divine omnipotence can effect any of them, and that divine goodness must have effected some one of them,

(3) he recognizes that, in fact, there has been in human history, first, an emergent trend and, later, the full realization of a solution that possesses all the traits determined or to be determined in a heuristic structure like this one.[32]

The existence of the solution will not sweep evil out of the world in the manner imagined by Marxists (who in this have been as utopian as any so-called utopian or "unscientific" socialists). The solution offers no magic cure for the blind spots of the dramatic subject. These blind spots, on the contrary, will continue to betray themselves in ordinary human failure as well as in the extremes of angelism and animalism. Group bias will urge replacing a single, universally accessible solution by a multiplicity of solutions for different classes and different nations. General bias will continue to introduce and promote the counterpositions. Counterfeit and truncated versions of the solution will by no means be excluded.

The solution will nevertheless be effective. It will generate its heroes, mainly saints. Should the solution turn out to be absolutely supernatural, there will result a heightening of the tension that arises whenever the limitations of lower levels are transcended. A mere humanism would then be excluded; on the other hand, an integral humanism, including the transformative potential of the absolutely supernatural, would be a goal both possible and in some sense requisite.

Lonergan left it to the reader to identify the solution that actually obtains. There is no doubt, however, about what the specifications for the solution intend. *The divine revelation known to us from Bible and Church—especially as highlighting the death and resurrection of Christ, the salient traits of the Church, and the transformative role of faith. hope and love—is the divine solution to the problem of evil.* Elsewhere and more recently, he has identified the solution with "scriptural doctrine," which, understanding suffering and death as the result of sin, inculcates the transforming power of Christ who, in us as in himself, makes suffering and death the way to resurrection and life. This transformation may be named "the law of the cross."[33] In his last work (from 1972 to 1982) the key premises of the argument we have been reviewing (*Insight*, chapter 20) have found repeated confirmation, but with new accents. *Insight*, ch. 20 deals not with method as such but with "special transcendent knowledge." The last writings deal with method, with how to get underway, the accent falling less on solutions than on the horizons within which problem, argument, and solution can make sense. Again, the late writings exhibit an intense interest in relating the "plateaus" of cultural development to the reality of human progress. The first such plateau, reached in antiquity, had to do with the drive of practical intelligence to master nature and social organization; the second, also reached in antiquity, dealt mainly with differentiations and developments of speech; the third, in modernity, bore on human understanding, on the transition to interiority, and on dealing critically and dialectically with such ideals as "enlightenment" and "emancipation."[34] Lonergan has, moreover, repeatedly called attention to the connective tissue that relates self-transcendence, religious faith, man's good and God's glory. "Most of all," he concludes, "faith," placing human effort in a friendly universe, "has the power of undoing decline."[35]

Primarily and directly the force of the argument presented here focuses on the sources and shape of the problem of evil and, much more at length, on specifications of the shape of a solution. Second, it heightens the awareness that the solution available through divine revelation genuinely meets the problem in its essential aspects, despite the unending whine of secular intellectuals in the modern West who simultaneously blame God for the lack of a solution and, on the same basis, deny that God exists. (Again, there is the muddled variation that exculpates God, having reduced him to finite dimensions, an imaginary god of impotent good will.)

"The human problem" or "the human dilemma" may be variously defined, but the definitions worth serious consideration have to do not just with suffering pain or injustice or death, but with "evil" in the full sweep of the theme. This becomes problematic in the rigorous and technical sense of the world—"the problem of evil"—only when the issue of God has found a resolution in the affirmation of God, bearer of the claim to be at once all-powerful and all-good. (Without God, evil would be a "problem" only in the sense of a massive, dispiriting fact. This, in fact, is the way in which the referent of the phrase is often understood today.) The realism of the solution is underscored by contrast with all the schemes by which secular thinkers from Condorcet through Marx to the present have reduced the dimensions of evil to a far lesser disorder than that envisaged by pagan thinkers such as Plato and Aristotle, who, though they took slavery (for example) for granted, had a more acute sense of the ravages of moral evil than those moderns who fully expected to wipe out all evil by magic, be it psychological, or educational, or economic, social, and political.

No matter how serious the thinking of these moderns in the sense of its serious themes (or in the sense of its possibly grave consequences for the human race, if adopted), this thinking has radically lacked the realism about solutions exhibited here.

It should be noticed that Lonergan's specifications for the solution take their point of departure from the functioning of the human subject and human society. The dramatic subject, with his liability to individual bias, the group with its liability to group bias, society installed in the illusion that its own commonsense way is sheer realism, absolutely assure the emergence of evil as fact. The assurance is a statistical expectation. And whoever suspects that this is a weak description of the problem of evil, that there is a gap between, on the one hand, the merely defective functioning of the human being as dramatic subject and of society as a society of dramatic subjects liable to scotosis and bias and, on the other, the problem of evil precisely as beyond the human power to cope with it—in other words, whoever thinks that Lonergan may have *underplayed* the dimensions of evil—has a way, direct and simple, of settling the matter, namely, by mounting an attempt to master in himself/herself those purported elements of the human dilemma epitomized by "scotosis" and the several modes of "bias." The more resolute the effort at this mastery, the solider will be the assurance of Lonergan's realism about evil, too. It will turn out that the referent is the same, whether conceptualized as scotosis and bias or as the seven deadly sins.

The starting point of the entire effort of reflection is not, to be sure, Adamic sin and its impact, the principal cause, in Paul's view, of the situation confronting humankind (Rom 5:12-19). Paul followed the Bible. The question, "Is there a solution for man?" could not emerge among the Hebrews as an issue; for, well before the Greeks they had already abundantly met it with their affirmation of "the living God." There was, however, a second question, which bore on God's purpose, plan, design, secret (*ʿēṣāh/mĕzimmāh/maḥăšābāh/sôd/rāz* : *boulē/dialogismos/mustērion*), the revelation of which the whole New Testament announced and celebrated. What was God's way of meeting the dilemma of man? The biblical answer was bound up with the figure of Jesus Christ. Though materially identical with "the solution" sought by Lonergan, the biblical and especially Pauline solution does not provide the terms in which to discuss cultural progress and decline. The problem as Lonergan conceived it overlaps here and there with Pauline terms, but does not coincide with them. On the other hand, Paul, ignoring "human nature" and "statistical necessity," arrives at inferences of his own and a new context in which to set the fact of divine intervention. The contrary-to-fact alternative is a destiny of eschatological death. Transcendental reflection moves on a different plane. It provides us with resources allowing us to deal realistically, in terms of human impotence and divine resourcefulness, with the deepest dimension of human progress and decline.

## V. The Reversal of Decline Concretely Considered

We might return for a moment to our three starting points: the relativism scored by Allan Bloom, the baffling phenomenon of deep unhappiness on the part of apparently successful men, and Pauline/Lonerganian views on the causes of decline.

Relativism grows from many disparate roots. It may arise as a principle of suspicion in response to extravagant claims. But no matter how inflated the claims that it would puncture, the relativist response is self-reversing. Meant to modify pretention, it ends in the pretention to subvert the real and the good. Hence its corrosive impact in theory and practice. As with all the counterpositions, its good intentions are futile. Its inevitable tendency is to accelerate the rhythm of decline. That it has destructively infected our civilization and culture is certain. A self-reversing error, it is nevertheless attractive and calls for repeated un-masking. Further consideration, in a word, has not only confirmed but deepened Bloom's judgment.

The disconcerting experiences of Mill, Skinner, and Tolstoy are now illuminated. The human being could not possibly find fulfill-ment in the things that these men envisaged (Mill and Skinner) or al-ready possessed (Tolstoy). Neither socio-political reform nor wide-spread psychological engineering nor personal fortune and achievement can assuage the deepest-seated hungers of the human heart. Happiness ties in with transcendent horizons and with some sense of access to "a solution" to the human problem. Meantime, unhappiness has a positive function, akin to the function of pain. As pain calls attention to physical needs violated or unmet, unhappiness calls attention to violated or un-met exigences of the human spirit.

By contrast, the above views of the causes of progress and the contrary causes of decline have, by this point, found solid support in historical, philosophic, and theological reflection. The effective func-tioning of human intentionality, which roots intellectual and moral vir-tue in the radical drive to intelligence, reason, and responsibility, and which includes the affirmation and love of God, represents just those positive elements imperfectly present to the thought of Mill, unequivo-cally lacking in Skinner, but strikingly realized in what emerged in the end from the anguished analysis in Tolstoy's *Confession.*

Prior to the final consummation of history, the solution of the human problem lies in that central but still fragmentary revelation of the divine plan for the fortunes of the world: God's own saving act, on behalf of every human being, in the death and resurrection of his Son, made Christ and Lord; the gift of the Spirit and the Spirit's renewal of human minds and hearts.

If thinking about decline is realistic and concrete, it is an im-mediate inference that *in the reversal of decline the Church will be deeply involved.* In "Healing and Creating in History," Lonergan attrib-uted "healing" but not "creating" to the Church of the late Empire—so the Church indeed lived on, "but in a dark and barbarous age . . . "[36] When in the fourth and fifth centuries the situation called for the dis-covery or invention of "a higher viewpoint," the alternatives for the civ-ilization of the late Empire being to achieve this or perish, that civilization perished.

That the failure should be charged in significant measure to the Church does not hinge solely or even mainly on the privileged social position of the post-Constantinian Church. It hinges mainly on the fact that the Church was charged with the substance of what we have been calling "the solution" and, indeed, was partly identical with that solution. (The extraordinary flowering of the high Middle Ages would offer a brief but brilliant intimation of this.) But this situation—the Church charged with the solution and partly identical with it—obtains today as certainly as it obtained in the fourth and fifth centuries or in the high Middle Ages. If the world no longer looks to the Church to fulfill this task, and if the Church has any lesser understanding of its mission, something is awry not only with the world but with the Church. Pope John XXIII diagnosed a major shortcoming of the Church as a falling behind, which would have to be met by an *aggiornamento* (updating) and *un balzo innanzi* (a forward leap). "So there is a sin of backwardness, of the cultures, the authorities, the individuals that fail to live on the level of their times."[37]

Apart from the matter of time and backwardness, there is in the Christian sensibility of the contemporary West a marked dissociation of the currently favored (biblical) language of religion (kerygma, covenant, election, redemption, judgment, parousia, etc.) from the currently favored language of human problem (alienation, anxiety, loneliness, frustration, self-destruction) and solution (trust, growth, confidence, success, wholeness, freedom). Consequently, there is a dissociation of consciousness, conation, responsibility, commitment, between the two.

Finally, while a continuum doubtless obtains between the reality of the solution to the human problem and the reversal of human decline, there is equally a discontinuum between the defining spheres of religion and culture, as well as between *the unicity of the solution and the multiplicity of both civilizations and cultures.* The task of theology is defined by the need to mediate between all these discontinuous elements. Four aspects of the task thus come immediately to the fore: *aggiornamento* or updating; a needed correlation of idioms; distinguishing and relating culture and religion; and mediating one solution to many cultures.

For present purposes we may limit consideration of updating

to an up-to-date grasp of human authenticity: its components, its task, its models. First among its components is religious conversion: the primacy among all one's loves of the love of God. This is first in the sense that the growth of human authenticity commonly follows a certain order of impact: the impact of religious commitment on a morally good life, and the impact of a morally good life on fundamental philosophic and existential judgments. The second component, the wellspring of a morally good life, is the habitual preference of values to satisfactions, when they conflict. The third component is most realistically conceived in negative terms: as a withdrawal from intellectual inauthenticity, or the break with picture-thinking. This is a condition of the judgments that fix on *positions* (basic options in harmony with the way human beings function in fact) and repudiate *counterpositions* (basic options at odds with the way human beings function in fact). At mid-century "authenticity" had a vogue as an existentialist buzzword. Now, newly defined by the threefold conversion specified above—religious, moral, intellectual—its real vocation in the world comes to light: to secure the active human share in the divine-human collaboration designed that the world have life and have it abundantly.

Human authenticity, then, is a hinge on which the divine-human collaboration turns; and it is the key to the reversal of decline. Aristotle grounded ethics on the phenomenon of "good men." Nor did he think that what that phrase referred to was unknown. "Actions," he said, "are called just and temperate when they are such as the just and temperate man would do."[38] Have we never known such men and women? Ordinary public opinion is far from infallible, yet there is a certain continuity between public praise and blame and the models of human authenticity. We look to the just, the brave, the generous, the moderate, the wise for guidance; we tend to agree, even when we know little of the matter, with the views of authentic persons: with, for example, the late Andrei Sakharov on war and peace, with Jacques Cousteau on the environment, with Mother Theresa on the love of God and man. Moreover, we tend to trust the quite fallible judgments of such persons, as of others to whom we attribute human authenticity, more in view of their realized authenticity than in view of their particular competences.

The swift and thoroughgoing change that swept eastern Europe in 1989, besides offering its share of models, dramatically illustrated what Vaclav Havel, echoing Alexander Solzhenitsyn, called in

*The Power of the Powerless* (1978),[39] the difference between "living within the truth" and "living within the lie." Havel had argued that authentic existence was a revelation of truth: the lone individual who simply decides to live in the truth threatens with collapse the whole world of appearances and lies. Such existence was accordingly charged with incalculable power. Suddenly, a set of favorable historic conjunctures showed how right Havel had been.

The correlation of the Bible and of its religious idiom with the present sequence of reflections is by no means artificial. "Problem" and "solution" are colorless heuristic terms. In biblical literature and especially in the Pauline letters they are represented (on the side of "problem") as transgression, bondage, enmity, condemnation, and death; and (on the side of "solution") as atonement, redemption (=liberation), redemption (=acquisition [to God/Christ]), reconciliation, justification, life/new creation.

Among the fundamental contexts in which culture and religion are distinguished and correlated is that of values.

> *Vital values*, such as health and strength, grace and vigor, normally are preferred to avoiding the work, privations, pains involved in acquiring, maintaining, restoring them. *Social values*, such as the good of order which conditions the vital values of the whole community, have to be preferred to the vital values of individual members of the community. *Cultural values* do not exist without the underpinning of vital and social values, but none the less they rank higher. Not on bread alone doth man live. Over and above mere living and operating, men have to find a meaning and value in their living and operating. It is the function of culture to discover, express, validate, criticize, correct, develop, improve such meaning and value. *Personal value* is the person in his self-transcendence, as loving and being loved, as originator of values in himself and in his milieu, as an inspiration and invitation to others to do likewise. *Religious values*, finally, are at the heart of the meaning and value of man's living and man's world.[40]

Religion, in short, is among the meanings and values that inform a way of life and that it is the function of an adequate cultural criticism to discover, acknowledge, validate. In one respect it is the most fundamental of these meanings and values, for it has to do with the the the relation of human beings to *the ground* of meaning and value.

Lastly, it is the task of theology to mediate between religion and culture, and the task of Christian theology to show how the solution of the human problem might pervade and transform any given culture. The solution is one, but theology, in accord with the diversity of related cultures (as in the contemporary West) must be many—related, ultimately coherent, but many.

This pluralist theological task is among the most crucial elements of the Christian task. Nevertheless, the scope of the Christian task is far greater than that of theology. It is to sustain, pervade, transform the perennial human task of building, rebuilding, sustaining the human order, creating the conditions in which Jack and Jill can marry, enjoy a modicum of economic and social security, raise children and send them to decent schools, worship God without interference, share according to their resources and preferences in the life and direction of the communities they live in, and, in short, have a chance to live and die in human dignity. In one sense the Christian task is simply defined: to bring into the world, or to bring to bear on the world, as full a human and Christian authenticity as the individual Christian can attain. It is to be the salt of the earth and a light to the world.

This is service on the model of the Servant who went to his death as a ransom for all. When the terms of the issue of cultural breakdown and decline are radicalized, the issue is instantly complicated by patterns of data (e.g., the consciousness of sin) that, since they do not fall within the patterns familiar to the secular analyst, call for a new differentiation of consciousness—call for it, but perhaps without the call's being squarely met. For, in the societies of our time there flourish systematic ways of reducing such patterns of human experience to psychic, social, or even political maladjustment. In any case, the present reflections are mainly addressed to those who, whether reluctantly or cheerfully, have abandoned the spurious hope that a civilization in decline may find adequate resources for the reversal of decline in the human potential movement; or in Wittgensteinian or Heideggerian versions of wisdom; or in a Leavisite cultivation of literature and the arts; or in the social sciences, or in "science and technology." For those who are on the track of the solution or have found it, the question is: what can we, the Church, singly and collectively do? First, contrary to the example of the Church of the Late Empire, we may take full account of the issue. There is a question of fact: are we in the West confronted at the present time by a civilization in decline, "digging its grave with a relentless consistency"? There is a moral question: do we have any role or responsibility in defending not just the Christian but the human cause? Do we have a role in sustaining our own civilization? It was not a question entertained in the earliest, most classic Christian sources, prior to the emergence of Christian cultural forms. In the era of Augustine when the situation of the late Empire was critical, the issue might have become thematic and have mobilized Christian energies, but it did not do so adequately. Still, in this context the word of Martin Buber holds truer than ever: "the meaning of the phenomenon of Jesus for the world of the nations remains, in my view, the authentic gravity of Western history."[41]

Who, then, if not *those for whom the phenomenon of Jesus remains the source and center of the gravity of Western history*, are equipped to sustain the civilization that has made this history? True, Christians cannot measure up to and meet the task of building and rebuilding by themselves, alone; but without the contribution of Christians and Christianity the outlook would be bleak. The West will not be argued out of self-destruction. Provoked, it will only quicken the pace of its grave-digging.

Just as decline is not itself some anonymous abstraction unconnected with actual human subjects, so what radically effects the reversal of decline is not some other anonymous abstraction equally unconnected with human subjects. It is precisely human authenticity operating in individuals, in groups, in society at large. Forces favoring this authenticity are family and school, the humanities and social sciences, public philosophy and religion. Elements of this authenticity pertain to interiority as cognitive and interiority as existential. If human authenticity qualifies human subjects individually and in groups, its primary field of operation is social. Insofar as the Church has a key role in the reversal of decline, it is as a world-wide self-constituting community equipped to serve.

For, the Church is a structured, outgoing process "not just for itself but for mankind."[42] It is a consciously redemptive process, recreating and healing the world. It has at its disposal such resources as the methodical use of dialectic: a primary use that aims at an alienation-

free and so ideology-free doctrinal posture, and a secondary use that ze-
roes in, first, on human studies (including the social sciences) in the
quest of discerning *positions* and differentiating them from *counterpositions*; and, second, on social process and the social situation in the
quest of sound social policy. All these uses of dialectic aim at a discerning liquidation both of alienation and of its rationalization in ideology.[43] The last-mentioned use, moreover, prepares discerning social policies whether for the Church or for other institutions in the world.

World process is for the most part spontaneously operative,
but a crowning part of it, the conduct of human life in the world, is the
product of acts freely and deliberately placed. The goal of arresting and
reversing decline is reached only by action within this historical process. The primary realization of the reversal of human decline—the
events of cross and resurrection, which, precisely because they are the
core of the divine solution to the human problem, are *normative*, i.e.,
"the *economy*" or "the *law* of the cross"—took place within this historical process. Likewise the countless dependent, secondary realizations
of this pattern have taken place and continue to take place within history.

There are, however, many points of departure for reductionism
vis-à-vis the solution. It would hardly be appropriate to prolong the
present discussion by trying to anticipate and deal with even a few of
the most likely of them. Still, by way of conclusion, it may be worth-
while at least to mention one reductionist account, not only prominent
but inevitable today. It is rooted in nineteenth-century thought and,
though its proximate basis is variable, it often takes a point of departure
precisely from the locating of the solution *within history*, for it posits a
contradiction between "normative" and "historical." Or, independently,
it may reduce the normative to non-normative via "symbol." In either
case *economy* or *law* is reduced to symbolic paradigm. The cross, one
striking thematization of "transcendence," becomes one paradigm
among many.

This issue will hardly find a lasting resolution today by the observation that it flatly contradicts the scriptures. A more telling observation will be that this reasonable-seeming proposal (all religions and philosophies are hailed and honored not only for their contributions to the
solution of the human problem but as identical with an adequate solution) cannot be the divine solution to the human problem, because it

does not meet the requisite of being universally accessible. At first, nothing could seem more accessible than this wide-open, supremely pluralist formula. But, in fact, the proposal is one more invitation to wisdom, i.e., to philosophic or religious thought. All such invitations are beyond the reach of the vast mass of human beings. This seemingly generous-spirited pluralism therefore cannot be—it certainly is not— the solution, but is one more among the *dialogismoi* (1 Cor 3:20) or illusory ideas that Paul repeatedly advises us to dismiss.

In conclusion, we should underscore the need to keep this line of thought in context. The spheres in which decline must be reversed are many. They are irreducible to religion. But by its capacity for sublating moral and intellectual life,[44] life in Christ is a vital source of the authenticity requisite to the reversal of every kind of decline—a source of the authenticity of scientists and scholars, of technical and political elites, of a cosmopolis recovering its instinct for sanity and for quality.

The reversal of decline is a massive task. But, just as in its integrity it envisages a more than merely human good, so it is a more than merely human task. In our world as it actually is, redeemed and re-created, the task belongs to that "new and higher collaboration" which, contrary to the aggressive secularism of our current avant-garde, cannot be reduced to an esoteric sideline cultivated by eccentrics. On the contrary, while it is "principally the work of God," it includes and transforms the whole life of the human race.

## NOTES

1. Allan Bloom, *The Closing of the American Mind* (New York: Simon and Schuster, 1987).

2. The story of Mill is cited by Jacques Barzun, "Toward the Twenty-First Century," in Barzun, *The Culture We Deserve* (ed.) Arthur Krystal (Middletown: Wesleyan University Press, 1989 ) 161-183, at 174-175 .

3. Skinner wrote in a personal journal: "Sun streams into our living room. My hi-fi is midway through the first act of *Tristan and Isolde*. A very pleasant environment. A man would be a fool not to enjoy himself in it. In a moment I will work on a manuscript which may help mankind. So my life is not only pleasant, it is earned or deserved. Yet, yet, I am unhappy. " See *Time* 98 (Sept. 20, 1971), 61.

4. Leo Tolstoy, *My Confession* in *Lyof N. Tolstoï. Vol. 17* (New York: Scribner's, 1904) 1-75, at 12-25.

5. Cited by Josef Pieper, "Fortitude, " in *The Four Cardinal Virtues* (Notre Dame: Notre Dame University Press, 1966) 121.

6. Bernard Lonergan, *Insight* (London: Longmans, Green, 1957; London: Longman, Darton and Todd, 1983) on progress and decline, including consideration of the social surd, xv, 234-236, 688-693.

7. Bernard Lonergan, *Method,* 55.

8. William Barrett, *Death of the Soul* (Oxford: Oxford University Press, 1986).

9. *Death of the Soul,* 157 .

10. Jacques Maritain, *Three Reformers: Luther—Descartes— Rousseau* (New York: Scribner's Sons, 1950 [original, 1925] ) 21.

11. Lonergan, *Method,* 357.

12. Jacques Barzun, "Twenty-First Century," (see above, note 2) 161.

13. Barzun, "Twenty-First Century," 162-163; emphasis added.

14. Leszek Kolakowski, *Main Currents of Marxism. I: The Founders* (Oxford: Oxford University Press, 1978; repr. 1988) 11-80.

15. Heidegger corrected this age-old idealist error only to fall into another, as Josef Pieper has observed: whoever makes temporality intrinsic to human existence "will find hidden from him not only the life 'beyond time' but also the very meaning of life *in* time." *On Hope* (San Francisco: Ignatius, 1986) 19-20.

16. Karl Jaspers, *Vom Ursprung und Ziel der Geschichte* (Munich: Piper, 1949, repr. 1983) 217-242.

17. *Death of the Soul* (see above, note 8) 140.

18. Karl Jaspers, *Notizen zu Martin Heideager* (Munich: Piper, 3rd ed. 1989) pp. 62, 191. The issue is put positively in Lonergan's essay, "The Subject," in *A Second Collection* (eds.) W. F. J. Ryan and B. J. Tyrrell (Philadelphia: Westminster, 1974) pp. 69-86, where, precisely in function of reference to the concrete self (84), the primacy of the existential is affirmed in a sense sharply distinguished from pragmatist, Scotist, Aristotelian, and Kantian as well as from twentieth-century phenomenological and existentialist thought.

19. See Bernard Lonergan, "*Insight* Revisited," in *A Second Collection,* 263-278, at 271-272.

20. Ibid., 272.

21. *Insight* (see above, note 6) 234.

22. See, for example, Mortimer Adler, *Six Great Ideas* (New York: Macmillan, 1984) 92-98; 212-227.

23. Milovan Djilas, *Conversations with Stalin* (Harmondsworth: Penguin, 1963) 91.

24. Josef Pieper, *Über das Ende der Zeit* (Munich: Kösel, 1950);

E.T., *The End of Time* (New York: Pantheon, 1954) .

25. See B. F. Meyer, "A Soteriology Valid for All, " in *The Early Christians* (Wilmington: Glazier, 1986) 114-158.

26. These texts on the coming restoration of Israel are treated in the short, classic monograph of E. L. Dietrich, *SWB SBWT. Die entzeitliche Wiederherstellung bei den Propheten* ( Giessen: Töpelmann, 1925).

27. Meyer, *Early Christians*, 149-150 .

28. Lonergan, *Method*, 101.

29. Lonergan, "The Subject" (see above, note 18) 85-86.

30. See Sebastian Moore, "For a Soteriology of the Existential Subject," in *Creativity and Method: Essays in Honor of Bernard Lonergan, S.J.* (ed.) M. L. Lamb (Milwaukee: Marquette University Press, 1981) 229-247.

31. *Insight*, 719-720.

32. *Insight*, 721.

33. Bernard Lonergan, "The Transition from a Classicist World-View to Historical-Mindedness," in *Second Collection*, 1-9, at end.

34. Bernard Lonergan, "Natural Right and Historical Mindedness" in *A Third Collection*, 169-183, especially 176-179 .

35. *Method*, 117.

36. Bernard Lonergan, "Healing and Creating in History, " in *A Third Collection*, 100-109, at 108 .

37. Bernard Lonergan, "Dialectic of Authority, " in *Third Collection*, 5-12, at 8.

38. *Nichomachean Ethics* II,iii,4; 1105b.

39. Václav Havel, "The Power of the Powerless," in *Václav Havel. Living in Truth* (ed.) Jan Vladislav (London: Faber and Faber, 1987) 36-122, at 55-57.

40. Lonergan, *Method*, 31-32, emphasis added.

41. Martin Buber, *Deutung des Chassidismus* (Berlin: Schocken, 1935) 60-61.

42. Lonergan, *Method*, 363-64.

43. Lonergan, *Method*, 365; cf. 357.

44. See Lonergan *Method*, 241-43.

11

# THE TEMPLE AT THE NAVEL OF THE EARTH

In the course of his encounter with Israel, Jesus of Nazareth drew on a wide range of ancient Near Eastern and biblical resources to intimate, specify, commend, defend particulars of his public mission, or the mission as a whole. Toward the end of his life, as the prospect of refusal took on clearer contour, he drew (unambiguously in private, in the mode of paradox in public) on the imagery of king and sanctuary. Acknowledged by Simon as the Messiah, Son of the living God (Matt 16:16), he followed in the line of classical messianic prophecy: as the anointed Davidid of the end-tlme he would build (*oikodomesŏ/ᵓebnê*) his temple/sanctuary. He would build it, moreover, on the rock of Simon!

The image recurred probably on the occasion of the challenge, in the wake of Jesus' cleansing of the temple, to "give us a sign "; he answered:

> Destroy this sanctuary/and after three days I will build it.[1]

In the ancient imagery of the anointed son of David/son of God (2 Sam 7:13-14; 1 Chron 17:12-13; Ps 2:7; 89:27; 110:3.; cf. 4QFlor 11) Jesus would build the house of God (2 Sam 7:13-14; 1 Chron 17:12-13; Hag 1:1-2; 2:20-23; Zech 6:12-13), i.e., the new temple/sanctuary that belonged to the end of time.

In this privileged imagery—pristine, vital, classic—lay a comprehensive revelation of the mission of Jesus. The gospel record as a whole makes it clear that in his view the real referents of the imagery of biblical promise—Zion, or cosmic rock and, on it, God's gleaming temple of the end of the days—were his chosen disciple, Simon (Matt 16:18) and the messianic remnant of believers, his *ekklēsia/ᶜēdtāᵓ*) or *kenista* (Matt 16:18). Jesus' offered, as a comprehensive description of his mission, the bringing into being of the new, eschatological, People of God.

It is not possible—it is flatly impossible—to register the force of these images and the reality that they mediate without assembling in one's own mind and imagination the elements at least of the tradition of ancient Israel on the temple built on Mount Zion, and its climax in the life and mission of Christ: what "temple" first meant and then what it came to mean to Israel through the psalm liturgy, the oracles of the prophets, and the dramas of history; finally, what Jesus designed the imagery of king and sanctuary to mean to his audience (and, in principle, to us). Hence this concluding essay in three parts. Part I tells the story of the Jerusalem temple. Part II enters into the meaning of temple imagery as it developed in the course of the centuries. Part III deals, first, with the story of Jesus with respect to the temple; second, with how the Church, the product of the handiwork of Jesus, in the era of 30-60 A.D., offers in the gospels not only a revelation of Jesus, but a compelling, if low-key, revelation of itself.

# I. The Story of the Jerusalem Temple

The temple of Jerusalem in its successive embodiments had a lifetime of a thousand years. It entered the life of Israel against opposition and exited from it in disaster. It began with myth, which makes it suspect, but has ended in symbol, so winning perennial meaning.

There was no temple in ancient Israel. Like the establishment of the monarchy, the building of the temple was a novelty. Both belonged to the assimilation of horizons and institutions from the surrounding world. They came into Israelite history as foreign bodies, imposing but ambiguous. Both met and overcame religious resistance; and though the destinies of the two institutions were not identical, they were deeply intertwined.

This tie between temple and king has held even for the afterlife of the temple in the messianic hope of Jews and in the christology of Christians. Before that nameless soldier from the troops of Titus, "urged on by some unseen force" (as Josephus put it),[2] hurled a firebrand through a golden aperture of the sanctuary building (A.D. 70), the temple had already begun its career as pure symbol, first among the Essenes, then among the followers of Jesus. Soon afterward it would

enter onto a life of pure symbol in rabbinic Judaism. So the temple out-
lived even itself. It lives on as the Bible lives on, vital beyond calcula-
tion. As a theme of biblical theology, moreover, the temple is a winged
synechdoche, inevitably bringing with it into present consciousness the
whole story of biblical Israel and the heart of the story of Jesus. Like
"covenant" or "kingship" or "reign of God," "temple" is central to biblical history and finds a kind of eschatological culmination in the New
Testament. It belongs among the most charged of Jesus' own symbols.

Since we rehearse and renew the story of the temple first of all
for ourselves, we do so in a way that connects with our own sense of
the real, i.e., in what is called the critical mode. This, to be sure, is not
the way in which Jesus, as a lifelong listener in the Synagogue, took in
the story of the temple. We shall recall much of this straightforward
biblical record in part two, where the themes and motifs of the temple
are reviewed in their substance with little critical apparatus.

## A. *Before the Monarchy*

Texts dealing with resistance to David's purported plan to
build a temple attest the religious stance characteristic of premonarchical Israel. This stance was rooted in Israel's conscious identity as the
people of YHWH; that is, it was first of all rooted in the covenant and
in the historical prologue to the covenant: the escape from state slavery
in Egypt.[3] Second, it was rooted in the entry into this covenant of tribes
resident in Canaan (Josh 24).[4] Third, it was rooted in several generations of existence as a tribal confederacy without a king.

Granted the justice of scholarly objections to the claim that
"covenant" might adequately comprehend the whole thematic content
of the Bible, and granted that our knowledge of the history behind the
most ancient covenant formulas of the Old Testament—the history of
the children of Abraham from the patriarchs (Genesis) to the covenant
at Shechem (Joshua 24)—remains fragmentary and often imprecise,
there are still solid grounds for affirming that the institution to which
the word "covenant" (*běrît*) refers was ancient and seminal. Without
reference to "covenant" the idiosyncrasy of classical Israel is artificially
opaque, whereas granted the covenant tradition, what certain data we
have become more easily understandable and more coherent. In fact,
the most ancient poems and sagas reveal an Israel congruous with later

history. The denial of the antiquity of the covenant tradition is in certain rigorously delimited particulars a forward step but, as an undifferentiated thesis, it remains an exaggeration and distraction.[5]

Among the oldest units of biblical literature are such premonarchical poems as the song of the sea (Exod 15) and the song of Deborah (Jgs 5), both of which attest the tribes' allegiance to YHWH. Ancient cultic texts such as the Sinai theophany and the decalogue, exhibiting diverse elements, some relatively early, others relatively late, present themselves as explanatory of this allegiance: a covenantal bond effectively sealed Israel's premonarchical identity as the covenanted people of YHWH.

Covenant seals identity. What this means emerges from the historical prologue or antecedent history of Josh 24:2-13, for here the salient traits of YHWH and Yahwism come to the fore. YHWH is powerful not in some limited locale but everywhere: "across the river" (24:2-3), in Canaan (24:3), in Egypt (24:5-6), at the Reed Sea (24:6-7), again in Canaan (24:8-13). He "gives" the land of Canaan to his own (24:13), making Balaam bless, not curse, the sons of Abraham (24:9-10), and driving the kings of the Amorites "from before your face" (24:11-12). In brief, he disposes of everything as he chooses.

Correlative to this power and gracious initiative is the call for allegiance ("service," see ʿābad 14 times in vv. 14-24) to YHWH alone (Josh 24:14-15) and the response (Josh 24:24):

> YHWH our God will we serve/and we will harken to
> his voice!

This parallels the still more ancient first commandment: "Thou shalt not worship gods of another nation against my right!" Finally, it finds a powerful echo in the confession,

> YHWH our God, YHWH our one God! (Deut 6:4).

In all three instances (the first commandment, the Shechem covenant, the confession of Deut 6), the imperative of exclusive cult is a response correlative to YHWH's love in action: he alone saved Israel. Likewise correlative to his transcendent initiative and power is the original form of the second commandment, i.e., the prohibition of making an image of YHWH. This prohibition removed YHWH from the conceptions of myth and the practices of magic; it confirmed him as the God who, so far from being immersed in natural process, transcended all nature and ruled all history.

A segment of recent scholarship (i.e., since about 1970) has produced a countercurrent to the syntheses produced by the schools of Alt and Albright.[6] Historical critique, called on to date the origin of given traditions, to separate early from late strata, and to recover the probably original form of given texts, often finds itself at an impasse. An example of basic importance has been the debate on the character of early Yahwistic cult between the school of "salvation-history" (Alt, Noth, von Rad; Albright, Mendenhall, Cross, Freedman et al.) and the school of Myth and Ritual (Volz, Mowinckel, Engnell et al.). Both groups have been able to point to substantial masses of data, the first to the covenantal formulae and sources of epic history, the second, to the psalm literature and prophetic oracles.

Our present interest fixes even more on the second complex of data than on the first. This, of course, signifies no commitment to or preference for the Myth and Ritual account of early Israelite cult. If there has been no clear winner in this debate, neither has contemporary skepticism succeeded in making both sides losers. Despite great confidence and continuing vogue, social-scientific analysis has not thrown more than a glimmer of light on early Israel and its establishment in Canaan.[7] Successful elements of explanation include at least the philological and literary side of the analysis of covenant, of Hebrew epic traditions, and the correlation of kingship themes with Near Eastern nature polytheism.

Israel does not fit well into any ancient Near Eastern pattern of sacral kingship ideology. It nevertheless came to share with the Canaanites a set of kingship motifs that functioned to support political arrangements in Israel after the time of David.

Did this sharing with Canaan first come about in the premonarchical late-second millennium? Or with the Jebusite cultic legacy of Jerusalem? Or as a part of an archaizing revival all through the Near East in the sixth and fifth centuries B.C.?

Among these options the outer limits span half a millennium. Substantial historical issues and numerous interpretative questions turn on which option is given preference. (All choices are likely to prove incomplete, and no choice, it seems, entirely excludes the possibility of turning out to have been mistaken.)

What has just been said of the YHWH-reigns theme holds also for numerous other themes of importance to our inquiry. Often we cannot find grounds for the resolution of such questions and are obliged to leave the matter bracketed; in this short outline there is hardly room for reconstruction, anyway, even where possible. Though we can date the advent of monarchy to Israel and specify some few causes and some few results, it is hardly possible to reconstruct the life of Israel in the eras of Saul, David, Solomon, and Rehoboam.

The following is what seems reasonably probable with respect to the tribal league. Its unity was religious. Devices to secure political unity were minimal. Even in emergency situations such as war not all the tribes rallied to battle (Jgs 4:15-17). The much discussed question of whether Israel was a twelve-tribe amphictyony has centered, first, on whether there was a common sanctuary serving as focal point for the tribes; second, on whether the biblical lists of twelve tribes (Num 26; Gen 49) are ancient. The existence of a single central sanctuary is uncertain in the sources, though a wooden chest, "the ark (ʾărôn) of God" (1 Sam 3:3; 4:4-5,13,19,21 etc.) or "of YHWH (1 Sam 5:3-4; 6:1-2,10; 7:2 etc.) apparently did serve as a focal point. A full account of the origin and function of the ark is unavailable to us. Most think that it was conceived as a kind of pedestal for the invisible presence of YHWH; hence, a majority interpret the holy of holies as a podium-shrine.[8] Normally kept in the sanctuary at Shiloh in central Palestine, the ark was also carried into battle as an emblem of the nearness of YHWH to the tribes and their cause. In the language borrowed from the Canaanite celebration of Baʿl, YHWH was described as going, mighty, to war:

> He spread apart the heavens and descended,
> a storm cloud under his feet.
> He rode a cherub and flew,
> he soared on the wings of the wind.
> He shot forth his arrows and scattered them,
> lightning bolts he flashed and put them in panic
> (2 Sam 22:10-11,15; Ps 18:10-11,15 [EVV 9-10,14]).[9]

The ark may, then, have served as the functional analogy to the central sanctuary in an amphictyony. Numerous scholars have urged that it was central to the great harvest festival (the Autumn new year) where covenant renewal took place in pre-monarchical Israel; in pre-Exilic and even perhaps as early as pre-monarchical Israel the harvest festival was the setting of the new year celebration of YHWH's reign.[10] Here Israel celebrated its God, YHWH of hosts, and, despite participation at the tribal level in Canaanite fertility rites, here YHWH reigned over his people.

The tribal confederacy derived its distinct identity from covenant with YHWH but, as indicated above, the covenant did not prevent significant borrowings from Canaanite religion. There is no doubt about the impact of the Canaanite mythology of ꜣEl and Baꜥl on theophanies and other biblical texts.[11] These borrowings, which antedated the monarchy, provided ancient Israel with a language forged by nature polytheism. The native tradition of the self-revelation of YHWH to Moses and of the covenant with YHWH at Sinai transformed this language (much as Yahwism was to transform the myth materials of Gen 1-11) in the fire of a single allegiance to a peerless, transcendent God. (This subtly subverted, without ceasing to take for granted, the notion that other gods existed. Positively, YHWH was the object of distinctive allegiance.)

At the tribal level a process of assimilation of non-Yahwistic cult and cult-saga to Yahwism is discernible in numerous texts of Genesis and Exodus. This one-way assimilative syncretism was recurrent at the level of the national religion as well if, as is probable, the adoption and adaptation to Yahwism of Canaanite ritual—in particular that of the great Autumn festival—goes back to early Israel, i.e., to the tribal confederacy. This probably favored the transition to monarchy and the centralization of the cult of YHWH in Jerusalem. (Under Jeroboam, essentially the same cult competed for allegiance, but at other, still older, cultic centers, Bethel and Dan.)

Clues to the existence of a pre-Exilic Autumn festival—at once a seasonal festival (harvest and new year) of the agricultural community exalting YHWH's triumph over the forces of chaos, hence his "reign," and a memorial and renewal of the covenant among the tribes and with YHWH—are scattered in biblical tradition. That there was an agricultural Autumn festival is not in doubt. Festal calendars in both the J tradition (Exod 34:22) and in that of E (Exod 23:16) indicate an Autumn feast at the turn (tĕqûpāh) or end (ṣēꜣt) of the year. Now, as John Gray has shown,[12] there is a tradition of the reign of God, correlative to the Baꜥl myth of Ras Shamra, attested in Ps 86; 1 Kings 8:2; Isa 52:7; Nahum 2:1. Were these two streams of tradition related? Did the great

Autumn festival in Israel celebrate the reign of Yahweh? A Yes in middle range probability commends itself. The final yield of the debate has been a greater awareness of the probability that certain biblical motifs, which we might otherwise have failed to correlate, really did and do belong together. They include creation and conservation; the regularity of the seasonal cycle; the judgment of God that exhibits his rule over this cycle as over the world; and, as eschatology began to exploit the temple's liturgical riches, the correlation of these motifs with the future (the end of the days/ʾaḥărît hayyāmîm) that YHWH in his own time would bring into being.

## B. *Saul, David, Solomon*

When the historiographical ideal of national history became dominant in Europe (namely, in the nineteenth century) biblical scholars became keenly intent on tracing the history of the institutions that forged the national state. (In the Bible this history of the coming to be of the state in ancient Israel is in significant part—though not wholly, of course—court-propaganda for the absolute monarchy of Solomon.)

There were abortive moves toward monarchy even prior to Saul (Abimelech, Jgs 9; cf. Jephthah, Jgs 11); only when political necessity—the threat to the tribes posed by Philistines settled on the southern Mediterranean coast of Canaan—imposed a new defence organization did the move come to term. The elders of Israel came to the prophet Samuel at Ramah and said, "Give us a king to govern us like all the nations" (1 Sam 8:5). The disadvantages of monarchy were outlined by Samuel:

> These will be the ways of the king who will reign
> over you: he will take your sons and appoint them to
> his chariots and to be his horsemen. . . . He will take
> your daughters to be perfumers and cooks and bakers. He will take the best of your fields and vineyards
> and olive orchards . . . He will take the tenth of your
> grain and of your vineyards. . . He will take your
> menservants and maidservants, and the best of your
> cattle and your asses . . . He will take the tenth of
> your flocks, and you shall be his slaves
>
> (1 Sam 8:11-17).

To insist on having a king was to "reject your God" (1 Sam 10:19) who had "brought you up" out of "the land of Egypt."

Nevertheless, monarchy, having political point and popular support (e.g., 1 Sam 8:19-20), arrived under the prophet Samuel's reluctant patronage in the person of Saul, son of Kish, of the tribe of Benjamin.

Like the major judges, Saul was a charismatic hero. In the sources on his rise to power he bore the title "commander" (*nāgîd*, 1 Sam 9:16; 10:1) namely, of the tribal militia, though "king" (*melek*) was often used of him (1 Sam 15; 18; etc.). Saul's kingship (*mĕlûkâ*, 1 Sam 14:47) was founded on a covenant made in Gilgal (1 Sam 10). He had a guard but no personal army. No provision was made for dynastic succession. When he and his sons died in battle with the Philistines, David—a protege but no relative—succeeded him.

How was it that David became Saul's successor? David had early entered the service of the king and distinguished himself by military skill and valor. His abilities and ambitions led to his expulsion from or abandonment of the service of Saul. He thereupon developed his own personal army and publicly established himself as an alternative to the king. At the deaths of Saul and his sons, David became king of Judah. The story of his rise to kingship over Israel is one in which shrewdness and self-interest are operative, yet—miraculously, by the charism of the truly magnanimous man—without undermining a genuine nobility on David's part. It is played out against the backdrop of a barbarian culture sometimes reminiscent of the Homeric heroes. Soon David was the conqueror of Jerusalem, king of all Israel, and in control of most of Palestine, Syria, and Transjordan.

The rise-of-David narratives are interwoven with a sequence of traditions on the ark (1 Sam 4:1-7:1; 2 Sam 6). The story of the ark was made to correlate with the story of David: the question was how the ark got to Jerusalem.

Urushalem, the ancient city of the Jebusites (a Canaanite people settled on the central highlands), was built on "the eastern hill," south of what is now the temple mount. Because this hill was lower than its western counterpart, it was long thought not to have been the site of Urushalem/Zion/the City of David (later called Ophel). But the fact that the eastern hill was fed by the only stream in the vicinity practically settled the matter, and modern archaeological excavation has definitively confirmed this view.

Jerusalem had had no tribal associations with the Hebrews prior to David. It was among those urban strongholds that had held onto their independence through the history of Israel's tribal confederacy. This very fact, together with the excellent defensibility of the site, made it the more attractive to David. Since, to the tribes, David consciously represented a new and suspect beginning, his first effort was to legitimate his kingship and capital. The bringing of the ark to Jerusalem was a virtuoso step in this direction.

But David was not to build a temple for YHWH-and-ark. (The present form of the tradition notwithstanding, the idea may never have occurred to him.) Whether David remained, in intention as well as in fact, within or almost within the transitional framework of the kingship of Saul, is difficult to say. There is no decisive evidence against it, but it depends on  tentative reconstruction.

Saul had not been succeeded by an heir. On his own initiative, David's commander, Joab, had dispatched the champion of the house of Saul, Abner, son of Ner (blood-feud, cf. 2 Sam 3); then Saul's son Ishbaal (=Ishbosheth) was betrayed and killed by his own officers (2 Sam 4). This liquidation of the house of Saul naturally served the advantage of David, a fact tacitly supposed as evident by the Solomonic writer.

## C. *The Temple of Solomon*

The stunning and brilliant piece of court history—the earliest history-writing among the rich inheritances of Byzantine and European civilization—known as "the succession to the throne of David" (2 Sam 6—2 Kgs 2), brilliantly recovered by Leonhard Rost, endorsed and confirmed by Gerhard von Rad, gives the Solomonic court version of how Solomon succeeded to the throne of his father.[13] It is, no doubt, religious history, and indeed "elective" history, but unlike the religious and elective history that preceded it, it fully recognized the workings of creaturely causality in an ongoing cause-and-effect sequence. Solomon inherited his father's throne despite a status of having been several times removed from the likelihood of succession. That most mysterious compound of divine and human causality that fixes the attention of theologians of history is consciously objectified for the first time. The court historian presents it not as a puzzle but as the marvel of YHWH's divine guidance of history. The admirable density of this history has elicited a wide variety of interpretations and of evaluations. Here we shall be satisfied merely to remark that the story could not have happened without the will, ambition, and devices of the Queen Bathsheba, of the prophet Nathan and, no doubt, of the seemingly passive figure of Solomon himself.

As the bringing of the ark to Jerusalem had been a virtuoso act on David's part, his son's building of the temple was a bolder act, more heavily charged with consequence for the story of Israel. It was well known that David, though he established a cult place in Jerusalem (on Araunah's threshing floor [2 Sam 24], which would serve as the site of the temple), had built no permanent sanctuary in which to house the ark. Solomon and his court attributed to David as much of the novelties of kingship as they could, but not the temple. The oracle of Nathan, however, attributed—perhaps in accord, perhaps in discord with historical fact—the desire to build "a house of cedar" for the ark of God (2 Sam 7:2-3). Ps 132 celebrates David's will to "find a place for Yahweh, a tent-shrine for the Bull of Jacob" (v. 5). There is no sign here that David desired to build a permanent *temple* for YHWH. As we look again at the opening verses of the oracle of Nathan, the same conclusion seems to hold.[14] What is not in doubt at all is that the Solomonic writers made David bear the burden of at least having planned to introduce a temple into the cultic life of Israel. If the cult of YHWH set Israel apart from the surrounding peoples, the system of king and temple still made it comparable to them.

Built by Phoenicians (1 Kings 5), the temple was surely of a type familiar to the Levant, though we have no contemporary example from other lands to nail this supposition down. Comparable to Solomon's sanctuary in three parts: *ʾûlām* (=porch or vestibule); *hêkāl* (=sanctuary, "holy place"); and *debîr* (=back chamber, "holy of holies") is the temple at Tell Tainat (ninth century, Syria), though we do not know what the functions of the tripartite division at Tell Tainat were.[15]

A fundamental literary problem in dealing with biblical data on Solomon's temple lies in settling the genre and provenance of the description in 1 Kings 6-7. Is this a text which, like others on the era of Solomon, was contemporary with the era it depicted, i.e., contemporary with the building of the temple? The question is still without a sure answer.[16] We do know that this tripartite sanctuary (*hêkāl*) was a thing of splendor. Its interior was panelled with cedar, lighted by windows, out-fitted with a rich (largely gold) cultic apparatus.

The sanctuary was 30 yards long, 10 yards wide, and fifteen yards high. We cannot describe the façade of the sanctuary whether of Solomon's temple or of Herod's. There were two columns of bronze be-fore the façade, with decorated capitals, Jachin (*yākîn*, "he will estab-lish") and Boaz (*bōʿaz*, "in strength"), words that may have introduced fuller inscriptions. Before the sanctuary stood the altar of holocausts and other appurtenances of sacrificial cult. The temple made a splendid impression.

The king's palace and other royal buildings—the House of the Forest of Lebanon, the Hall of Pillars, and the Hall of the Throne—were even more impressive, were more extensive and took a longer time to build.[17] This in itself is an index to how the combination of tem-ple and monarch originally fit together. It would be excessive to call the temple the chapel of the king. Nevertheless, the monarchy, with its pomps and works, provided the context in which the temple had its place.

The classic positive representation of the sense of the temple is provided in 1 Kgs 8 by the account of the installation of "the ark of the covenant of YHWH" in the inner chamber, the holy of holies, of the sanctuary of YHWH, followed by the filling of the sanctuary with the bright cloud signifying YHWH's presence and by the prayer of Solo-mon's dedication. Aware that the heavens could not contain the Lord God, the king was abashed that the same God had willed to take his place on earth in the sanctuary of the temple. The motifs of this Deute-ronomistic prayer are: the now fulfilled promise of YHWH to David that his son would build the house for the name of YHWH the God of Israel; entreaty to fulfill the rest of the promise to David, that the line of David would never die out from the throne of Israel; entreaty that YHWH hear the prayers of king and people when they pray "toward this place"; prayer to judge Israel in justice, condemning the guilty and vindicating the righteous; prayer that YHWH forgive the sin of the peo-ple, and bring them back to the land he had given their fathers; that YHWH hear their prayer in days of drought, famine, seige, and hear the foreigner from a far country come "for Thy name's sake" in order that "all the peoples of the earth may know Thy name and fear Thee" (1 Kgs 8:43); and the prayer ends with the dominant and finally overarch-ing theme of the confession of the elect people in exile precisely for its sins.

The anti-monarchy, anti-temple conservatism of the tribal league had accented the mobile presence of the ark of YHWH and the tent of revelation (ʾōhel môʿēd),[18] contrasting it favorably with the stability of a temple (2 Sam 7:5-7). Formerly, YHWH had been at home in any tribe; this flexibility would now come to an end. When we add thereto the altogether understandable recoil from the oppressive new social arrangements associated with monarchy, court, military and landed aristocracy, we form some notion of the victory of the temple. For, the temple won out. We see this despite the split of the monarchy and the tactic of Solomon's former prefect of forced labor, Jeroboam, now king of the northern tribes and rival to Solomon's son Rehoboam, of setting up alternative cultic centers by renewing the sanctuaries of Bethel and Dan.

Some prophets had nothing to say of the temple. But that it was well established may be inferred from the fact that, following the blank in our knowledge of prophecy in the southern kingdom after Solomon, Isaiah saw in the twin realities of the covenant with David and the temple of Solomon the essence of the cult of Yahweh and the faith of Israel. Among changes of orientation we should name that from the Exodus wilderness to Jerusalem. In early poetry Yahweh comes from Sinai (Deut 33:2; Jgs 5:4-5; Ps 68:8); now he shines forth from Zion (Ps 50:1-3).

## D. *From the Death of Solomon to the Destruction of the Temple*

Dynastic succession was not so thoroughly established that Rehoboam could claim the throne exclusively by right of inheritance. The council of the tribes had to endorse him. It corresponds to this situation that when the split between north and south actually took place ca. 922, Jeroboam carefully kept the style of his own kingship in tune with the style of Saul. Solomonic tradition, as we have already observed, had taken a different tack, namely, toward absolute monarchy, with a confirming ideology to vindicate it. The election of David was loosened from the constraints of its historic context and highlighted as a divine vow, an eternal decree, that absolutized monarchy, house of David, and temple on Zion. This was, of course, politically dangerous; inevitably the Solomonic era was transitional. Social engineering gave impetus to the break with tradition. Figures who represented bonds with the old order (Abiathar, Nathan, Joab, and others) ceased to figure on the scene of the court. Reminders of the tribal league went into eclipse.

If the old covenant tradition, as seems probable, had made its way into the Autumn New Year festival, the festival featured such themes as the renewal of the two-way conditional covenant of the tribes with YHWH. (Originally, the festival had been simply agricultural, celebrating the imposition of divine order on nature, the guaranteeing of the agricultural year.) With the penetration of historical motifs the feast became more properly Yahwistic. Solomon's kingship, court, and temple now impinged on the liturgical year in a new way, bringing a competing set of mythological ideas into play: identification of the divine triumph over chaos with the foundation of monarchy and temple.

It is sometimes forgotten that the monarchical state brought prophecy, too, its great age. Among its features was the transition from the thunder of theophanies to God's favoritism for the poor and afflicted, the crushed and lowly in spirit. This, as we shall presently have occasion to notice, represented a deepening of the Israelite sense of God and his will. YHWH did not thereby become the lonely transcendent; he remained the Lord of history.

Isaiah (ca. 742-701), probably by birth an insider to the Judean establishment, possibly a cultic prophet, represents a field of vision in which king and temple function as center of gravity of the faith of Israel. Ben Ollenburger has recently argued, mostly on the basis of Isaian oracles, that YHWH's claim to kingship over Zion functioned to impose limits on the Davidic-Solomonic ideology of kingship.[19] Isaiah, in short, appealed to Zion symbolism, in the consciousness of its premonarchical roots *against* the pretentions of the monarchy.

That the prophets' conception of revelation drew, like that of numerous earlier traditions of Hebrew epic history, on pre-monarchical, Canaanite resources may be illustrated from the scene of the call of Isaiah (Isa 6). The scene offers a glimpse of "the Council of YHWH," modelled as it was on the Canaanite "Council of ʾEl." Numerous scholars have invoked 1 Kgs 22 (treating early ninth century), a brilliantly colorful text in which the prophet Michaiah, son of Imlah, called on to advise the king of Israel (Ahab) in league with the king of Judah (Jehoshaphat) on a prospective war against the Aramaeans, says:

> Listen now to the word of YHWH: I saw YHWH
> seated on his throne, with all the host of heaven in at-
> tendance on his right hand and his left. YHWH said,
> "Who will entice Ahab to go up and attack Ramoth-
> Gilead?" One said one thing and another said anoth-
> er, until a spirit came forward and standing before
> YHWH, said, "I will entice him." "How?" said
> YHWH. "I shall go out, he answered, and be a lying
> spirit in the mouths of all his prophets" . . . You see,
> then, how YHWH has put a lying spirit in the mouths
> of all these prophets of yours . . .

The prophet presents himself as listening to the plans of the divine court until some matter is settled; only then may he announce: "Thus says YHWH . . . " When Jeremiah railed against false prophets, he posed the rhetorical question (Jer 23:18):

> For which of them has stood in the Council of
> YHWH, has attended to his word, and announced it?

Ps 32 evokes the court of heaven and YHWH's judgment on the gods. So, in Isa 6, Isaiah is in the temple of Jerusalem, but he is also ecstatically privy to the heavenly council of the gods. As YHWH addresses the council: "Whom shall I send? Who will go for us?" Isaiah, his lips purified by an altar-ember, cries out, "Here I am, send me!" Thus, the prophet, champion of the covenant with David, receives his hard, judgment-laden mission.

The scene supposes a correlation between the earthly temple and the heavenly temple where YHWH presides over his divine court. Mythological conceptions of the temple were accordingly alive and functioning in ancient Israel. Conservatives skeptical of the existence of these conceptions in the pre-Exilic period have by and large lost the debate. Three points in particular define the temple-mythology that obtained from the beginning: (1) the temple was the microcosm or epitome of the world; moreover, the building of the temple was consciously charged with motifs parallel to the priestly account of the creation of the world. (2) The temple bound together the diverse levels or "stories" of the universe: the abode of YHWH above the firmament, the world that the temple epitomized, and the netherworld that belonged to the waters under the earth. (3) The temple, finally, was the navel of the earth, source of order, life, fertility for the world at large. We shall consider these themes at greater length below (part two).

Do they prove that classical Israel was immersed in mythic modes of thought (as described, for example, by comparatists of religion such as Eliade and others)? The question, it seems, has yet to receive a fully differentiated and fully satisfactory answer. What blocks a straightforward "yes" is the core conviction recurrently attested in prophetic oracles, songs, and proverbs that all events on earth fulfill the plan (ʿēṣāh/mĕzimmāh/maḥăšābāh) of YHWH. Should he withdraw his breath, mankind would crumble into dust (Job 34:14f.). Every animal in the forest is his and he knows every bird in the mountains (Ps 50:10f.). Mythical thinking supposes an absolute sphere of archetypes, independent of gods and men, that Eliade names *illud tempus*. Despite numerous phenomena parallel with extrabiblical myth-literature, there seems to be no biblical counterpart to *illud tempus*, probably because all that happens accords with and originates in and subsists at the pleasure of the will, counsel, plan of YHWH. What in the nature polytheism of the Near and Middle East and in ancient Mediterranean paganism generally is grounded mythically, in the mythlike elements of biblical thinking is grounded in a rudimentary conception of Providence.

To return to our historical framework: the fall of the Northern Kingdom of Israel to the Assyrians took place (722) in the course of Isaiah's career (742-701). The Northern tribes thereafter vanished from biblical history, if not from biblical memory. Themes of restoration in Ezekiel and in the intertestamental era would maintain the hope of their restoration to Israel, the twelve-tribe people.

The drive of Yahwist reformers to the centralizing of cult in Jerusalem doubtless originated among Jerusalem priests. It found effective expression in "the book of the Law" (an early version of Deuteronomy) found by the high priest Helkiah in the temple (2 Kgs 22:4-10). It became the basis of king Josiah's cultic reforms toward the end of the seventh century.

At this historical point we might pause to insert into Israel's political history an effort to synthesize the lines along which religious sensibilities developed in Israel. Without conniving with ideology-like claims of absolute uniqueness, we should acknowledge that the development was distinctive. Let developments in Greece serve as a foil for comparison and contrast. Bruno Snell showed how the Greeks progressively discovered human intentionality.[20] This took place through the step-by-step assembly of the elements of mind and heart. Homeric heroes objectified the springs of action, as, responding to gods or goddesses, they shaped their goals. Then the lyric poets objectified human feelings. Then the tragedians gave expression to the interplay of human conflict, decision, and destiny. Then the philosophers pondered reflexively the elements of this intentionality . . . .

The Hebrews, by contrast, were intent on the discovery, not of the intentionality of man, but of the way, the goodness, the good pleasure of God. They did not so much assemble elements or parts, as register successive deepenings of human subjectivity with respect to God. The ninth-century scene of Elijah on Horeb (1 Kgs 19:9-18) represented an experience of the numinous in a mode altogether new to faith in Yahweh, leaving behind the theophanies of Sinai and the adaptations of Yahweh to the storm-god, Baᶜl. This was, of course, far more than a change of imagery. YHWH was not in the hurricane, not in the earthquake, not in the fire. The revelation said how YHWH was present to the world. There was no need of great phenomena. A whisper was enough; silence would do. YHWH was transcendent in a new way and somehow thereby present "to us" in a new way.

The revelation to Elijah at Horeb spelled the end of the first phase of Israel's religious subjectivity, which bore the stamp of Sinai, of borrowings from ᵓEl and Baᶜl, and of the building of the temple of Solomon. At the mouth of the cave of Horeb, it opened a new, second phase, which was to take its stamp from the prophetic movement and, perhaps most of all, from the powerful currents of the theology of Isaiah. A primitive naiveté that simple-mindedly counted on YHWH and his election or singling-out of Israel as a claim on lavish blessings would yield to the recognition that a sinful and unrepentant people could expect disaster on "the day of YHWH."

This second moment in the nation's life was marked by the breakdown of familial, tribal, and ethnic solidarity and the proportionate rise of individualism. (Such was the opening of the era that Karl Jaspers called "the axis-time" of human history.[21]) It took a specifically biblical form in the prophets: not the windfall of boundless blessings but a new sense of moral responsibility. The disaster of exile branded the lesson of this reversal on the body of Israel for ages to come.

The third movement in the life of the nation was defined by Israel's response to the Exile and, in particular, by the legacies of the Exilic and post-Exilic prophets, notably Jeremiah, Deutero-Isaiah, and Ezekiel. These three, together with the work of the Deuteronomistic historians of the seventh and sixth centuries, and with the Priestly redaction of the Pentateuch, provided key orientations for the post-Exilic life of Israel. Ezra and Nehemiah, and such prophets as Trito-Isaiah, Hagai, and Zechariah, belonged centrally, i.e., influentially, to this moment. We shall presently return to it with a view to exposing how the entry of apocalyptic or absolute eschatology had an all-transvaluing impact on Israel's post-Exilic legacy.

Not human intentionality, we said above, and not the discovery of human powers as in Greece, but rather a heightening of religious consciousness, shaped Israel's lines of historic development. They followed upon a cumulative set of ascertainments touching human need. They sharpened the awareness of "flesh," i.e., of man as sinful creature. They came to focus on his misery as a client of God. The enhancement of human existence turned neither on human wisdom nor on human power, but on God—and so on "faith." Isaiah addressed the king, but what he said held for the whole people:

> If you do not stand firm in faith, you shall not stand
> at all (Isa 7:9).

At bottom this issue of faith and non-faith, to be sure, came down to a fault-line in the make-up of man. There was a problem that lay in his powers:

> The heart is of all things the most crooked, it is be-
> yond remedy (Jer 17:9).

Prophetic hope was predicated on an unlikely escape, the escape of man from the crassness of his own heart. In the second and third phases of Israel's biblical journey hope turned on renewal, a new heart and a new spirit (Jer 31:33-34; Ezek 36:26-27). The building of the temple belonged to phase one in this evolving history, and corresponded to the first century of Solomon's temple. The epiphany at Horeb (Elijah at the mouth of the cave) corresponded in certain particulars to the role of classical prophecy up to the depredations of the Neo-Babylonian, Nebuchadnezzar. Finally, Ezekiel's vision of restoration would preeminently stamp the third phase of Israel's development, which we shall sketch in more detail.

This phase corresponded to the half-millennium of the temple of Zerubbabel (begun in 537, resumed in 520, dedicated in 515, and rebuilt by Herod, beginning in 20/19 B.C.). The prophets' recognition of human need, deepened by the shock of Exile and a new consciousness of sin, penetrated the psyche of Israel. There was an extraordinary discovery of human depths in the transition from the preaching of the Levites (Deut 5-12) to the Deuteronomistic History (Deut-2 Kgs): a national confession of sins laid at the feet of YHWH. This confession was a lasting monument, in its first edition reflecting the reform of Josiah (640-609), and finally reflecting the Exile itself.[22] It abominated the violation of the great commandment, naming this violation idolatry, the sin of Jeroboam. It celebrated the election of David and Jerusalem. It was also a penitent's act of hope. Simultaneously, there was the emergence and development of powerful prophetic themes: a deeply positive stance toward the afflicted (*ʿăniyyîm*) and the poor (*dallîm*), the crushed (*nidkāʾîm*) and the lowly (*šĕpālîm*). A kind of prelude to the destruction of the temple (Zeph 3:11-13):

> I will remove from your midst your proud boasters
> and you shall no longer flaunt your pride on my holy
> mountain.
> I will leave in your midst a people afflicted and poor;
> the remnant of Israel, they shall take refuge in
> YHWH's name.

This third of the successive phases in the deepening of human and especially religious subjectivity had something of an open-ended character from the refusal of Israel to find a true and definitive restoration in the Judean restoration of the end of the sixth century and succeeding years. The scriptures were more and more read as still open to fulfillment, increasingly pointing to the future.

The neo-Babylonians under Nabu-kudurri-usur (biblical Nebuchadnezzar), after pressuring Judah and exiling its leadership, destroyed the city of Jerusalem and the temple of Solomon in 587. The monarchy and court, the temple, its sanctuary and accoutrements (ark, cherubim, and the like) all fell victim to this catastrophe. But long before the end of the Exile prophets in Judah and Babylon were already laying new foundations for Israel.

## E. From the Exile to Titus

A post-Exilic text (Trito-Isaiah) presents the new theme of the poor in these terms:

> These are the words of the Lofty and Exalted One
> who dwells in eternity, whose name is Holy:
> I dwell in a high and holy place
> and also with the crushed and the lowly in spirit,
> to revive the spirit of the lowly
> and to revive the spirit of the crushed
>
> (Isa 57:15).

The tangle of human experience left God's way *(derek)* opaque. Still, he grounded the hopes of his afflicted people. It was to be not an event, but a vision—Ezekiel's vision of restoration—that would shape the post-Exilic era. The mountain of Sinai was transposed to Zion—an Isaian theme, now central to Ezekiel—charged with symbol: "a mountain high and steep" (Ezek 17:22), belonging to "the heights of Israel" (Ezek 17:23) recurrent in the prophecy of the new Exodus (Ezek 20:40) and, above all, in the chapters on restoration (Ezek 40-48). It is here "a very high mountain" (Ezek 40:2) of revelation and restoration. Even before restoration Israel had been set "in the midst of the nations" in the center of the earth: encircling her are the lands (Ezek 5:5). What defines salvation? The return of the divine presence to Zion, the cosmic mountain. For, the whole point of the new Exodus is the perfect worship of YHWH. Themes of paradisal restoration are copious: flowing streams signaling fertility and healing; the site of the earth-navel; restoration of the Davidic king.

The accent on the temple need not be conceived in reductionist terms. On the contrary, it lifts "building" into the sphere of the transcendent.[23] The vision of restoration was granted to Ezekiel at a moment midway to the Jubilee year that was to mark the return from Exile. Internally, restoration consisted in "a new heart" and "a new spirit" (Ezek 36:26); externally, in the whole vision of Zion restored (Exek 40-48). Can Ezekiel's prophetic view, drawing as it does on many currents of tradition, lay claim to thematic coherence? A solid case can be made for it.[24] Now *all Israel* is made heir to the promise to David. The Davidid, a shepherd to be made prince *(nāśî²)*, would preside over all the tribes engaged in the perfect worship of YHWH.

The heritage of Ezekiel, to be sure, did include certain ambiguities. A first such ambiguity lay in the prophet's exclusive accent on the restoration of Israel. What is to be said of the Creator-God's relation to the world?[25] A second ambiguity lay in the relation of Ezekiel's vision to the reality of Israel's history. On the one hand, the temple of Ezekiel was a visionary reality that represented one side of the restoration to come (the other side being the divine creation of a new heart and new spirit, Ezek 36:26-27, when God would cleanse Israel "of all your iniquities," 36:33). Now, the prophet implicitly called on Israel to realize this vision in the actuality of history—in its totality far beyond the power of the human subject. The solution assumed by the prophet was to envisage human agency as instrumental to the good pleasure, will, intentions of God.

Israel did what it could. The temple of Ezekiel, for example, became the model for the rebuilding of the temple under Zerubbabel, as the correlation of measurements between Ezekiel's description and the sources on the temple of Zerubbabel (e.g., 1 Maccabees and the excerpts from Hecataeus of Abdera in Josephus's *Against Apion)* indicate.[26] But many of the heirs of Ezekiel were beset by the temptation to set aside that more central issue, the burden of radical human need, the problem of the heart of stone (36:26) incurable by human resources and human effort.

Response to the Exile was exceedingly diverse. For some the disaster was a judgment on the people for having failed to cultivate the cult, not of YHWH, but of the gods of the triumphant nations! On the other hand, the dominant note was the acknowledgement of sin against YHWH, the confession of sins, and hope of restoration. Restoration themes flourished, and they would set the stage for post-Exilic life.

We have observed that for some the themes of restoration found fulfillment in the Jerusalem theocracy brought into being in the fifth century by reformers such as Ezra and Nehemiah. For others, who would prove to be decisive, restoration themes were held in reserve for the future. This played into the power of apocalypticism when it broke surface, namely, at least as early as the third century.

At this point we must briefly take account of this movement, which prompted an all-transvaluing permutation of the consciousness of Israel. It would alter perspectives on the temple along with every other inheritance from the past. This revolutionary change of horizon

and field of vision had its at first seemingly innocent literary manifesta-
tion in a new type of consolation literature, typified by divine revelation to a chosen figure. Building on and supernaturalizing biblical prec-
edents, the Book of the Watchers (which would eventually constitute
the first chapters of Henoch) seized on fascinating fragments of myth.
In time, however, the crucial matrix of apocalypticism from the stand-
point of the history of religions, would turn out to be an absolute eschatology. This was already implicit in myth-motifs such as the slaying of
the sea-dragon. But the implicit would burst its traditional integuments
and peak in an affirmation of divinely guaranteed definitive *life*. This
comprehended the resurrection of the dead.

Among the new possibilities that entered into Israel's view of
the world was a goal for the nation's historic life: a restoration that
would be not only climactic but *definitive*. For this would follow a
judgment that would itself be definitive, and it would be followed in
turn by the divine gift of definitive life: eternal life, a life morally con-
tinuous but physically discontinuous with the life of the present. Great
reversals, such as the reversal of fate of the Servant in Deutero-Isaiah
(Isa 52:13-15; 53:11-12), were now magnified beyond Israel's wildest
dreams. H. L.Ginsburg, in an article on the oldest interpretation of the
suffering Servant[27] showed how the new consciousness of a life beyond
the life of this world was shaped, in Daniel 12:2-3, by the Isaian heritage. The Servant became the type of those heroes of wisdom, the
*maśkîlîm*, whose destiny would be

> to shine like the bright vault of heaven. . .
> like the stars for ever and ever (Dan 12:3).

Here were awesome and ineffable perspectives! There was one plan of
God, one story of Israel and mankind, one final judgment, one gift of
eternal, *risen* life. All the old ambiguities were swept away in these
stunning new ascertainments. The future—the time of affliction, the
judgment, the restoration of Israel—would have an absolute character.
Hence, all those elements that belonged to these themes were themselves transformed. The new covenant, new temple, new cult, were en-
dued with a certain uncanny, transcendent quality. Prosaic restoration
themes were transformed. The eye of hope was peeled for great things:
a new creation that would totally and definitively reverse the disadvan-
tageous position of Israel vis-à-vis the nations.

Before following up on these perspectives, we must first return to the pre-apocalyptic era of post-Exilic Israel. The work of rebuilding the temple began soon after 538 (decree of Cyrus), was interrupted, then resumed in 520, and it was finished in 515. The dramatic moments in its history were three profanations, that of 167, Antiochus Epiphanes (rededication by Judas Maccabaeus); that of Pompey in 63 B.C.; and that of Titus which put an end to the temple in 70 A.D. By the time of the second profanation, apocalyptic perspectives had begun to impose themselves.

A high point in the non-apocalyptic history of the temple theme belongs to the later history of the second temple. It was the long effort of the rebuilding of the temple under Herod. Among the truly great builders of the ancient world, Herod made the announcement of the rebuilding of the temple to the people of Jerusalem, whom he assembled for this purpose in the temple court in 20 B.C. Despite their initially skeptical lack of enthusiasm, the king was bent on achieving one of the great building feats of ancient times. He would do it, moreover, in a way calculated to allay the fears of his most rigorously conservative critics.

By comparison with the temple of Solomon the temple of Zerubbabel has often been disparaged, but the evidence for the alleged inferiority is not altogether clear. In any case, the rebuilding program of Herod was such that the temple had never been more impressive. Herod kept the design of the temple, but changed the proportions. With great "Herodian" blocks of rock he built up and enlarged the temple platform, raising double colonnades in white marble round the entire pavilion. He rebuilt and refurbished the fortress Antonia. The sanctuary and other buildings in the center of the pavilion were rebuilt in splendor, the façade of the sanctuary covered with gold and the interiors decorated in cedar. To the observer the temple created an impression dominated by gold and white marble.[28]

The substance of Herod's building program was finished in about a decade, but the details of ornamentation were an ongoing affair, keeping priestly craftsmen busy until A.D. 62. Ironically, the war that would bring the temple to ruin broke out four years later. Long in coming, it was devastating in impact. As early as the opening paragraphs of his great *Jewish War*, Josephus urged that Titus had not wanted the temple put to the torch. In the summer of 70, the gates of the city having already been breached, Titus held a camp conference with his lieutenants, which ended with the decision not to destroy the sanctuary. Josephus writes:

> It had, however, been committed to the flames by God long ago: by the turning of time's wheel the fated day had now come, the 10th of Loös, the day which centuries before had seen it burnt by the king of Babylon . . . .[29]

## II. Temple Themes and Motifs

### A. *The Canaanite Connection*

Canaanite ʾEl, the father-god, had his Tent of Assembly in the Amanus mountains of the far north, and there the Bull, the King, the Eternal One of the hoary beard sat in council with his consort ʾAsherah, and other wives, with his son Ba'l and other children, other gods.

Such was 'El, the One of the Mountain, consort of ʾAsherah, the Lion Lady (= ʿAstart) who may or may not have been the one and the same as Tannit, the Dragon Lady (=ʿAnat).[30] ʾEl's abode was

> . . . at the sources of the two rivers
> in the midst of the fountains of the double-deep.[31]

At the foot of the cosmic mountain in the north the cosmic waters welled up. Cosmic mountain, cosmic waters, and sanctuary—this is the language of the sacred. The world somehow had its bases in this sphere. In Canaanite myth it is not clear that the world itself was conceived as a mountain,[32] but it did have several cosmic mountains. Apart from Amanus, the mountain of the father-god ʾEl, there is Zaphon, the Mountain of Ba'l. Their peaks were divine habitations; from their foundations flowed the water that was the condition of the life of the world. The language used in the mythological texts found at Ras Shamra made the mountain-sanctuary a point of meeting, of union, between the underground waters below and the heavens above. The divine temple effected a kind of cosmic harmony. The poetry of the late second millennium can be astonishing:

> The speech of wood and the whisper of stone,
> the meeting of heaven with earth,
> of the deeps with the stars.[33]

To coordinate heaven and earth belonged to the temple's functions.

It is difficult to delineate with certainty how much of the cosmic conceptions common to the ancient Near East attached to the temple of Jerusalem from the start, what elements accrued to it in the course of time, what elements never were part of the Israelite understanding of the temple. The particularities of this debate between maximalists and minimalists have a certain relevance to our topic, but it is quite limited.

Samuel Terrien's 1970 essay, The Omphalos Myth and Hebrew Religion,[34] followed in the line of classic monographs by W. H. Röscher[35] and A. J. Wensinck[36] on the conception of the navel of the world among the Greeks and the Semites, and applied it to the Jerusalem temple in an effort to see just how much of the vast and seemingly disparate biblical data on the temple could be organized in terms of the navel idea. It was Terrien's thesis that the myth of the navel of the earth,

> far from being an incidental aspect of worship at the temple of Jerusalem, constitutes in effect the determining factor which links together a number of its cultic practices and beliefs that otherwise appear to be unrelated.[37]

These included snake-worship, chthonian rites, the solar cult, male prostitution, and bisexuality.

Minimalists who have taken up these questions after 1970, e.g., Richard Clifford[38] and Shemaryahu Talmon,[39] have indicated or implied skepticism respecting Terrien's proposal. It is true that the relevance of certain particulars has not been proved in the proper sense of the term. It is not even agreed, for example, that the Hebrew word *tabbûr* (Jgs 9:37), which biblical translations render "navel," originally carried that meaning. And the word *tabbûr* is applied to Jerusalem no earlier than the sixth century (Ezek 38:12). In view of the passage in Ezek 5:5,

This is Jerusalem:
In the midst of the nations I set her
and encircling her are the lands,

it might seem overly rigorous to insist that the last *t* be crossed and last *i* dotted before attributing the navel idea to Ezek 38. That is, though the Ezek 38 passage does not have an immediately surrounding set of indices supporting the navel idea, there is the text in Ezek 5, which offers a certain extrinsic support for the probability of the "navel" theme in Ezek 38. (Alternative version of *tabbûr*: "high plateau"). Moreover, in the tribal allotments in Ezek 47:13-48:29 we have indirect but persuasive evidence of navel ideology. Ezekiel, at the very end of this text (48:25-27), assigns the northern tribes Issachar, Zebulon, and Gad to the south of Jerusalem, so positioning "the city" in the exact center of the land, "as befits the 'navel of the earth'."[40] Finally, though on a one-by-one basis one cannot prove the relevance of all Terrien's data to the navel idea, some parts do cohere, and there is no doubt that others accrued to the temple in the course of time. The minimalists seem to start ahead on points; soon their case sags. And by the time we arrive at the end of the whole tradition—among the rabbis, in the New Testament and among the traditions of early Christian pilgrims—the maximalists have easily got the better of the argument. Debate is most relevant to the temple of the earliest period, where in some measure it remains irresolvable.

What we can say is that in common with the Phoenician world of the late second millennium the Hebrews of the age of Solomon and later cultivated common Near Eastern cosmic imagery. They ascribed a privileged place to the national temple. The world was made up of "firmament" (*rāqîaʿ*)—"that inverted bowl we call the sky"; "dry land" (*yabbāšāh*); and primeval deep (*tĕhôm*). Sun, moon, and stars were set in the firmament. The bases of the land were sunk in water. Mountains bound together sky, land, and subterranean sea. Each of the stories of the universe had its appropriate order.[41]

The oracle of Nathan, 2 Sam 7:5-16, highlights the motif of the building of a house for YHWH. The oracle as a whole meant one thing in the days of David, a second in those of Solomon, a third to the Deuteronomistic History, and a fourth to post-Exilic tradition. The differentiation between the first two falls outside our immediate interest;

the tendency of the Deuteronomistic Historians was to soften the lines
of Solomonic emphasis on the unconditionality of the oath to David; finally, post-Exilic tradition read the text as the supreme source of royal
messianism. Key terms occur in part two (the promise) of the oracle,
vv. 12-14a:

> When your days are fulfilled
> and you lie down with your fathers,
> I will raise up your offspring after you,
> who shall come forth from your body,
> and I will establish his dominion.
> He shall build a house for my name,
> and I will establish the throne of his dominion
>       forever.
> I will be his father and he shall be my son.

The messianic reading of the text either took Solomon to be a type of
the Messiah or else referred the lines not to Solomon but directly to the
Messiah. There is a messianic valorization of this text from Qumran
(4QFlor, where, however, David's son's building of the house of God, a
motif that had proved historically prominent and potent, is allowed to
drop for reasons peculiar to the Qumranites). The main point: the promises to David encompass the Messiah, son to David and to God; consequently, messianic expectation outside Qumran took this figure—like
Solomon, like Zerubbabel—as the chosen, destined builder of the temple.

The historic sense of the text assigns the building of a house
for Yahweh to the moment when David has rest from all his enemies.
Now this moment had arrived, according to the prayer of Solomon.

> But will God indeed dwell on the earth?
> Behold, heaven and the highest heaven cannot
>       contain Thee,
> How much less this house which I have built!
>                        (1 Kings 8:27).

Meantime, YHWH (Solomon recalls) has chosen David's "house" in
the sense of dynastic lineage. And so the temple was made to fit centrally into the scheme of primitive cosmology. In mythical terms its site
was on the world's highest mountain; at its foot were the springs of wa-

ter for the dry land and at its peak the dwelling place of God on earth.
Directly above was the heavenly abode of him

> who sits above the circle of the earth (Isa 41:22).

Elements of Near Eastern cosmology are unambiguously highlighted in the dream of Jacob (Gen 28) that revealed

> a stairway set up on the earth, its top reaching
> heaven. And lo, messengers of God were ascending
> and descending it: and lo, YHWH stood above it: . . .
> and Jacob was afraid and said, 'How awesome is this
> place! This is none other than the house of God, and
> that the gate of heaven!' (Gen 28).

Doubtless as early as the age of Solomon, Mount Zion began
to be invested with the properties of paradisal myth such as we see it in
Genesis 2, and was celebrated as such in the Autumn and Spring cult.
The liturgy of "songs of Zion" probably antedated Isaiah. It survives in
some of the oldest psalms.

YHWH reigns! Where does YHWH reign? From his throne in
the innermost chamber of the sanctuary of the temple. Something of the
old tradition of the league of tribes was perpetuated in the procession of
the Ark to its place in the inner chamber of the sanctuary of Solomon's
temple. (The Spring new year, derived from Mesopotamia, yielded in
time to the Autumn new year, as among the Canaanites and Egyptians.)
Here YHWH was "enthoned on cherubim," winged beasts carved in
wild olive wood, whose wings spread from wall to wall in the inner
chamber.

His reign was his renewal of the cycles of nature, a seasonal
reimposition of divine rule over the cosmos (Pss 47; 93; 96; 98; cf. 46;
95). From his sanctuary on Zion YHWH secured Israel from its enemies (Pss 20; 46; 47; 48; 93; 97; 98), for he was not only Lord of Israel,
but Lord over all nations on earth (Pss 47; 48; 96; 99).

Despite Zion's unimpressive height (dwarfed by the Mount of
Olives to the east) it was destined, in clear accord with motifs in Canaanite mythology, to become the highest of all the mountains of the
world (Isa 2:2). Isa 14:13 makes reference to ᵓEl's abode in the Amanus
"in the far recesses of the north." The transferal of motifs from ᵓEl's

abode to YHWH and Zion is evident in the prophets and psalms. Perhaps the most extraordinary case of identification of Zion with (ʾEl's) cosmic mount of assembly is in Ps 48:3, where—all geography to the contrary notwithstanding—Zion, YHWH's holy mountain, is specified as "the far recesses of the north."[42] Ezek 47 offers the supreme exaltation of the motif of the springs at the foot of the mountain and from under the temple. Isa 33:21 evokes Jerusalem, where the water appears in its transcendent reality:

> There we have YHWH in all his majesty
> in a place of rivers and broad streams;
> but no galleys will be rowed there,
> no stately ships sail by.

Again, Joel 4:18 [EVV 3:18] promises,

> a fountain will spring from YHWH's house
> and water the wadi of Shittim.

This is reserved for the eschaton, when YHWH will become king over all the earth: "on that day, summer and winter alike, running water will issue from Jerusalem, half flowing to the eastern sea and half to the western sea" (Zech 14:8). If the Massoretic text of Ps 46:5 is accurate, it alludes to "the stream whose channels gladden the city of God." The psalms typically celebrate Zion in extravagant terms. It is God's "holy mountain, the fairest of heights" and "joy of all the earth" (Ps 48:3 [EVV 2]).

In 1985 Jon Levenson offered a compelling account of the sequence and polarity in biblical tradition of Sinai and Zion.[43] In so doing, he likewise presented a cogent argument for the role of cosmic-mountain motifs from early in the tradition. This holds in particular for the early adoption of the theme of the temple as a minature of the world. The argument runs as follows. First, such is the thrust of the symbolism realized by the Phoenician Hiram for King Solomon (1 Kgs 7:23-26). In common Canaanite myth the sea embodies chaos and its defeat validates the kingship of the divine victor and the building of his royal palace/temple. In the light of this myth

> it is not surprising to find a model of the sea, now

utterly tame, within the Temple precincts. YHWH is
enthroned near the tangible symbol ["the sea" of 1
Kgs 7:23] of the legitimacy of his cosmic sovereignty, established in protological times (Psalm 93).[44]

Furthermore, 1 Kings 7 offers several other examples of cosmic symbols. The twelve oxen or bulls (v. 25) probably symbolize the months
of the year; as grouped in threes they represent the four directions or
corners of the world. "The arboreal and vegetative symbolism along the
rim of the sea recalls the primal paradise [identified with the cosmic
mountain]."[45] In sum, temple symbols suggest that the temple itself is
not only an antitype modelled on the heavenly temple (1 Chron
28:11f.), but represents the world itself in essence.

    If, as later Jews and Christians alike maintained (possibly in
accord with age-old temple ideology), the temple site specified the
point from which God created the world, the building of the temple
mirrored the very act of creation. Compare the motifs of "finishing,"
"seeing," what had been finished, and "making sacred" in Gen 2:1f.;
1:31; 2:3 and, respecting the tent of revelation or meeting, i.e., the os-
tensible model of the sanctuary of the temple, in Exod 39:32,43; 40:9).
As the creation took seven days, the building of the temple took seven
years, and both culminated in the theme of "rest" (Gen 2:2; Ps 132:14;
cf. 1 Chron 22:9; Isa 66:1).

    The presence of God defined the central meaning of the tem-
ple sanctuary. This, as biblical tradition copiously attests, was "the
house of God" where he (or his "name") dwelled. The theme of presence, to be sure, has been a source of perplexity to many biblical scholars in our time, for many have shared in the philosophic confusions that
make the theme baffling. Does not presence imply quantity? But is
God, like us, bodily? If he is near here, is he not far from there? And if
God is not bodily, how can he be here or there, far or near, present or
absent? Oblivious of these conundrums, the psalmist affirmed

        YHWH is near to all who call on him,
        To all who invoke him in truth (Ps 145:18).

That he was present in his house, that from this presence and house
came all the blessings of life and fertility to the whole world, was the
unshakable conviction of YHWH's people.[46]

Of maximum significance is the holy mountain as goal of the great pilgrimage feasts. Those from all lands of exile shall say: "One and all were born in her" (Ps 87:5), for everyone, no matter where he was born, would recognize in Zion his true home (Ps 87:7). From Zion God summons the whole earth "from the rising of the sun to its setting" (Ps 50:1), and the reign of God evokes the image of "the princes of the peoples gathered together with the people of the God of Abraham" (Ps 47:10 [EVV 9]), for all the ends of the earth shall remember and turn to YHWH (Ps 22:28 [EVV 27]; cf. Ps 86:9), bringing their offerings to the temple court (Ps 96:8-10; cf. Ps 68:30 [EVV 29]). These texts give some indication of how powerful a resource of meaning temple ideology was, together with its complements, e.g., the application of cosmic-mountain motifs to Zion.

We shall now switch to the Greek world and look to Homer for indications of how cosmological motifs took root in the Greek world. Greek temples, such as those of Miletus and Delphi, were heirs of age-old cosmological tradition.

## B. Navel of Sea, Navel of Earth

Long held captive by a doting nymph on a wooded island in the foaming sea, Odysseus, as the Odyssey opens, is yearning to die. His captor, Calypso, is the daughter of Atlas (Odys. 1.53-54):

> who knows the depths of every sea, and himself
> holds the high pillars keeping apart earth and heaven.

If Atlas thus sustains the order of the world, where should he dwell but at the center of the world? In any case his daughter Calypso lives

> on a sea-girt isle, where is the navel of the sea
> (Odys. 1.50).

When Hermes comes to the island to tell her that the gods have resolved to let Odysseus go free (5.43-58), he finds her in a broad cave (5.58) in the center of a luxuriant wood (5.63f.). There is a fragrant fire on the hearth (5.59) and the nymph is going back and forth before the loom, weaving with a golden shuttle (5.62). Around the cave trails a great vine laden with grape clusters (5.68f.). From four fountains at the cave's mouth water flows in four directions (5.70f.).

These images appear to belong to a schematic whole. The navel of the sea (*omphalos thalassēs*, 1.50) is the cosmic center. Regularly associated with it are the wood (=tree=pillar) and the subterranean water whence flow four rivers (like the four rivers that water the earth from Eden according to Genesis 2:10-14, or the four streams of Mesopotamian art, or the four rivers that descend the four buttresses of Mount Meru in Indian tradition). The weaving at a loom images the rolling course of time; the sun is a cosmic shuttle.[47] Both the fountains and the cave in the center of the wood evoke access to the netherworld (as does Atlas's knowledge of the depths of every sea) and the figure of Hermes evokes commerce with the world of the celestial gods.[48]

Even before his seven-year stay on Ogygia with Calypso, Odysseus (as he would recount to Alcinous and the Phaeacians) had known Aeaea, Circe's island (10.135), wooded (10.150) and "surrounded by the boundless deep as by a crown" (10.195). Circe is the daughter of Helios (=the Sun) and granddaughter on her mother's side of Oceanus (Primeval Water, i.e., the great river that encompasses the earthdisk (10.138f.). Like Calypso, she sings as she goes back and forth before the loom, weaving "a great imperishable web" (10.221f.). At her direction Odysseus would make his way to the house of Hades (10.490f.), there to learn from the blind seer Teiresias the "measures" of his return to Ithaca (10.540).

That Circe and Calypso are counterparts is suggested by their lineage and description. Divine nymph, Circe is a peculiarly sacral figure, adept of sorcery (e.g., 10.233-243) and mystagogy (10.490-493; 505-545; 572f.). That her isle, like that of Calypso, is the cosmic center is suggested by its being the point of departure for the way to Hades (10.570-574) and the point of arrival for the return (12.1-3). The world navel, we have already observed, is the appointed place of access to both the celestial world and the netherworld. Though Hermes is often mentioned in the Odyssey, and depicted at some length when he leads the spirits of the slain wooers into Hades (24.1-202), he is represented as passing between heaven and earth only on his errands to Calypso and to Circe. In 10.307f. we are told:

then Hermes departed to high Olympus through the
wooded (meson an' hyléessan) isle . . .

The passage of Hermes to and from both the isle of Calypso
(5.43-58) and the isle of Circe (10.277-308) hint of the navel of the
earth, point of access to the abode of the gods. The passage of Odysseus from Circe's isle to Hades and back adds the suggestion that it is
equally the point of access to the abode of the dead.

Homer did not invent but inherited such cosmological images
as the earth's navel and its attendant motifs. Our interest, however, is
not in where he derived it from, but simply in its presence in the poem.
Comparatists have located the imagery of the navel of the earth not
only in Near Eastern and Mediterranean sources, but all over the world,
notably in China and India.

It would be mistaken to suppose that every temple in antiquity
bore the claim to be the navel of the earth. It would be another mistake
to think that this mythological conception exhausts the significance of
the temple, and a third to suppose that it is the navel motif that assures
the primacy of the "sacred" among the functions of temples in the ancient world.

Still, we know from the second- and first-millennium temples
how the Near and Middle East shared, in whole or part, these cosmic
conceptions, including the navel-of-the-world mythology. The temple
of Jerusalem was invested from the start with mythological significance. At least by the time of Ezekiel the temple-city of Jerusalem was
conceived as the navel of the earth. At a later date we see that this conception included the motifs of the cosmic rock not only as foundation
stone of the (world) sanctuary/temple, but as lid over the netherworld.
The mountain where the temple stood was thought of as hollow; in its
depths lay the netherworld.

It is worth noting that in Ps 9 "the gates of death" are played
off against "the gates of Zion" (vv. 13-14) and that later tradition, both
Jewish and Christian, for many centuries kept alive a center-of-the-
world interpretation of Ps 74:12 on God "working salvation in the
midst of the earth." Isa 19:24 speaks of Israel as "a blessing in [the
midst of] the world." (The motifs, however, are admittedly neither clear
enough nor strong enough to settle matters in dispute.)

The translators of Ezekiel into Greek rendered *tabbûr* in Ezek
38:12 by *omphalos*/navel. They thus underscored a conceptual scheme

bearing on the presence of God. Without the slightest weakness for nature religion, Ezekiel (the first to convert "paradise" motifs into motifs of future hope) pressed cosmic conceptions and images into the service of "divine presence" and "divine salvation."

In the mid-second century B.C. there is an instance of logopoeia or allusion to cosmological motifs in the symbol of the cosmic tree: "I saw, and lo, there was a tree in the center of the earth . . . (Dan 4:10). The image introduced the dream of king Nebuchadnezzar, which Daniel would interpret to the king's dismay.

In the late second century B.C. the Essenes produced the work now known as the Temple scroll. It exhibits a number of striking features: words of God, especially those cited from Deuteronomy, are transposed from third-person to first-person, and the same holds for non-Biblical parts of the scroll; the text is given over in large part to divine commands for the building of the temple and the organization of the cult; above all, the scroll provides data on holiness-ideology in the late second century and later and the role of the temple in that world of meaning.

The scroll makes up for a kind of lacuna. The Torah had not given instructions on the building of the temple; the scroll makes good this lack. It follows with probability that the temple in question in the scroll is not an ideal future temple; it is the temple for time and history. It specifies how the temple would be, now, if it were to accord wholly with the plan and will of God. The proper reading of the key text in col. 29, however, is still disputed and tentative.[49] Here, it seems, the scroll alludes to a new temple that God will build on "the day of Blessing/ [new] Creation" (col. 29). We shall not summarize nor, least of all, attempt to resolve the exegetical dispute. The main interest of the temple scroll for us lies in its witness to a theme that is not peculiar to the Essenes but holds for all Judaism: the theme of holiness (which, we should recall, was often treated in a way quite independent of the theme of "new creation," and of a new spirit and new heart solving the problem of the heart most crooked, or heart of stone). The temple is the center and matrix of the holiness of both land and people. Holiness—the quality of the sacred and the elect, the singled-out or set apart— emanated, so to speak, from the center outward in concentric circles from the holy of holies to the holy place (*hêkāl*), the altar and court of the priests, to the court of Israel, the court of women, the temple court, the temple mountain, the holy city, and finally to its environs.

Ethiopian Enoch 26:1 attests Jerusalem as "the middle of the earth." The Samaritans claimed the same for Gerizim. The images that gathered around the cosmic rock—first identified with the rock on which the altar of holocausts was built, then with the foundation rock of the holy of holies—made up a complex that comprised the gates of heaven above, the sanctuary, the cosmic rock, the gates of the netherworld below.

In rabbinic and later Judaism the cosmic rock—site of creation, of paradise and the tree of life, source of the rivers of the world, proof against the deluge—was identified with Zion; with the altar of holocausts, and simultaneously with the rock-altar on which Abraham was about to sacrifice Isaac and with the altar of Melchizedek. Later, the cosmic rock was identified with the foundation rock (*ʾeben šĕtiyyāʾ*) in the holy of holies. It bore the house and throne of God and was the destined locale of the judgment of the world. Or the rock was Abraham ("the rock from which you were hewn," Isa 51:2), whose feet braved the subterranean waters . . . Again, the tradition made the twelve patriarchs the rock.

The first Christians, meanwhile, were sure they knew the veritable rock: a disciple chosen for that role by Jesus. In the following Christian centuries tradition transferred the whole apparatus of imagery (cosmic rock, site of creation, of the sacrifice of Isaac, of Melchizedek's priestly functions, site of the coming judgment) to Golgotha. *Here* was that sacred center where God, my King of old, worked salvation in the midst, i.e., in the innermost-center, of the earth (Ps 74:12)—an extremely rich tradition, which, however, belongs to an era later than the one that occupies us.[50]

## III. Jesus and the Temple

### A. *Historical Critique*

The first move in the public life of Jesus did not touch the temple of Jerusalem; it was activity as a "baptizer" (John 3:22-26) within the context of the baptism-movement sponsored by John ("the baptist,"=*ho baptistes/matbelana* ).[51] From the start Jesus took his stand outside the lines of the religious establishment. The prophets of Israel may be similarly differentiated, some working from within, others from without, the current establishment. John was clearly an outsider, and Jesus took his stand alongside John.

When John was arrested, Jesus withdrew to Galilee, where he launched the proclamation of the reign of God. Of itself, this proclamation did not situate him within or without the religious establishment. The ambiguity quickly found an at least partial resolution in the provocations of Jesus on the Sabbath halaka (scribal lore).

Jesus stood in opposition, not to the Sabbath, but to the scribal prescriptions that were meant to define its perfect observance. What was under attack was the claim of the halaka to an identity in practice with the Torah of Israel. The attacker, by affirming the Sabbath (e.g., Mark 2:27), showed that Israel and its traditions were not under attack. Even when he struck the note of transcendence this prophet managed at the same time to specify the object of critique: not the Torah (cf. Mark 10:17-31=Matt 19:16-30=Luke 18:18-30; Mark 12:28-34=Matt 22:34-40=Luke 10:25-28; etc.), not the truth of the election of land, people, and temple (though he made it clear that they remained open to final definition) but the pretentions of the halaka.

There were two great ascertainments which Jesus, like John before him, called on his listeners to grasp. First, he announced a break in the times. The measures of time appointed for Israel's waiting were now, at this moment, filled to the brim. The Law and the prophets held sway up to the day on which John stepped into the light of history. From then onward there was a new time, which from his own, later, independent vantage point he denominated by "the reign of God" (cf. Matt 11:12-13).[52]

Second, Israel stood in need. The outsider, Jesus, looked on the Israel of his time as aimlessly wandering: "The sight of the crowds moved him to pity: they were like sheep without a shepherd, harassed and helpless" (Matt 9:36; Mark 6:34). Of the scribes he said: "They are blind guides!" (Matt 15:14). A two-line proverb-type saying in three-beat rhythm followed:

> If the guide of a blind man is blind, they both will fall
> in the ditch (Matt 15:14; Luke 6:39).[53]

His entire public life dramatized this view of Israel: the scribes did not function as a leadership planted by God. Of itself this may seem mild, but:

> Any plant not of my heavenly Father's planting—
> there is One who will uproot it!
> (Matt 15:13; divine passive).

On the other hand, without recourse to titular claims, Jesus implicitly called on Israel to recognize *in him* the shepherd of Israel.

What exactly was it in the halaka of the scribes that drew Jesus' harsh attack? There have been numerous answers. We have thus far emphasized a remotely conditioning factor in the critique: removal of the blocks or blindspots that would keep Israel from recognizing him for what he was, and cultivating the conditions and dispositions that would allow his contemporaries to find in him God's chosen agent of definitive restoration. The halaka, we should remember, was already well underway toward what it would become in rabbinic Judaism, namely, the crowning element of a complete religious system. "Complete" implies "offering little or no room for discontinuous elements in the coming eschatological completion." There was no room for a completion that could not be inferred from the past, but rather would require a new revelation.

John came urging that Israel was called on *to respond, now, with repentance and baptism.* This prophetic call had a potent popular impact, but it failed to win a positive response from Israel's religious elite (Mark 11:30-33=Matt 21:25-27=Luke 20:4-8; Matt 3:7-9=Luke 3:7-8; Matt 11:18=Luke 7:33; Matt 17:12; 21:32). Why not? Were they not on the side of repentance, amendment, preparation for God's judgment? They were. But they conceived of all these things as part and parcel of a self-sufficient system. John demanded more. He demanded something that the scribes were not familiar with in advance: himself, his role, his rite. *That* was the problem. For these resourceful, confident, well trained scribes a prophet like the Baptist, or a prophet like Jesus—anyone who claimed to bring to Israel from God a new, crowning revelation—ran the risk of seeming (as, for example, the temple would later come to seem) dispensable, an accessory, optional extra. Neither John nor Jesus successfully resolved the radical problem grounded in this disparity of horizons between themselves and the scribal elite of their time. That elite knew all about "the evil impulse," but in the common view it was not equivalent to the kind of radical human problem which, if unresolved, might put the destiny of Israel in jeopardy. Indeed, the Torah had somehow already met the whole range of human problems. The resources of Torah and halaka, which included the means of making expiation for the forgiveness of sins, were fully adequate. In short, it was hardly possible to entertain two such ideas as, first, a destiny of salvation for all but a few reprobates among the children of Abraham and, second, the hazardous situation of one in deep present need—a situation supposed by such statements as "unless you repent, you will all likewise perish" (Luke 13:3).

Jesus' critique of this scribal elite, however, was many-sided. Drawing on a later Christian problematic, some critics have thought that his target was the illegitimacy of "casuistry" and "merit." This seems unlikely. It is true that casuistry can be put to irreligious uses, but false that casuistry is intrinsically corrupt. Jesus, too, considered moral and cultic questions to vary concretely in accord with circumstances (Matt 5:22-23; compare Mark 2:19 and its parallels with Matt 6:17-18 on fasting; or, the great variety of ways in which Jesus deals with "the righteous"). The fault he found with the scribes was not, it seems, a matter of method. As for the issue of merit, it calls for an understanding of Palestinian Jewish suppositions, which simply did not entertain the possibility that reward (*śakār/misthos*) be removed from the relations between God and man. Jesus did not recoil from the category of reward, but approved and adopted it. True, he did not linger on the details of "reward." And in accord with biblical and Judaic tradition generally, he set all God's rewards within an all-commanding context of gratuity.

Neither was Jesus' critique of the halaka a fundamentalist repudiation in principle of the role of reason, of explanatory commentary, summary, reformulation, and the like. He, too, offered these things. He, too, for example, was willing to reduce the commandments to the love of God and the love of one's fellows. To restate the issue at hand in concrete terms, consider the repeated Sabbath conflicts in the opening of Mark's gospel (*Mark 1:21-28*=Luke 4:31-37; *Mark 1:40-45*=Matt 8:1-4=Luke 5:12-16; *Mark 2:23-28*=Matt 12:1-8=Luke 6:1-5; *Mark 3:1-6*=Matt 12:9-14=Luke 6:6-11). The critics of Jesus are presented as having a systematic point to make, and they make it in the climactic fourth episode. It could not be God who was acting in these cures, for *if God were at work, the cures would not contravene the Sabbath halaka.* Only an intellectual elite could generate this kind of fanatic confidence in itself and in its system—the confidence to interpret a miracle of mercy as the infraction of a law. Jesus could appeal to the onlookers', i.e., ordinary people's, religious common sense. Sabbath or not, there had to be something awry with a system that forbade, that found itself driven to the position of preventing, acts of love and mercy. There was something awry with a sanctification of the Sabbath that worked like a stranglehold. Nor is this blind exaggeration an illusion on our part, retrojected into antiquity. It is confirmed by the even more extravagant form of Sabbath halaka attested among the Essenes.

Moreover, the Synoptic tradition provides further evidence that we have not misconceived the conflict between Jesus and the scribes, for purification issues followed the same lines. The distinctive emphases of the halaka positively subverted what the biblical tradition as a whole endorsed as indisputable values, "the weightier demands of the Law" (Matt 23:23). The original meaning of Jesus' paradox on "sins of speech" makes the point. What is the real meaning of "defile"? Is it to be found in food laws (which Jesus, in fact, accepted)? [55]

> Nothing that goes into a man from outside can defile
> him but [only] what comes out of a man defiles him.

The critique bore on the blindness evidenced in shifting the accent from defilement in the crucial moral sense (as in sins of speech, a particularly powerful theme in Jesus' words) to the exceedingly meticulous avoidance of ritual impurity cultivated, not by Jews in general, but by the religious elite.

The halaka of the scribes—precisely insofar as it converted the codes of the Bible into a comprehensive system conspicuous, in Jesus' view, for its lack of proportion, and repeatedly found to contradict the values that it was designed to protect—was a solid bone of contention between him and the professionally holy. So far as I can judge, it was not a general principle or theory that fed Jesus' critique of the halaka but a whole series of particular judgments. Nor does it seem that he rejected the halaka root and branch down to the last detail. (He behaved in accord with halakic prescriptions for the celebration of the Passover.) This does not undermine the critique, which remains severe, but it does tell us something of the character of the critique that is worth mention. He knew the halaka not as a traditionalist but as a sovereign eschatological judge.

The critique Jesus directed against the halaka of the scribes had a flip-side: his positive conception of the dawning eschaton. We shall first offer some observations on the logic of his proclamation of the reign of God; second, on the kind of personal role that he assumes with reference to it.

Israel itself—the elect people, temple, land, tradition—was central to the suppositions of John and of Jesus. Here were two prophetic figures that not only did not share the scribal view of the whole as essentially complete, but took the initiative in forcing the issue. Both affirmed Israel as open to completion and in positive need of that completion. Both presented themselves as appointed to the task of that completion, as indispensable to it, and destined to realize it.

"The reign of God," it has been long recognized, had several uses among the Jews of antiquity. Jesus adopted this phrase in the sense of the happy ending that God had promised would crown the story of Israel. The "happy" note is struck in Synagogue prayers for the reign of God ("put away from us sorrow and sighing," "and they shall all be satisfied and refreshed in Thy goodness"). As in Isaiah 52, the proclamation of the reign of God was supremely good news. To Jews of Jesus' time it was news of the happy ending. God would right every wrong. Israel would not only put aside all sorrow and sighing, not only be satisfied and refreshed: "They shall take joy in Thy reign!"[56] Jesus named the signs: the blind see, the lame walk, the deaf hear, the dead are raised, news of salvation is broken to the poor (Luke 7:22=Matt 11:5). The "Today" pronounced by Jesus was the proclamation, at a Synagogue service, of the fulfillment of the scriptures. "Today" was the day of blessing (Luke 4:21). Despite the lack of this or that particular kind of fanfare, his presence signalled the moment of Israel's bridal celebrations (Mark 2:19), the renewal of the world (new garment, new wine: Mark 2:21-22=Matt 9:16-17=Luke 5:36-38).

These joyous motifs belong to the "logic" of proclamation of the reign of God. The same is true of numerous thematic correlates of God's reign. Inevitably, these correlates came to light, not in one dramatic moment, but step by step across the whole story of Jesus: (new) covenant (Mark 14:24=Matt 26:28=Luke 22:20), (new) assembly of God's people (Matt 16:18), new law (Matt 13:4-8; cf. Mark 10:5-9), under a new king and shepherd, who was also emissary, physician, teacher, and master-builder of a new sanctuary.[57] These thematic correlates should not be misconstrued as merely *coherent* with the proclamation;

the proclamation goes beyond merely setting up the conditions of their intelligibility and appropriateness. It suggests or implies them. What is left initially ambiguous and open is the personal role of Jesus with respect to the total scheme of God's reign.

Still, copious gospel data on what we might call the "style" of Jesus cumulatively and convergently diminish the ambiguity. Style can be subtle, in some ways intangible, in others decisive. In the story, for example, of the cure of the paralytic (Mark 2:1-12=Matt 9:1-8=Luke 5:17-26) the issue of Jesus and the forgiveness of sins had to do (not, obviously, with the question of whether Jesus was divine, but rather) with a certain radical religious independence on his part. Indeed, this ran all through his public ministry. Within the limits of the story of the paralytic the force of this authoritative independence makes itself felt despite the lack of a full explanatory account of it. Despite Jesus' low-key style in the matter of "claiming," the scribes were acute in sensing here Jesus' implicit shift of authority to his own person. This kind of extravagant independence would break the monopoly of the system, with its center in priesthood and temple.[58] This particular issue (Jesus' independence with regard to the forgiveness of sins) was probably recurrent, for he seems to have repeatedly pronounced people's sins to be forgiven.[59]

The hallmark of Jesus' style lay in combining ordinary manner with extraordinary matter. It is authority assumed rather than insisted upon. Authority is legitimate power; and what legitimizes power is authenticity.[60] Einstein's authenticity as a physicist is what gave him authority, that is, power acknowledged by other scientists as worthy of collaborative follow-up. Analogously, the whole issue of Jesus hinges on his authenticity, i.e., on his truly being what he claimed to be. Modesty of manner, the first component of Jesus' style, has a bearing on this authenticity. So, too, does his implicit but extraordinary claim, which became more and more overt and explicit with the unfolding of events.

Why was it not spelled out from the start? At one time the common answer was: to avoid the danger of misinterpretation in political terms. Formulated with the appropriate qualifications and nuances, this answer still holds, but it does not meet the question fully. The full answer has to do with an economy of revelation. Over and above the concrete, specific need to avoid misinterpretation as a revolutionist, Jesus exhibited a discerning realism about how the acceptance of God's word was conditioned. What was needed was not learning nor intellectual gifts (Matt 11:25 =Luke 10:21), nor a flamboyant "sign from heaven" (Mark 8:11=Matt 16:1; Luke 11:16; cf. Matt 12:38-39=Luke 11:29; John 4:48; 6:30), nor stunning preternatural messages (Luke 16:30-31), but a heart open by the grace of God to the prophetic word on its merits (Matt 11:26=Luke 10:21; Matt 16:17; cf. John 6:44).

Early in the story it is supposed that prior to his sharing in the baptismal rite sponsored by John, Jesus had lived an externally ordinary life as a craftsman (*tektōn*, Mark 6:3; cf. Matt 13:55) in a Galilean village, Nazareth. His education was, no doubt, that typical of an ordinary villager.[61] He attended the Synagogue with his fellow villagers and shared in the usual pilgrimages to Jerusalem. This impression is supported by the anecdote of his later appearance in the Nazareth Synagogue and the reaction to it of the people there (Mark 6:3-4=Matt 13:54-56; cf. Luke 4:21c).

But Jesus was no ordinary man. After the arrest of John he announced the consummation of time and history in the language of God's reign. He taught "with authority." He drew on the imagery of salvation; he worked miracles; he placed symbolic acts in the manner of the ancient prophets.[62] He announced the fulfillment of the scriptures, and the only scriptures whose fulfillment he held in abeyance (in private or esoteric instruction) was the future dominated by "the Son of man." In time it would become clear that he himself would fill that role.[63] Eventually, he made the issue of his own status thematic: Who do men say that I am?

We are thus led to Simon's confession of Jesus at Caesarea Philippi and to the thematic bond between "king" and "temple." First, we shall deal with the intention of the Matthean text and with its historicity. In all the Synoptic gospels the scene of the confession at Caesarea Philippi has a certain pivotal significance. The readership has been instructed from the outset in the messianic identity of Jesus; the Caesarea Philippi scene depicts the figures in the story as they slowly catch up with the readership on the truth about Jesus.

Jesus is the one who presses the issue: who do men say that I am? This, moreover, is followed by: And who do you [plural] say that I am? Simon answers: You are the Messiah (Son of the living God). Jesus' response to Simon, in Matthew, is to give him the name *Kêphā²/* Rock, rendered into Greek as *Petros*=Peter. There follows his instruction to keep his messianic identity secret. The next text, a distinct pericope, presents a prediction of his coming repudiation, passion, death, and glorification; Simon's rejection of this notion; and Jesus' silencing of Simon. The two pericopes are bound together by multiple ties, and function in the story as a unity.

Since our main interest is the relation of this scene to "Jesus and the temple," the accent falls on the words of Jesus:

> (17) Blessed are you, Simon Bar-Jona,
> for flesh and blood has not revealed [this] to you,
> but my Father in heaven.
> (18) And I say to you: You are "Rock" (*Kêphāʾ/ Petros*/Peter) and on this rock I will build my Church and the gates of Hades shall not prevail against it.
> (19) And I will give you the keys of the reign of heaven and whatever you bind on earth heaven will bind and whatever you loose on earth heaven will loose.[64]

The three verses are themselves one unit. There are, however, three parts, to which the verse divisions correspond. Each part begins with a thematic statement that is then unpacked by the following couplet. Each couplet exhibits antithetic parallelism. The whole is dominated by the image of the cosmic rock: atop it the sanctuary is built; beneath it the netherworld rages in vain. The hinge on which this dominant image turns is "Messiah," that Son of David and Son of God who is destined to build the temple. The meaning, then, is that the true temple of the last days, built on the faith-confessing Simon/*Kêphāʾ*/Peter, is the new (messianic!) people of God.

From the oracle of Nathan (2 Sam 7) the bond between "Son of David" and "building the temple" had become classic. The same should be said of the bond between "temple" and the imagery of the holy mountain or cosmic rock. How credible it is that this was an authentic word of Jesus probably turns most of all on whether it is credible that he should use this kind of symbolic language. The cumulative impact of the mass of traditional symbols drawn on and exploited by Jesus may come as a surprise: salvation as wedding, banquet, harvest, new wine, new world-garment, vine and vintage, fig tree and fig leaves, sunlight and darkness, lamp and bushel. The savior as shepherd, physician, teacher, householder, fisherman, king. All these images are classic symbols. Here we have builder, rock, and building.

In dealing with historicity, we should distinguish between the substance of these words and their formal composition. That the substance of the saying derives from Jesus is indicated by a datum common to the gospels: Jesus gave the name *Kêpha'*/Peter to Simon. That the composition of the saying is from after Jesus is indicated by some of the expressions used.

We learn from all four gospels that Jesus gave the name *Kêpha'*/Peter to Simon (Matt 16:18; Mark 3:16; Luke 6:14; John 1:42). No rationale for this name other than that offered by Matthew has ever been made even minimally probable. John offers a quasi-parallel to Matthew on the charged giving of the name (John 1:42): "You shall be named Cephas."

That the actual composition of vv. 17-19 derives, however, from Matthew or, more probably, from Synoptic or Matthean tradition is indicated by "Father in heaven" in verse 17 and by "the reign of heaven" in verse 19, neither of them phrases used by Jesus.[65]

In terms of temple motifs, we must take up the scene of the entry into Jerusalem, cleansing of the temple, a clearly climactic moment in Jesus' relation to the temple. The cleansing of the temple, however, belongs to a whole set of contexts. Immediately, there is the before-and-after context: the entry into Jerusalem leading up to the cleansing, and the challenge of authorities at the temple following the cleansing. This complex itself belongs to the latter part of the public life of Jesus, the sequence that the Caesarea Philippi scenes initiated. The hallmark of this sequence is the consciousness of the danger of repudiation. Jesus anticipated, in the mode of provisional prophecy,[66] repudiation by the leaders of the nation and in their wake by the nation itself.

The challenge is to penetrate to the inside of the complex event of entry, cleansing, and encounter with authorities. Since the initiative was entirely on Jesus' side, the question is, what was he up to? Respecting his purposes in general, there is a first straightforward observation: Jesus was not a reformer. His controlling proclamation (the reign of God has drawn near) and its follow-up might include a few elements of immediate reform, but reform as a controlling category implies ongoing history, whereas the thrust of Jesus' career bore on the consummation of history. There were aspects of Jesus' mission in which "reform" played a real but minor role; for example, his blanket dismissal of Mosaic legislation on divorce (Matt 19:1-12=Mark 10:1-

12) involved a reform of practice, but its root was the presence of the eschaton in the person and mission of Jesus—hence the eschatological return to the norm of paradise. Clearly, "the presence of the eschaton" altogether transcends the category of mere reform.

Neither, on the other hand, was Jesus a revolutionary.[67] In his view it was not revolution that would establish the reign of God. Rather, God's reign "comes," "draws near," "appears"; one "enters into" it, or "accepts" or "inherits" it. And if one "seeks after" or "attains" it, this is not by arms but by faith and hope, a longsuffering trust in God.

What categories, then, might be positively appropriate to him? It is clear that, like John, he was a "preparationist," his whole effort bent on making Israel ready for the end. And, like John, he was a "a fulfiller," intent on bringing the scriptures to realization.[68] The categories that historical-Jesus research has commonly appealed to in order to interpret the entry and cleansing (reformer and revolutionary) are accordingly most improbable from the start; we are better advised to begin by looking for clues in the themes of "preparation" and "fulfillment."

Moreover, we should take account of what we know of "Jesus and the temple." This amounts to two facets of the same expectation. He affirmed the prophecies of salvation with their end-time imagery of Zion and the temple—belonging to the eschatological themes that the "pilgrimage of the peoples" evoked.[69] But contrary to the common conviction of his contemporaries, Jesus expected the destruction of the temple in the coming eschatological ordeal (Mark13:2=Matt 24:2 =Luke 21:6). The combination seems contradictory. How could he simultaneously predict the ruin of the temple in the ordeal and affirm the end-time fulfillment of promise and prophecy on Zion and temple? The paradox is irresolvable until one takes note of another trait of Jesus' words on the imagery of Zion and temple, namely, *the consistent application to his own disciples of Zion- and temple-imagery*: the city on the mountain (Matt 5:14; cf. Thomas, 32), the cosmic rock (Matt 16:18; cf. John 1:42), the new sanctuary (Mark 14:58; Matt 26:61). The mass of promise and prophecy will come to fulfillment in this eschatological and messianic circle of believers.

To summarize the heuristic clues: we should approach the complex "entry-cleansing-encounter with authorities" in the light of *preparation* for the reign of God, and, despite dark prospects for the temple, in the guarantee that all eschatological prophecy on the temple would come to *fulfillment*.

Did Jesus undertake this dramatic gesture in the despairing conviction that it was futile? The answer turns on how we are to interpret his prophecies of repudiation and death and of the ordeal that would engulf Israel, the capital city, and temple. Among the numerous clues, there is one that seems to me close to decisive. It derives from the earliest Christian history. The post-Easter Church of Jerusalem depicted in the first chapters of the Acts of the Apostles quite clearly took Jesus' dark, grim predictions of the eschatological ordeal to have been provisional. This would hardly have been possible if they had thought that Jesus intended his prophecies of the ordeal in an absolute sense. In the light of this and other data[70] it is highly probable that Jesus himself understood his own dark images (of death, of the ordeal, of the destruction of capital and temple, and so on) in conditional terms. The condition was, of course, Israel's non-response to his last call. When he placed the prophetic acts of entry and cleansing, he had by no means given up hope of a positive response from Israel.

What, then, did he intend? Contemporary analysis of "the communication situation" differentiates Sender, Receiver, Code, Contact, Context, and Message. We may apply these analytic tools to the event at hand. Sender: Jesus (and his disciples). Receiver: those present on the scene and all those who would hear of it. Code: biblical eschatology, accent on Zechariah. Contact (attitude toward sender): varied (sympathetic, antipathetic, curious). Context: several contexts overlap, as has been said above and will be reiterated below. Message: this depends on the answer to the question, what did Jesus intend?

In the light of the impending consummation, Jesus intended *to elicit from Israel-on-Passover-pilgrimage positive responses to his claim to mediate the messianic restoration of Israel.* He intended the winning over of adherents to the remnant of Israel destined for restoration. How might this intention find realization? First, by a public act of messianic fulfillment. The entry into Jerusalem purposely evoked classic messianic tradition (Zech 9:9) on the king of peace, seated not on a war-horse but on an ass. The temple-cleansing that followed recalled the end of the book of Zechariah: "No longer will any trader be seen in the house of the LORD of hosts" (14:23). Finally, the riddle with which Jesus responded to those who demanded authorization for his acts ("Destroy this sanctuary and after three days I shall build it") recalled Zech 6:12, "Here is the man whose name is Branch; he will branch out from where he is and rebuild the temple of YHWH."

    The code in which, at this point, Jesus communicated with a divided Israel, those who hailed him, those who opposed him, those who wondered about him, was messianic and especially Zecharian tradition. The basic message of the entry into Jerusalem was: the Messiah is here! What was the message of the cleansing? First, outrage at irreverence toward the sacred. But there was more to the matter than that.

    Briefly to reconstruct the event: Jesus left Bethphage (*et Tur*, on the summit of the Mount of Olives) on "the foal of an ass"; he descended the Mount of Olives hailed by his disciples and other Galilean pilgrims, swiftly joined by others acclaiming him. Prospects of success, prospects of failure: both were real. His choice of resources was bold and deft. He conjured up the nation's most compelling traditions at a moment when receiver-competence was at its peak. Once arrived at the temple court, his disciples secured the gates (Mark 11:16), allowing no use of the court as a short cut. He himself overturned tables, drove animals and merchants alike from the temple platform (Mark 11:15-17=Matt 21:12-13=Luke 19:45-46; cf. John 2:14-17).

    The entry into the temple precincts, filled as it was with messianic meaning (not only the symbolic act of Jesus, but the indication of its being understood), provided an advance interpretation of the cleansing as a messianic act. The word of Jesus, (according to the Markan text, primitive vis-à-vis those of the parallels, as we shall see below), reads: "Is it not written,

> My house shall be / a house of prayer for all peoples?
> You have made it / a den of robbers!

How can you so desecrate the holy house of God? The desecration lay in where the commerce of exchange (coinage, birds, and animals) was taking place, namely, in the temple precinct itself. This was the element of reform and correction in the event. It was typical of Jesus that he refused to take the tolerant view of this abuse. We should remember that whereas he allowed what the scribes forbade (e.g., on Sabbath observance), he also forbade what they allowed. Unlike the scribes, he did not acquiesce in any of life's routine disorders—the routine use of oaths (Matt 5:34-37), routine verbal abuse (Matt 5:22). He warned that the heedlessly slanderous word would be remembered at the judgment (Matt 12:36-37). He put an end to taken-for-granted concessions to human frailty like divorce and remarriage (Matt 19:3-12=Mark 10:2-12). In brief, he found fault with the shifts and dodges of average carnal man, which Israel, like the world at large, simply accepted as part of the human condition. He was especially sensitive to irreverence (Matt 23:16-22).

The tendency observable in all four gospels was not to enhance but to downplay the event (probably to forestall any temptation to interpret Jesus as a revolutionary). Thus, Mark represents Jesus as acting alone, despite the fact that the prohibition expressed in Mark 11:16 ("He would not allow anyone to carry anything through the temple"; cf. the similar rabbinic prohibition of using the temple pavilion as a shortcut, *m. Ber.* 9:5), in view of the many gates (at least eight) required the collaboration of his disciples. Both Matthew and Luke have further reduced the event, each giving a two-verse account and neither acknowledging the causal nexus of the event to the conspiracy against and arrest of Jesus (contrast Mark 11:18). Finally, John has altogether removed the cleansing scene from the prologue to the passion story.

The literary structure, which has not been entirely suppressed in the gospel redactions, indicates the basic symbolic dimension of the event. As acclamation of the king was followed in Near Eastern tradition by royal restoration of cult, so here the motif of messianic acclamation was followed by *eschatological* restoration of cult.

With this observation we return to the texts chosen by Jesus. Matthew and Luke show that it served their purposes to keep "house of prayer" and to leave aside "for all peoples." That this was an omission is most probable. There are many, many biblical texts that show the temple as holy and to be revered—a place of divine presence, of cult, of prayer. Jesus picked the one great text that related the holiness of the temple ("house of prayer") to its eschatological future ("for all peoples"). It is possible but unlikely that he (or, for that matter, the Matthean and Lukan traditions) picked this "gentiles" text, but dropped the reference to the gentiles. Why then did Matthew and Luke drop the allusion? Did they think that it was simply irrelevant? Did it strike them as unfulfilled prophecy? The Markan text, in any case, presents the implicit promise that the promises on the temple will be kept.

The word of Jer 7:11 ("Has this house, which is called by my name, become a den of robbers in your eyes?") censures the self-contradictory conduct of Israel. You break all the commandments, cried Jeremiah; then, putting your trust in the temple, you cry, "we are saved!" Jesus fixed atomistically on this indignation (cf. John 2:17).[71]

"Restoration of cult" epitomizes the event. At a pragmatic level the restoration had an element of immediate reform, clearing the temple pavilion of commerce and shortcut-takers. The event was moreover charged with symbol. The restoration of cult symbolized here has been variously interpreted. Many years ago, Bengt Sundkler argued that, inasmuch as the temple stood as symbol of the world, its purification prefigured purification of the world (i.e., by the redemptive death of Jesus).[72] It is at least true that the restoration of cult must relate in some fashion to the death of Jesus. But the restoration of cult signified by the cleansing of the temple would remain opaque, open, incomplete to the disciples until the Last Supper was reconsidered in the light of the risen Jesus.

Temple authorities swiftly confronted Jesus and demanded a sign authorizing "these things" (John 2:18; cf. Mark 11:27-28=Matt 21:23=Luke 20:2). His response was the temple riddle. An approximate reconstruction:

> "Destroy this sanctuary and after three days I will
> build it,"

(cf. Mark 14:58; Matt 26:61; John 2:19).[73] The imperative "destroy" (John 2:19) has conditional force; the three-days reference is an idiomatic expression for "short time" and a symbolic expression for the time of the ordeal; the building of the sanctuary, implicitly messianic, bears on the messianic community transformed in the reign of God.[74]

The riddle—with its central image of the sanctuary streaming light on the world—was not the last word of Jesus, but it was among his last words. There had been many earlier words on the consummation and its earthly preparation. He had said that his death would be a ransom (Mark 10:45=Matt 20:28; cf. Isa 43:3-4); at the final earthly Passover with his disciples he would define his death as expiatory offering (Mark 14:24=Matt 26:28; Luke 22:20; John 6:51; cf. 1 Cor 11:24) and covenant sacrifice (Mark 14:24=Matt 26:28; Luke 22:20; cf. 1 Cor 11:25). But if the temple riddle was not Jesus' last word, it became a haunting refrain. First, it was spoken in the shadow of the temple-sanctuary, a prophetic riddle; then it was spoken before the Sanhedrin, a garbled piece of false testimony ("I shall destroy . . . ); finally, it was spoken beneath the cross, the taunting of a loser. But Golgotha did not put an end to the story of Jesus and the temple. The centurion spoke the last word of all: "Surely this man *was* God's Son!" (Mark 15:39=Matt 27:54=cf. Luke 23:47).[75]

## B. The Handiwork of Christus Faber

The Easter experience of the disciples validated for them the word of the Centurion. Hence, the story of Jesus and the temple not only went on; it is still going on. Jesus himself identified sanctuary/ temple with his own (for he would build it) community of the saved, transfigured in the reign of God (Mark 14:58=Matt 26: 61). This, then, would be the final destiny of his own ("my") community, built on *Kê-phā*/Rock/Peter (Matt 16:18).

Our own final question is: what can we learn both of the Messiah and of the messianic house of God by reflection on the gospels in just those terms? Jesus left a "voluntary association" on earth. This was his work. What kind of work was it? And what does his leaving it tell us? He has answered both questions in the mode of indirection. His work stands in the image of the sanctuary of the last days, built by the royal architect and master-builder. It is the house or dwelling place of God. It is meant for the end of time and the reign of God. This Church, bloodied like its builder for its witness to a divine mission, bears the imprint: Christ made me. For all its sins, the Church bears in its living selfhood the signature of the messianic artisan.

But the image of builder and building is at most an index to an answer. What exactly did Jesus leave behind as his work? An appropriate answer is found in appropriate evidence, here first and foremost in the set of gospel stories that Jesus' associated followers have bequeathed to us. Primarily, they tell us about him, but in some ways they tell us just as compellingly about themselves, how they understood themselves, what made them tick.

In some deep, not immediately specifiable way, they understood themselves to depend on Jesus. The stories are about the past, but they reveal that the storytellers took the figure they tell about to be, even now, the magnetic center of their lives.

The setting of the stories is Israel in the era of Tiberius (14-37 A.D.), when the Prefect Pontius Pilate (26-36 A.D.) administered Judea and Samaria. The story begins with the rugged figure of John the Baptist, whose public appearance in the wilderness of Judea dated from the year 28 A.D. In him "prophecy" in a classic sense returned to Israel after long absence.[76]

The earliest Christian community remembered the burden of John's prophecy, the imminence of divine judgment. In this he had called on all Israel to repent, confess its sins, perform a rite of immersion symbolizing a washing, and await the appearance of the mysterious figure who would be God's agent of judgment. Those who tell this story in this way are clearly persuaded that John, now dead, had been an authentic prophet of the end, his message "from heaven." The fact that years had passed between the word of the prophet and this telling of his story, and that meantime the end had not come, has not disillusioned the storytellers. Why not? To offer a good answer, we must follow the story further through the career of Jesus, his arrest, execution, and resurrection.

Jesus enters the scene. When he immersed himself in the water of the Jordan, the Holy Spirit came down on him like a dove,[77] and a voice addressed him: "You are my beloved Son..."[78] This was immediately followed by the Spirit's urging Jesus into the wilderness where, undertaking a complete fast from food, he gave himself over to prayer. At the end of a weeks-long period during which he was sustained like a mystic, he had an encounter with Satan: Satan's effort (as Jesus interpreted it) to pervert the true or authentic fulfillment of his mission.[79]

The middle, or substance, of the story is made up of Jesus' words and acts: his proclamation of the reign of God; his promises that those who accepted his word and lived by it would share in the reign of God; his teaching about what "the reign of God" really meant; his cures and exorcisms, which did the same; the miracle of the multiplication of loaves, which again did the same; his graciousness toward all, conspicuously including the notorious sinners whom he welcomed to his table; the sending of disciples to bring his message first to all Galilee, in time to every town and village in Israel; the repeated warnings that sudden judgment would mean the ruin of the blasé and indifferent; debate with the learned on his "authority" and mission.

The end of the story of the earthly Jesus was anticipated by a new moment: Jesus undertook to prepare himself and his followers for the worst. The worst was Israel's refusal. And the worst aspect of the refusal was what? Suffering and death for Jesus and his disciples? No. He spontaneously recoiled from all those dreadful and ironic elements of refusal, and they figured in the instruction of his followers, but they are not the key, so to speak, to this new moment in the story.

The key was a risk that had always been inescapably bound up with the character of his mission. The point of Jesus' mission had been restoration—object of the hopes of the prophets and the prayers of the Synagogue. Now, to reject the mission of Jesus was to miss out on its offer. In the view of Jesus and his followers, this was Israel's rendez-vous with its own destiny.

Anyone for whom this, as a category, is meaningless, may find some difficulty in grasping the force of the texts on the coming disaster. But even a complete outsider to the hopes of Israel should be able to form an idea of what it might mean—to one bound heart and soul to his people, which he took to be God's people—that they should be on the point of losing out on their appointed place and role in the plan of God.

Jesus' response to this prospect was to create new conditions of success. He would give his own life for Israel and the world; he would train his disciples to bring this new factor into play by carrying on the mission throughout the ordeal or tribulation—it would be fierce but brief—to be opened by his death, and to be closed by his vindica-tion and the advent of God's reign.

The last part of the story was dominated by a final symbolic act, the cleansing of the temple; by a last confrontation with the relig-ious elite in Jerusalem; a last Passover with his disciples; the arrest, trial, and execution of Jesus as one who claimed to be "the king of the Jews."

Finally, the key condition of the "what made the story-tellers tick" took place: the appearance of the risen Jesus to men and women of his entourage.

This set of meetings (we refer to it under the rubric "the Easter experience of the disciples") had a clearly transformative impact on them. It transformed their understanding of the status and destiny of Je-sus: God had raised him from the dead. It dramatically vindicated his mission. They took his resurrection from the dead as entailing his exal-tation as Messiah and Lord (not, to be sure, because of any anterior bond between "resurrection" and "messiahship," but because *vindica-tion* of the messianic role that Jesus had implicitly claimed, inevitably seemed to them to entail this exaltation). Correlatively, they took them-selves to be the messianic community in which they, first-fruits of Is-rael, had reached eschatological restoration. Furthermore, they experienced Easter as forgiveness and reconciliation with their messianic Lord;[80] as the missionary mandate of the risen Christ;[81] and as the beginning of the fulfillment of the promises and prophecies of Jesus.

We should accordingly distinguish between foreground and background in the telling of the story of Jesus. In the foreground there was the memory of Jesus, richly various, image succeeding image—a meal celebrating the conversion of a tax-collector, a debate with some scribes, the exorcism of a madman—while in the background was the habitually-impinging awareness of his realized destiny (rejection, crucifixion, death—all reversed, transfigured by resurrection). Frequently the play of awareness between foreground and background generated irony, piquant or pungent. Those who recounted the threat of Antipas, mediated by Pharisees (Luke 13:31-33), were conscious of the later silence of Jesus before this same Herod (Luke 23:5-11). The narrators of the multiplication of loaves well knew the story of Jesus' creative variation on the Passover liturgy that "founded" the eucharist and, of course, they regularly shared in the eucharistic liturgy.

These early Christians did not work out theoretical accounts of the disparities, such as the gap between eschatological scenario and actual history. Some resources assuredly were ready to hand. They were fully conscious of the category of provisional prophecy.[82] Their pneumatic experience was radically confirmatory of their heritage from Jesus. They were not faced with crises of cognitive dissonance. They were, above all, a believing community, which under sustained pressure first from Jewish, then from pagan, power centers, proved to have within it whatever heroic resources were necessary for their survival.

A sane critique of the many texts that in the heady heyday of New Testament form criticism had been assigned an origin among the appearances of the risen Jesus has now persuasively replaced them among the stories of the earthly Jesus.[83] Behind and alongside this form-critical *faux pas* was an authentic grasp of the uncanny that did typify these texts. An example is the story of Luke 5:1-11, a miraculous catch of fish in the Lake of Galilee and its impact on Simon:

> "Depart from me, O Lord, for I am a sinful man"
> (Luke 5:8).

This was a consciously ordinary man's response to encounter with an order of goodness that stood outside the sphere of ordinary persons, places, and events.

This kind of experience was recurrent, and the gospels framed it again and again. Sometimes it is the disciples who register the presence of the authentically sacred, sometimes others—the crowd, or a sinner stunned by Jesus' compelling graciousness (Luke 19:8).

Correlative to the aura that thereby accrues to the figure of Jesus is the awe in which the storytellers hold him. Nevertheless, the tone of the narratives, story after story, is one of restraint, as if consciously intent on allowing the figure of Jesus to bring the same music to the listeners, hearers, readership—and let it resonate in their psyches—as it had brought to the narrators. This tone of confident sobriety is among the telling pointers to the group that has taken over the memory of Jesus, shaped it in words, projected it for "the many" to share.

It is wholly deliberate on the part of the tellers that all those present and future hearers whom the storytellers address, find themselves invited to recognize that they themselves are somehow in the story. They belong to "the many" who would come from east and west, the many (i.e., the countless "all") for whom Jesus gave his life as ransom, expiatory offering, and covenant sacrifice.[84]

The story told in the gospels—in scores of anecdotes, discourses, longer narratives—so turns out not only to present the figure of Jesus and to reveal the traits of the voluntary association that he left on earth, it also addresses the hearer/reader, inviting and summoning him/her. Are you with him? Then you are with us; we are with you. Join us. Come inside.

Join what? Jesus was habitually cautious, reticent, about names and titles whether for himself or for his followers, rarely relaxing a habitual shying away from them. Nevertheless, he did not hesitate to draw on a classical fund of images by which to describe his own mission and—not only the character, but the forordained status and role of—those gathered round him. He thereby characterized his "voluntary association" in the scriptural language of the flock that he, the shepherd, gathers; as the invited wedding guests; as God's planting, the city perched on the mountain, and the family of the end-time.

> His favourite of all the images for the new people of God is the comparison of the community of salvation with the eschatological family of God. It is the substitute for the earthly family which Jesus himself and

> the disciples accompanying him have had to give up.
> (Mark 10.29f. par.)[85]

This conception serves remarkably to draw together seemingly disparate aspects of Jesus' language.

> In the eschatological family God is the father (Matt. 23.9), Jesus the master of his house, his followers the other occupants (Matt. 10.25). The older women who hear his word are his mothers, the men and youths his brothers (Mark 3.34 par.). And at the same time they are all the little ones, the children, indeed the *nepioi* of the family (Matt. 11:25) whom Jesus addresses as children, although in age they are adult.[86]

We are thus provided with a context in which to read the frequent references to Jesus' table-fellowship, for "the family of God appears above all in table-fellowship, which is an anticipation of the meal of salvation at the consummation."[87]

We focus our wondering on both Jesus and the Church. Since it was Jesus who brought the Church into being (by gathering his disciples, teaching them how to understand him and in this light to understand themselves), and since we are persuaded that we learn to understand the artisan in the light of his artifact and the artifact in the light of the artisan who brought it into being, our wondering shifts back and forth between the two. We have focused now on Jesus as bringing the Church into being, now on the Church as a revelation of the Jesus who created it.

This reciprocal revelation offers a unique access to that innermost selfhood and subjectivity that is the Church. The story that the gospels tell is consciously comprehensive: it includes the reader in the story—and not passively only. Again and again they implicitly converse with the readership. Those who are in the Church already are continuously encouraged to savor the poetry that runs through the Jesus-stories recollected in tranquillity. Those who are not in the Church are invited to come in, to be a part of the association that not only cherishes the memory of Jesus, but grounds its most personal and extravagant hopes on his risen life, and celebrates past, present, and future in the light of "Jesus is Lord!" Willingly or not, we are addressed, invited, summoned, encouraged, warned, enlightened by the voice of the narrators, but also of Jesus. In the story he is addressing the disciples, or crowds, or critics. But the reader, despite the great diversity of address- ees, finds that somehow all these words—to onlookers, close friends, critics—are also addressed to him: "Come to me, all who are weary. . ." "Do not be afraid, little flock . . . " "How clever you are at setting aside the commandment of God . . . "

It was unforeseen that the readership of the gospels should have extended across centuries. It was unimaginable to the first story- tellers that their audience would be counted in the hundreds of millions. Christians fondly hoped, as late as the sixties and seventies of the first century, to live to see the parousia. But no. The finished gospel redac- tions belong to the transition-period from awaiters of an early parousia to awaiters of a parousia whose day no one knows.

The revolt against Rome broke out in A.D. 66 and essentially ended in 70 when the city and temple were destroyed. Herod's great masterpiece, its final ornamentation hardly completed, vanished in the wreckage of war. In its stone, wood, and metal embodiment the temple and its history were finished. Judaism would rebuild on Torah and hala- ka, Synagogue and sage. In the course of time death came to the last Jewish Christians who had prayed at the temple. But from Jesus and the Jesus tradition it had already long since been clear to Christians that the temple of stone and gold belonged to "the time of the Law and the prophets." Two outsiders—John and Jesus—had ushered in a new era: covenant, people, code, temple, cult, all new. What this means we have learned from the gospels, the Church's essential story and storytelling, its self-revelation and revelation of John, Jesus, the disciples. The all- inclusive horizons that the gospels project invite their readers to discov- er how the temple of living stones lives on even now.

# NOTES

1. See below, note 73.

2. JW vi. 252.

3. Pioneer studies: George E. Mendenhall, "Ancient Oriental and Bib- lical Law," *Biblical Archaeologist* 17 (1954) 26-46; "Covenant Forms in Israe- lite Traditions," *Biblical Archaeologist* 17 (1954) 50-76;   Klaus Baltzer, *The*

*Covenant Formulary in Old Testament, Jewish and Early Christian Writings* (Philadelphia: Fortress, 1971).

4. Martin Noth, *Das System der zwölf Stämme Israels* (Stuttgart: Kohlhammer, 1930) with many successors and followers.

5. After spending many months laboriously working through the issue, I found a satisfactory account in F. M. Cross, *Canaanite Myth and Hebrew Epic* (Cambridge: Harvard University Press, 1973) 79-90, 265-273.

6. Cross, *Canaanite Myth*, 79-83.

7. See John W. Rogerson, "Anthropology and the Old Testament," in *The World of Ancient Israel: Sociological, Anthropological, and Political Perspectives* (ed.) R. E. Clements (Cambridge: Cambridge University Press, 1989) 17-37. The conclusion, however, is not Rogerson's, but mine, based in part on data provided by Rogerson and others in this volume.

8. This is almost universally acknowledged; but it is noteworthy, if strange, that Noth, Vincent, and Yadin dissent. See Theodor A. Busink, *Der Tempel von Jerusalem von Salomo bis Herodes*, two vols. (Leiden: Brill, vol. 1, 1970; vol. 2, 1980) I, 200.

9. Translation from Cross, *Canaanite Myth*, 159; see 158-159.

10. See John Gray, *The Biblical Doctrine of the Reign of God* (Edinburgh: Clark, 1979) 9-38.

11. Cross, *Canaanite Myth*, 13-75 on 'El; 91-194 on Ba'l.

12. Gray, *Biblical Doctrine*, esp. 2-22.

13. On the succession text, see Leonhard Rost, *The Succession to the Throne of David* (Sheffield: Almond, 1982); Gerhard von Rad,"The Beginnings of Historical Writing in Ancient Israel," in *The Problem of the Hexateuch and Other Essays* (New York: McGraw-Hill, 1966) 166-204; see 176-189.

14. Cross, *Canaanite Myth*, 21-211; 232-237; 241-244.

15. Jean Ouellette, "The Basic Structure of Solomon's Temple and Archaeological Research," in *The Temple of Solomon* (Missoula: Scholars Press, 1976) (ed.) Joseph Gutmann, 1-20, at 4-5.

16. Ouellette, 1.

17. Busink, *Tempel*, vol. 1, 129-151 surveys these questions. On the sanctuary of the temple, vol. 1, 162-218.

18. " ohel mô ed, which we can translate accurately as 'tent of the council or assembly' thanks to extrabiblical lexical material, was understood in P as 'the tent of the divine-human meeting,' that is, 'the tent of revelation'." Cross, *Canaanite Myth*, 300.

19. Ben Ollenburger, *Zion, the City of the Great King: A Theological Symbol of the Jerusalem Cult* (Sheffield: JSOT Press, 1987).

20. Bruno Snell, *The Discovery of the Mind* (Cambridge: Harvard University Press, 1953; repr. New York: Harper & Row [Harper Torchbook], 1960).

21. Karl Jaspers, *The Origin and Goal of History* (New Haven Yale University Press, 1953).

22. This refers to the first edition of the Deuteronomistic History. (On the two editions, see Cross, *Canaanite Myth*, 278-285.)

23. Jon D. Levenson, *Theology of the Program of Restoration of Eze-kiel 40-48* (Missoula: Scholars Press, 1976).

24. Levenson's case for thematic coherence in Ezekiel: see *Program of Restoration*, 57-73, 87-91, 95-101.

25. T. W. Manson, *The Teaching of Jesus* (Cambridge: Cambridge University Press, 2nd edition, 1935) 181: "[In Ezekiel's view] the restored Israel, purified by the fiery affliction of the Exile, is the Remnant which turns to enjoy salvation, whatever may be the fate of the rest of the world."

26. Joachim Jeremias, "Hesekieltempel und Serubbabeltempel," *Zeitschrift für die neutestamentliche Wissenschaft* 52 (1934) 109-112.

27. H. L. Ginsburg, "The Oldest Interpretation of the Suffering Servant," *Vetus Testamentum* 3 (1953) 400-404.

28. *JW* v, 182-237, esp. 201-205 and 222-224.

29. *JW* vi, 250.

30. Cross, *Canaanite Myth*, 30-34.

31. *Corpus des tablettes en cunéiformes alphabétiques* (Paris: Imprimerie Nationale, 1963) (ed.) A. Herdner, 4. 4. 21-22.

32. See Richard J. Clifford, *The Cosmic Mountain in Canaan and the Old Testament* (Cambridge: Harvard University Press, 1972) 9-25 for critique of the world-mountain (*Weltberg*) theme derived from former Mesopotamian studies. (Still, the redactor of the introduction to the Deuteronomistic History, Deut 1-3[4], conceives of the land of promise as "the mountain of the Amorites," "this mountain," etc.).

33. *Corpus des tablettes* (CTA) 3. 3. 19-22.

34. Samuel Terrien, "The Omphalos Myth and Hebrew Religion," *Vetus Testamentum* 20 ( 1970 ) 315-338.

35. Wilhelm Heinrich Röscher, *Omphalos. Eine philologisch-archäologisch-volkskundliche Abhandlung über die Vorstellungen der Griechen und anderer Völker vom 'Nabel der Erde'* (Leipzig: Teubner, 1913); *idem, Neue Omphalosstudien: ein archäologischer Beitrag zur vergleichenden Religionswissenschaft* (Leipzig: Teubner, 1915); *idem, Der Omphalosgedanke bei verschiedenen Völkern. besonders den semitischen* (Leipzig: Teubner, 1918).

36. A. J. Wensinck, *The Ideas of the Western Semites Concerning the Navel of the Earth* (Amsterdam: Muller, 1916).

37. "The Omphalos Myth," 317.

38. Clifford, *Cosmic Mountain* (see above, note 2) though noncommittal on Ezek 38:12 (135), accepts the navel motif for the LXX of Ezek 38:12 (183).

39. Shemaryahu Talmon, "*har, gibh‘āh*," *Theological Dictionary of the Old Testament* (Grand Rapids: Eerdmans, 1974- ) III, 427-447, at 437f. *Idem*, "The 'Navel of the Earth' and the Comparative Method," in *Scripture in History and Theology* [J. C. Rylaarsdam Fest-schrift] (eds.) A. L. Merrill and T. W. Overholt (Pittsburgh: Pickwick Press, 1977) 243-268.

40. Levenson, *Program of Restoration*, 118.

41. Rogerson, "Anthropology" (see above, note 7) at 23.

42. Cross, *Canaanite Myth*, 38. Levenson, *Sinai and Zion* (see note 43 below) 124f., following and improving upon Clifford, has offered a different translation,"the utmost peak of Zaphon," set in synonymous parallelism with "the city of the great King."

43. Jon D. Levenson, *Sinai and Zion: An Entry into the Jewish Bible* (Minneapolis: [Seabury] Winston, 1985).

44. *Sinai and Zion*, 139.

45. Ibid.

46. See Samuel Terrien, *The Elusive Presence. Toward a New Biblical Theology* (New York: Harper & Row, 1978). The positive conception of cosmic-mountain themes found in Levenson, *Sinai and Zion*, stands in contrast to Terrien's tendency to associate them rather with deviant, syncretistic features of temple practice. On the other hand, Terrien's *Elusive Presence* offers a rather full, dialectically balanced treatment of YHWH's "presence" to his temple, people, and world.

47. E. A. S. Butterworth, *The Tree at the Navel of the Earth* (Berlin: de Gruyter, 1970) 9.

48. Butterworth, *Tree*, 10f., 62, 118f.

49. See Johann Maier, *The Temple Scroll. An Introduction, Translation and Commentary* (Sheffield: JSOT, 1985) 32 (translation); 86 (commentary). Among participants in the exegetical debate: Yigael Yadin, David Flusser, J. Maier, B. Thiering, B. Z. Wachholder, D. Swartz, P. Calloway.

50. See the monograph of Joachim Jeremias, *Golgotha* (Leipzig: Pfeiffer, 1926).

51. Dalman, *Words*, 141.

52. Dalman, *Words*, 139-143.

53. ᵓ*in yidbar samyāᵓ lĕsamyāᵓ/tĕrêhôn napĕlîn begûmṣāᵓ*. Burney, *Poetry*, 133.

54. Jeremias, *Theology*, 147. "Casuistry" atomizes sin; "merit" makes it innocuous. Possibly; but it is not true that for Jesus all sins have the same weight, nor that there is no such thing as works of supererogation and perfection. See *Theology*, 210, for a more exact statement: "Why does Jesus reject the *Halakah*? Mark 7:6-8 gives the answer. It is because this lawgiving is entirely the work of men (v. 7) and contradicts the commandment of God (v. 8)."

55. The intended sense of Mark 7:15=Matt 15:11 is problematic on

several scores. Despite the fact that the text functioned in one stream of early Christian tradition to justify the abolition of clean-versus-unclean foods (Mark 7:19b; Rom 14:14), there are reasons (I have given them in Meyer, *Aims*, 149) for thinking that there was no intention here to dismiss this entire body of Jewish tradition. A full history of the text seems beyond us. The issue seems to me the sense of "defile": here, playing moral purity off against ritual purity, Jesus attacked the self-deceptlon involved in the exaggerated accent on and meticulous particulars of halakic treatments of ritual purity. The accent falls on the second line.

56. The citation on sorrow and sighing is from the eleventh petition of the Tephilla (or Eighteen Benedictions); that on being satisfied and refreshed is from the *Seder Rab Amram* 1. 29b. Both are cited from Dalman *Words*, 98. "They shall take joy . . . " is again from *Seder Rab Amram* 1.29b.

57. A full historical treatment of the "restorationist" side of "the reign of God," and so of such correlates of God's reign as: the (new) covenant, (new) people, (new) law, (new temple, (new) cult in Judaic literature is still lacking, despite excellent preliminary work in German New Testament scholarship (Dalman, Jeremias, Hengel, Betz, et al.). The above-mentioned thematic correlates are among the crucial data overlooked by current historical-Jesus research, much of it bogged down in ahistorical (non-eschatological) suppositions. Jesus is thus the more easily converted into a cynic sage, or a charismatic loner intent on, e.g., keeping Israel from sliding into a ruinous war with Rome.

58. Sean Freyne, *Galilee, Jesus and the Gospel* (Philadelphia: Fortress, 1988) 45f.; N. T. Wright, "Jesus, Israel and the Cross" in *The Glory of Christ in the New Testament* [G. B. Caird Festschrift] (Oxford: Clarendon, 1987).

59. Among texts which express or suppose Jesus' declaration of the forgiveness of sins: Luke 7:36-42, 47-48; Mark 2:5=Matt 9:2 =Luke 5:20 (divine passive); cf. John 20:23.

60. Lonergan, "Dialectic of Authority," in *A Third Collection* (ed.) F. E. Crowe (New York/Mahwah: Paulist; London: Chapman, 1985) 5-12.

61. On Jesus' education, see Riesner, *Lehrer*, 206-245.

62. Heinz Schürmann has made an excellent terminological proposal, one that hits off the distinctive note of Jesus' symbolic acts vis-à-vis those of the prophets: they are "fulfillment-signs" Erfüllungszeichen. See the essay "Die Symbolhandlungen Jesu als eschatolologische Erfüllungszeichen. Eine Rückfrage nach dem irdischen Jesus," *Bibel und Leben* 11 (1970) 29-41, 73-78, reprinted together with other essays relevant to the understanding of Jesus' symbolic acts in Schürmann, *Das Geheimnis Jesu. Versuche zur Jesusfrage* (Leipzig: St. Benno, 1972) 74-110; see esp. 88-89.

63. Jesus as fulfiller of the role of Son of man: Jeremias, *Theology*, 275f.

64. See Meyer, *Aims*, 185-197, 303-305. The phrases "heaven will bind" and "heaven will loose" render a divine passive and (behind Greek *en*) an Aramaic *b* of agent (not place). For a well-argued and perhaps equally probable alternative reading, see Stanley E. Porter, "Vague Verbs, Periphrastics, and Matthew 16:19," *Filologia Neotestamentaria* 1 (1988) 155-172.

65. The composition of vv. 17-19 is post-paschal, but probably pre-redactional rather than redactional: *Aims*, 305, note 52.

66. On this see Allison, *Ages*, 155-160.

67. There is, to be sure, a metaphorical sense in which Jesus decidedly is a revolutionary. Gerd Theissen in an incisive treatment, "Jesusbewegung als charismatische Wertrevolution," *New Testament Studies* 35 (1989) 343-360, exploited the analogy with revolution, showing how the ministry of Jesus corresponded to the revolution in values that delegitimizes an old regime and legitimizes a new, and how the advent of the reign of God was conceived as the actuality of the revolutionary change to be effected in fact. The eschatological restoration of Israel would indeed be "revolutionary" in both phases. It nevertheless remains true (as Theissen acknowledges) that Jesus' work could not be comprehended in the this-worldly terms of a revolution in the proper sense of the term.

68. On the theme of "preparation," see Meyer, *Aims*, 234-235; on the theme of "fulfillment," see especially chapter four above.

69. Meyer, *Aims*, 122-127.

70. See above, note 66.

71. It seems unlikely that Jesus fastened on the expression "robbers," as if the complaint were against the money-changers or merchants for short-changing their customers. Jeremiah's word (*parîsîm*) meant "violent ones." These might well be robbers, but the sense specific to "robber" is not required by the text. In rendering this text the Greek translators chose the word *lęs-tai*=robbers, bandits; the word later acquired the sense "revolutionaries." But they might as well have chosen other terms. *Pārîş* is not a common word nor is it commonly rendered by *lęstēs*. The sense "revolutionaries," in particular is irrelevant both to Jeremiah and to the gospels.

72. B. Sundkler, "Jésus et les païens," *Revue d'Histoire et de Philosophie religieuses* 16 (1936) 462-499. Though I adopted this reading in *Early Christians*, 64, it does seem to me that its probability hinges on how widely Judaism shared the view of the temple as symbol of the world—a not easily answerable question.

73. In the Synoptic gospels the entry and cleansing pericopes are followed by a question about Jesus' authority (Mark 11:27-33= Matthew 21:23-27=Luke 20:1-8). None of the Synoptists, however, immediately connects this question with the cleansing. Moreover, as it stands, the question about authority strikes a peculiarly undramatic, halakic note, as if Jesus' "authority" were the

authority to teach (*rĕšût*). John by contrast presents the cleansing as followed immediately by the Jews' demand for a "sign" in support of his intolerable pretention. It would seem at least to be in the middle-range of probability that John has retained the original context of the sanctuary riddle. On the issue of wording, it seems highly probable to me that the "I will destroy" is exactly what early Christian tradition repudiated, with excellent reason. (The only alternative possibility, which strikes me as altogether improbable, is that, since elsewhere the destruction of the temple is a part of "the ordeal," and since Jesus' task is to kindle the blaze that will be the ordeal, he might be regarded as remotely occasioning the destruction of the temple.)

74. Again, for Jesus "(new) sanctuary/temple"="(transformed) community." Hence, it was surely in and through the expectation of the pilgrimage of the peoples that Jesus anticipated the fulfillment of Isa 56:7. (The early Christian *hellēnistai* would find its fulfillment in the world mission. See Meyer, *Early Christians*, 67-83.)

75. On how to read this text, see Philip G. Davis, "Mark's Christological Paradox," *Journal for the Study of the New Testament* 35 (1989) 3-18, at 11.

76. There has been much discussion over the past generation of whether Jews generally, in the time of Jesus and before, were persuaded that prophecy had died out with Malachi and would return with the advent of the eschaton. Those answering in the affirmative seem to have the advantage in the ongoing argument. See above,

77. Jeremias, *Theology*, 52.

78. On the sense and connotations of "Son of God," dominant in the baptism and temptation accounts, there is, of course, a considerable literature. Perhaps "title," however, is somewhat misleading. Jesus is "Son," beloved, unique, first-born; God is *ʾabbāʾ*: as only a father knows his son, so only a son knows his father. . . (Matt 11:27). *ʾabbāʾ* is not exactly a title. It points to a sphere of intimacy that the coming into play of title-factors presupposes. The only instance I know of, in which *ʾabbāʾ* is used in Jewish literature as a way of addressing God is—perhaps significantly—the Targum on Ps 89:26 (par. 2 Sam 7:14). The son of David/son of the LORD so addresses the LORD. See Hans-Peter Rüger, "Aramäisch II, " *Theologisch Real-Enzyklopädie* III, 603.

79. Fritz Neugebauer, *Jesu Versuchung* (Tübingen: Mohr-Siebeck, 1986).

80. Jeremias, *Eucharistic*, 204, note 3.

81. The missionary mandate belongs to redactional texts, but this does not of itself settle the issue of historicity. The explicitly universalist character of the mandate is thoroughly suspect. See Anton Vögtle, "Die ekklesiologische Auftragsworte des Auferstandenen," in *Das Evangelium und die Evangelien* (Düsseldorf: Patmos, 1971) 243-252. But a reiterated mandate for

the mission to Israel is perfectly plausible, indeed probable.

82. Allison, *Ages* 155-160.

83. R. H. Fuller, *The Formation of the Resurrection Narratives* (Philadelphia: Fortress, 2nd edition, 1980) 160-167 offers a sober and cogent reconsideration of texts too easily assigned to an original setting in "the Easter experience of the disciples." (The one point on which I differ from Prof. Fuller relates to Matt 16:17-19, no part of which seems to me to have originated in the Easter experience.)

84. See above,

85. Jeremias, *Theology*, 169.

86. Ibid.

87. Ibid.

# NAMES: ANCIENT AND MEDIAEVAL

# NAMES: MODERN

# INDEX OF PASSAGES

## NON-CANONICAL TEXTS

Printed in Great Britain
by Amazon.co.uk, Ltd.,
Marston Gate.